First World War
and Army of Occupation
War Diary
France, Belgium and Germany

3 CAVALRY DIVISION
Headquarters, Branches and Services
General Staff Appendices to 1141
11 October 1914 - 30 November 1914

WO95/1142/1

The Naval & Military Press Ltd
www.nmarchive.com
Published in association with The National Archives

Published by

The Naval & Military Press Ltd

Unit 10 Ridgewood Industrial Park,

Uckfield, East Sussex,

TN22 5QE England

Tel: +44 (0) 1825 749494

www.naval-military-press.com

www.nmarchive.com

This diary has been reprinted in facsimile from the original. Any imperfections are inevitably reproduced and the quality may fall short of modern type and cartographic standards.

© **Crown Copyright**
Images reproduced by permission of The National Archives, London, England, 2015.

Contents

Document type	Place/Title	Date From	Date To
Heading	B.E.F. France & Flanders. Third Cavalry Division. Headquarters. General Staff. Operation Orders And Intelligence Summaries 1914 Oct To 1919 May.		
Heading	1914-1919 3rd Cavalry Division General Staff Appendis. Operation Order Etc. Oct 1914-May 1919		
Miscellaneous	G.S. 3rd Cavalry Division Oct. 1914		
Miscellaneous			
Miscellaneous	Orders sent by telephone to General BYNG, Commanding 3rd Cavalry Division, about 12 noon 10th October, 1914.		
Operation(al) Order(s)	Orders sent by telephone to General Capper about 12 noon. 10th October, 1914		
Miscellaneous	Orders sent by telephone to General WATT about 12 noon. 10th October, 1914		
Miscellaneous	To:- General WATT, Commanding Troops, Beernem	11/10/1914	11/10/1914
War Diary	To:- Major General T. Capper, C.B. D.S.O. Commanding 7th Division.	11/10/1914	11/10/1914
Miscellaneous	To:- Major General the Hon J.H.G. BYNG. C.B. M.V.O. Commanding 3rd Cavalry Division.	11/10/1914	11/10/1914
Operation(al) Order(s)	Operation Order No. 1 by Lt-Genl. Sir Henry Rawlinson, Commdg. IV Army Corps.	13/10/1914	13/10/1914
Miscellaneous	To:- Major General T. Capper, C.B. D.S.O. Commanding 7th Division.	15/10/1914	15/10/1914
Miscellaneous	Telephone Conversation.	17/10/1914	17/10/1914
Operation(al) Order(s)	Operation Order No. 2 by Lieut. General Sir H. Rawlinson Bart., C.V.O., C.B. Commanding IV Corps	18/10/1914	18/10/1914
Operation(al) Order(s)	Operation Order No. 3 by Lieut. General Sir H. Rawlinson Bart., C.V.O., C.B.	19/10/1914	19/10/1914
Operation(al) Order(s)	Operation Order No. 4 by Lieut. General Sir H. Rawlinson Bart., C.V.O., C.B. Commanding IV Corps.	20/10/1914	20/10/1914
Operation(al) Order(s)	Operation Order No. 5 by Lieut. General Sir H. Rawlinson Bart, C.V.O., C.B. Commanding IV Corps.	21/10/1914	21/10/1914
Miscellaneous	A Form. Messages And Signals.	24/10/1914	24/10/1914
Operation(al) Order(s)	Operation Order No. 6 by Lieut. General Sir H. Rawlinson, Bart. C.V.O., C.B. Commanding IV Corps.	25/10/1914	25/10/1914
Operation(al) Order(s)	Operation Orders No. 7 by Lieut. General Sir H. Rawlinson, C.V.O., C.B. Commanding 4th Corps.	13/11/1914	13/11/1914
Miscellaneous	Army Operation Order No. 8 By Lieut. General Sir H.S Rawlinson, Bart. C.V.O., C.B. Commanding IVth Corps.	13/12/1914	13/12/1914
Operation(al) Order(s)	Operation Order No. 9 by Lieut. General Sir H. Rawlinson, Bt. C.V.O., C.B. Commanding IVth Corps.	18/12/1914	18/12/1914
War Diary	Zonnebeke	17/10/1914	19/10/1914
War Diary	Moorslede	19/10/1914	20/10/1914
War Diary	St. Julien	20/10/1914	20/10/1914
War Diary	Goudberg	20/10/1914	20/10/1914
War Diary	St. Julien	20/10/1914	20/10/1914
War Diary	Hooge	21/10/1914	22/10/1914
War Diary	Zandvoorde	23/10/1914	23/10/1914
War Diary	Zillebeke	24/10/1914	25/10/1914

War Diary	Klein Zillebeke	26/10/1914	26/10/1914
War Diary	Zillebeke	26/10/1914	26/10/1914
War Diary	Zillebeke	27/10/1914	28/10/1914
War Diary	Klein Zillebeke	29/10/1914	29/10/1914
War Diary	Zillebeke	30/10/1914	30/10/1914
War Diary	Klein Zillebeke	30/10/1914	30/10/1914
Miscellaneous	A Form. Messages And Signals.		
Miscellaneous	From:- O.C. Officer Patrol Sent at O.C. Royal Dragoons,	10/10/1914	10/10/1914
Miscellaneous	From:- O.C. Cav. Patrol, The Royal Dragoons	10/10/1914	10/10/1914
Miscellaneous	A Form. Messages And Signals.		
Miscellaneous	A Form. Messages And Signals.	11/10/1914	11/10/1914
Miscellaneous	From:- O.C. Armed Master Poelcapelle.	11/05/1914	11/05/1914
Miscellaneous	A Form. Messages And Signals.		
Miscellaneous	To Headquarters 3rd Cav. Div.	16/10/1914	16/10/1914
Miscellaneous	From:- Major General Hon. J.H.J. Byng, C.O., M.V.C. Commanding 3rd Cavalry Division.	17/10/1914	17/10/1914
Miscellaneous	A Form. Messages And Signals.		
Miscellaneous	W.A. 1/17.X Zonnebeke. General Staff 3rd Cavalry Division	17/10/1914	17/10/1914
Miscellaneous	Intelligence.	17/10/1914	17/10/1914
Miscellaneous	A Form. Messages And Signals.	18/10/1914	18/10/1914
Miscellaneous	From. O.C. Royal Brigade.		
Miscellaneous	A Form. Messages And Signals.	19/10/1914	19/10/1914
Miscellaneous	From 3rd Cav. Div.	20/10/1914	20/10/1914
Miscellaneous	From 6 Cav. Div.	22/10/1914	22/10/1914
Miscellaneous	A Form. Messages And Signals.		
Miscellaneous	3 Cav. Div.	25/10/1914	25/10/1914
Miscellaneous	3rd Cav. Divn.	26/10/1914	26/10/1914
Miscellaneous	A Form. Messages And Signals.		
Miscellaneous	W.D. 9/26.X I.O.C. IV. A.C.	27/10/1914	27/10/1914
Miscellaneous	W.D. 8/26 X To G.O.C. 3rd Cav. Div.	27/10/1914	27/10/1914
Miscellaneous	G.O.C. 7 Cav. Bde.	27/10/1914	27/10/1914
Miscellaneous	C Form (Duplicate). Messages And Signals.		
Map			
Miscellaneous	C Form (Original). Messages And Signals.		
Miscellaneous	3rd Cavalry Brigade.	27/10/1914	27/10/1914
Miscellaneous	IVth Cavalry Brigade	27/10/1914	27/10/1914
Miscellaneous	A Form. Messages And Signals.		
Miscellaneous	W.D. 9/27.X GOC IV A.C.		
Miscellaneous	A Form. Messages And Signals.		
Miscellaneous	To The C.S.O. 3rd Cav Div.	27/10/1914	27/10/1914
Miscellaneous	A Form. Messages And Signals.		
Miscellaneous	3rd Cav Div.		
Miscellaneous	G.O.C. 2nd Cavalry Division.	27/10/1914	27/10/1914
Miscellaneous	A Form. Messages And Signals.		
Miscellaneous	Hd Qrs I AC Chateau E Houge	28/10/1914	28/10/1914
Miscellaneous	C Form (Original) Messages And Signals.		
Miscellaneous	G.O.C. Cavalry Corps.		
Miscellaneous	A Form. Messages And Signals.		
Miscellaneous	C Form. (Duplicate.) Messages & Signals.		
Miscellaneous	From 2nd Cav. Div.	29/10/1914	29/10/1914
Miscellaneous	A Form. Messages And Signals.	29/10/1914	29/10/1914
Miscellaneous	From 3rd Cav. Div.	29/10/1914	29/10/1914
Miscellaneous	From C. R.H.A.	29/10/1914	29/10/1914
Miscellaneous	From 3rd Cav. Div.	29/10/1914	29/10/1914

Miscellaneous	C Form (Original) Messages And Signals.	29/10/1914	29/10/1914
Miscellaneous	A Form. Messages And Signals.	29/10/1914	29/10/1914
Miscellaneous	Form 3rd Cav. Div.	29/10/1914	29/10/1914
Miscellaneous	C Form. (Duplicate). Messages And Signals.	29/10/1914	29/10/1914
Miscellaneous	Messages And Signals.	29/10/1914	29/10/1914
Miscellaneous	Messages And Signals.		
Miscellaneous	A Form. Messages And Signals.		
Miscellaneous	From 3rd Cav. Div.	29/10/1914	29/10/1914
Miscellaneous	C Form (Duplicate). Messages And Signals.		
Miscellaneous	Form 2nd Cav. Div.	30/10/1914	30/10/1914
Miscellaneous	A Form. Messages And Signals.		
Miscellaneous	From 3rd Cav. Div.	30/10/1914	30/10/1914
Miscellaneous	A Form. Messages And Signals.		
Miscellaneous	From To. O.C. Royals Klein Zillbeke	30/10/1914	30/10/1914
Miscellaneous	A Form. Messages And Signals.		
Miscellaneous	From 7th Cav. Bde.	30/10/1914	30/10/1914
Miscellaneous	From 3rd Cav Div.	30/10/1914	30/10/1914
Miscellaneous	C Form (Original) Messages And Signals.		
Miscellaneous	A Form. Messages And Signals.		
Miscellaneous	From 3rd Cav. Div.	30/10/1914	30/10/1914
Miscellaneous	A Form. Messages And Signals.		
Miscellaneous	C Form (Duplicate). Messages And Signals.	30/10/1914	30/10/1914
Miscellaneous	From To 3rd Cav. Div.	30/10/1914	30/10/1914
Miscellaneous	From To 3rd Cav. Div.		
Miscellaneous	A Form. Messages And Signals.		
Miscellaneous	From 2nd Cav. Div.	30/10/1914	30/10/1914
Miscellaneous	C Form (Duplicate). Messages And Signals.		
Miscellaneous	A Form. Messages And Signals.		
Miscellaneous	From 2nd Cav. Div.	30/10/1914	30/10/1914
Miscellaneous	From 3rd Cav. Div.	30/10/1914	30/10/1914
Miscellaneous	A Form. Messages And Signals.		
Miscellaneous	C Form (Duplicate). Messages And Signals.	31/10/1914	31/10/1914
Miscellaneous	A Form. Messages And Signals.	31/10/1914	31/10/1914
Miscellaneous	Hooge	01/11/1914	01/11/1914
War Diary	Ypres	02/11/1914	02/11/1914
War Diary	S Of Hooge	02/11/1914	02/11/1914
War Diary	Near Hooge	02/11/1914	03/11/1914
War Diary	Ypres	04/11/1914	05/11/1914
War Diary	3rd Kil. Ypres Mehin Rd	06/11/1914	07/11/1914
War Diary	Ypres	08/11/1914	20/11/1914
War Diary	Hazebrouck	21/11/1914	30/11/1914
Miscellaneous	Report on Operation for 12 noon	27/10/1914	27/10/1914
Miscellaneous	Hooge	01/11/1914	01/11/1914
War Diary	Ypres	02/11/1914	02/11/1914
War Diary	S of Hooge	02/11/1914	02/11/1914
War Diary	Near Hooge	02/11/1914	03/11/1914
War Diary	Ypres	04/11/1914	05/11/1914
War Diary	3rd Kil. Ypres Monin Rd	06/11/1914	07/11/1914
War Diary	Ypres	08/11/1914	20/11/1914
War Diary	Hazebrouck	21/11/1914	30/11/1914
Miscellaneous	My Dear General.	04/11/1914	04/11/1914
Miscellaneous	Report on operation 3rd Cavalry Division October 30th November 3rd 1914		
Miscellaneous	C Form. (Duplicate). Messages And Signals.		
Miscellaneous	A Form. Messages And Signals.		
Miscellaneous	C Form (Duplicate). Messages And Signals.		

Miscellaneous	
Miscellaneous	A Form. Messages And Signals.
Miscellaneous	
Miscellaneous	C Form (Duplicate). Messages And Signals.
Miscellaneous	A Form. Messages And Signals.
Miscellaneous	C Form (Duplicate). Messages And Signals.
Miscellaneous	A Form. Messages And Signals.
Miscellaneous	C Form (Duplicate). Messages And Signals.
Miscellaneous	A Form. Messages And Signals.
Operation(al) Order(s)	1st Army Corps Operation Order No. 30
Miscellaneous	
Miscellaneous	A Form. Messages And Signals.
Miscellaneous	G.O.C. 6th Cav. Bde.
Map	
Miscellaneous	C Form (Duplicate). Messages And Signals.
Miscellaneous	A Form. Messages And Signals.
Miscellaneous	Messages And Signals.
Miscellaneous	A Form. Messages And Signals.
Operation(al) Order(s)	3rd Cav. Div. Operation Order No. 18
Miscellaneous	A Form. Messages And Signals.
Miscellaneous	Messages And Signals.
Miscellaneous	3rd Cav. Div. Operation Order No. 19
Miscellaneous	A Form. Messages And Signals.
Miscellaneous	Report on Operation 3rd Cavalry Division
Miscellaneous	A Form. Messages And Signals.
Miscellaneous	
Operation(al) Order(s)	3rd Cav. Div. Operation Order No. 20
Miscellaneous	A Form. Messages And Signals.
Miscellaneous	
Miscellaneous	A Form. Messages And Signals.
Miscellaneous	G.S.O. I 3rd Cav. Div.
Miscellaneous	A Form. Messages And Signals.
Miscellaneous	Messages And Signals.
Miscellaneous	A Form. Messages And Signals.
Miscellaneous	To G.O.C. I Corps
Miscellaneous	A Form. Messages And Signals.
Miscellaneous	General Staff 3rd Cav. Div.
Miscellaneous	General Staff 3rd Cav. Division.
Miscellaneous	G/49 G.O.C. W.D. 2/7
Miscellaneous	
Miscellaneous	A Form. Messages And Signals.
Miscellaneous	
Miscellaneous	A Form. Messages And Signals.
Miscellaneous	? of the 2nd Life Guards Commanding Officer.
Miscellaneous	A Form. Messages And Signals.
Miscellaneous	Messages And Signals.
Miscellaneous	C Form. (Duplicate). Messages And Signals.
Miscellaneous	Messages And Signals.
Miscellaneous	A Form. Messages And Signals.
Miscellaneous	C Form (Duplicate). Messages And Signals.
Miscellaneous	A Form. Messages And Signals.
Miscellaneous	
Miscellaneous	C Form (Duplicate). Messages And Signals.
Miscellaneous	
Miscellaneous	A Form. Messages And Signals.
Miscellaneous	C. Form. (Duplicate) Messages & Signals.

Miscellaneous	A Form. Messages And Signals.		
Miscellaneous	C Form (Duplicate). Messages And Signals.		
Miscellaneous			
Miscellaneous	A Form. Messages And Signals.		
Miscellaneous	C Form (Duplicate). Messages And Signals.		
Miscellaneous	A Form. Messages And Signals.		
Miscellaneous			
Miscellaneous	To:- 1st Div., 2nd Div., 3rd Div., 1st Cav. Div., 3rd Cav. Div., Lord Cavan.		
Miscellaneous	A Form. Messages And Signals.		
Miscellaneous	W.D. 3/14	14/11/1914	14/11/1914
Miscellaneous	C Form (Duplicate). Messages And Signals.		
Miscellaneous	A Form. Messages And Signals.		
Miscellaneous	C Form (Duplicate). Messages And Signals.		
Miscellaneous			
Miscellaneous	C Form (Duplicate). Messages And Signals.		
Miscellaneous	G.152 G.O.C. I Ave.		
Miscellaneous	A Form. Messages And Signals.		
Miscellaneous	Messages And Signals.		
Miscellaneous	A Form. Messages And Signals.		
Miscellaneous	C Form (Duplicate) Messages And Signals.		
Miscellaneous	A Form. Messages And Signals.		
Miscellaneous	C Form (Duplicate). Messages And Signals.		
Miscellaneous	Messages And Signals.		
Miscellaneous	A Form. Messages And Signals.		
Miscellaneous	Messages And Signals.		
Miscellaneous	A Form. Messages And Signals.		
Miscellaneous	G.O.C. I.A.E. W.D.	18/11/1914	18/11/1914
Miscellaneous	A Form. Messages And Signals.		
Miscellaneous	Messages And Signals.		
Miscellaneous	C Form (Duplicate). Messages And Signals.		
Miscellaneous	A Form. Messages And Signals.		
Miscellaneous	G.O.C. I.A.C.	20/11/1914	20/11/1914
Miscellaneous	General Staff. 3rd Cav. Div.		
Miscellaneous	A Form. Messages And Signals.		
Miscellaneous			
Miscellaneous	A Form. Messages And Signals.		
Miscellaneous	C Form (Duplicate). Messages And Signals.		
Miscellaneous			
Miscellaneous	A Form. Messages And Signals.		
Miscellaneous	G.O.C. I AC	20/11/1914	20/11/1914
Miscellaneous	Ga.144. 19th AAA		
Operation(al) Order(s)	Operation Order No. 17. by Lieut-Colonel Sir Edmund Allenby. M.G.-B. Commanding Cavalry Corps.	09/03/1915	09/03/1915
Operation(al) Order(s)	Operation Order No. 18 by Lieut. General Sir Edmund Allenby, K.C.B. Commanding Cavalry Corps.	10/03/1915	10/03/1915
Miscellaneous	A Form. Messages And Signals.		
Miscellaneous	W.D. 2/11 III	10/03/1915	10/03/1915
Miscellaneous			
Miscellaneous	Headquarters, Cavalry Corps.	07/05/1915	07/05/1915
Miscellaneous			
Miscellaneous	Report on the part taken by the 3rd Cavalry Division, commanded by Brigadier-General D. Campbell vice Major-General Sir J. Byng, officiating in command of the cavalry corps, in the operation of April 22nd to May 4th.		

Miscellaneous	Summary of Operations of 3rd Cavalry Division during period 23rd April to 6th June, 1915		
Miscellaneous			
Miscellaneous	Summary of Operations of 3rd Cavalry Division during period 23rd April to 6th June, 1916		
Miscellaneous	Summary of Operation of 3rd Cavalry Division during period 23rd April to 6th June, 1915		
Miscellaneous	General Headquarters.		
Miscellaneous	3rd Cavalry Division G.735.	18/05/1915	18/05/1915
Miscellaneous	3rd Cavalry Division		
Map			
Miscellaneous			
Map	Situation At 12-45 p.m. 13th Mar. 1915		
Miscellaneous			
Map	Situation at 4-45 p.m.		
Miscellaneous			
Map	Situation at 4-0.9 a.m		
Miscellaneous			
Miscellaneous	3rd Cavalry Division. Appendix To G. 735		
Miscellaneous	Notes by the General Officer Commanding, 7th Cavalry Brigade, on Trench Line.		
Miscellaneous	Report by the Officer Commanding Leicestershire Yeomanry, on the Trench Line.		
Miscellaneous	Further report by Leicestershire Yeomanry (Lieut W.S. Fielding-Johnson) on the Trench Line.		
Miscellaneous	Report by 2nd Life Guards on Trench Line.		
Map			
Operation(al) Order(s)	Cavalry Corps Operation Order No. 3	20/05/1915	20/05/1915
Miscellaneous	W.D. 78 19 V G 769	21/05/1915	21/05/1915
Miscellaneous	150th Bde.	21/05/1915	21/05/1915
Miscellaneous	G.797	28/05/1915	28/05/1915
Miscellaneous	Headquarters, Vth Corps.	29/05/1915	29/05/1915
Miscellaneous	Headquarters, 3rd Division.	04/06/1915	04/06/1915
Miscellaneous	Reference 5th Corps Letter G.X 1245		
Diagram etc	Reference Zillebeke. Sheet 1/10,000		
Miscellaneous			
Miscellaneous	Narrative of Operations 25th/28th September. 1915		
Miscellaneous	3rd Cavalry Division.		
Miscellaneous	3rd Cavalry Division. App 1	19/09/1915	19/09/1915
Miscellaneous	Reference ? Sheet 5a Appendix 2		
Miscellaneous	3rd Cavalry Division. Appx 3	20/09/1915	20/09/1915
Miscellaneous	8th Cavalry Brigade. Appx 4	20/09/1915	20/09/1915
Miscellaneous	March Table Issued With G.285		
Operation(al) Order(s)	First Army Operation Order No. 95. Appx 5		

B.E.F. FRANCE & FLANDERS.

THIRD CAVALRY DIVISION.

HEADQUARTERS.
GENERAL STAFF.

OPERATION ORDERS AND
INTELLIGENCE SUMMARIES
1914 OCT TO 1919 MAY.

1142

B.E.F. FRANCE & FLANDERS.

THIRD CAVALRY DIVISION.

HEADQUARTERS.
GENERAL STAFF.

OPERATION ORDERS AND INTELLIGENCE SUMMARIES 1914 OCT TO 1919 MAY.

1142

1914-1919
3RD CAVALRY DIVISION

General Staff Appendices.
Operation Orders etc.,
INTELLIGENCE SUMMARIES
OCT 1914 - MAY 1919

Index

Headings in colour chalk have been added –

SUBJECT.

G S 3rd Cavalry Division
Oct. 1914

No.	Contents.	Date.
	Messages.	

1

Orders sent by telephone to General BYNG,

    Commanding 3rd Cavalry Division,

  about 12 noon 10th October, 1914.

---

1. You are to march this afternoon to THOUROUT, to be there before dark, and push patrols to S.S.W., and S.E.

2. General WATT with the troops of 7th Division now about BRUGES moves this afternoon to the cross-roads S.W. of BEERNEM to arrive there before dark.

3. CAPPER will be withdrawing from GHENT tonight and will arrive at AELTRE by daylight tomorrow.

4. The Commander of the French troops in GHENT has been asked to conform and move to WYNGHENE.

5. Information from LONDON just received that another German Reserve Brigade is moving via ALOST towards GHENT.

6. Before moving off, call up this H.Q. for final instructions, and on arrival at THOUROUT report your telephone number.

                                    (Initialled)   R.A.K.M.

Orders sent by telephone to General CAPPER
about 12 noon. 10th October, 1914.

----

1. You are to withdraw tomorrow night from GHENT to AELTRE and be there by daylight 12th October.

2. General WATT with his Battalions now at BRUGES and the Divisional troops with him moves today and will be at the cross-roads S.W. of BEERNEM before dark.

3. BYNG with 3rd Cavalry Divn. moves this afternoon to THOUROUT to be there before dark.

4. Inform French Commander that G.O.C. would like him to conform and move to WYNGHENE.

5. The force has come under the orders of Sir John French, whose instructions have not yet been received.

6. Information from London just received that another Reserve German Brigade is moving via ALOST towards GHENT.

7. On arrival report Telephone number.

(Initialled) R.A.K.M.

Orders sent by telephone to General WATT
about 12 noon 10th October 1914.

---

1. You are to move (with your 3 Battalions and the Divisional Troops with you) this afternoon to the cross-roads S.W. of BEERNEM, to arrive there before dark.

2. General Capper will be withdrawing from GHENT tonight and will arrive at AELTRE by daylight tomorrow.

3. Byng with the 3rd Cavalry Divn. moves this afternoon to THOUROUT to be there before dark.

4. The Commander of the French troops in GHENT is being asked to conform and move to WYNGHENE.

5. Information from London just received that another Reserve German Brigade is moving via ALOST towards GHENT.

6. Before moving off call up this H.Q. for final instructions, and on arrival at BEERNEM report your telephone number.

         (Initialled) R.A.K.M.

To :-

General WATT,

    Commanding Troops, BEERNEM.

                             IV Corps H.Q.
                             VILLA DORIS
                               OSTEND.
                             11th October 1914.

1. You will move the troops under your command tomorrow morning to COOLSCAMP, the road junction 2 miles W.S.W. of WYNGHENE will be clear for you by 10 a.m.

2. General Capper with the troops in GHENT will be moving tonight via AELTRE to THIELT, reaching the latter place tomorrow (12th October) afternoon.

3. The 3rd Cavalry Divn. moves tomorrow morning from THOUROUT and OOSTCAMP to the neighbourhood of ROULERS.

4. On arrival at COOLSCAMP you will again come under the orders of Major General Capper.

5. Reports to be sent to Corps' H.Q. at OSTEND until further orders. You will maintain communication continuously by telephone with Corps H.Q. until you rejoin General Capper's command.

                           (signed) R.A.K. Montgomery,
                                     B.G., G.S.
                                     IV Corps.

To :-

Major General T. CAPPER, C.B. D.S.O.
Commanding 7th Division.

Headquarters IV Corps
VILLA DORIS
OSTEND.
11th. October, 1914.

1. The troops under your command in GHENT will move during tonight and tomorrow via HELTREE to THIELT, the leading troops to reach THIELT before dark tomorrow (12th Oct.) evening.

2. The transport of the Forces to be sent back clear of GHENT before dark today.

3. The 3rd Cavalry Divn. moves tomorrow morning to ROULERS.

4. The troops at present under the command of Brigadier General WATT, now at BEERNEM, move tomorrow morning to COOLSCAMP and will again come under your orders.

5. Reports to be sent to Corps Headquarters at OSTEND until further orders. You will maintain communication continuously by telephone woth Corps Headquarters.

R.A.K. MONTGOMERY,
Brigadier-General, General Staff.

Issued at 3.50 p.m.

To :-

    Major General the Hon. J.H.G. BYNG, C.B., M.V.O.
    Commanding 3rd Cavalry Division.

                                  Headquarters IV Corps
                                          VILLA DORIS
                                              OSTEND.
                                        11th October, 1914.

1.   Move the Cavalry Divn. tomorrow (12th Oct.) morning to ROULERS, line of protection ZONNEBEKE - LENDELEDE.

2.   General CAPPER, with the troops under his command in GHENT, will march tonight via HELTREE to THIELT reaching the latter place before dark tomorrow evening.

3.   The troops now at BEERNEM under Brigadier General WATTS will march tomorrow morning to COOLSCAMP. The road WYNGHENE - SWEVEZEELE - COOLSCAMP is to be cleared for this column by 10 a.m.

4.   Reports to be sent to Corps Headquarters at OSTEND until further orders. You will maintain communication continuously by telephone with Corps Headquarters.

                                            R.A.K. MONTGOMERY
                                    Brigadier-General, General Staff.

<u>Issued at 4.15 p.m.</u>

Copy No........

Operation Order No.1
by
Lt-Genl. Sir Henry Rawlinson, Commdg. IV Army Corps.

Headqrs. IV Army Corps
Hotel de Ville, ROULERS.
13th October, 1914.

1. The IV Corps will move tomorrow to YPRES.

2. The Force will move as follows :-

   (a) The 3rd Cavalry Division, furnishing a strong Advanced Guard of one Brigade, will proceed by the road ISEGHEM - ROLLEGHEMCAPPELLE - DADIZEELE - BECELAERE - YPRES. The head of the main body to cross the main ROULERS - LILLE road 2½ kilo. S.E. of MOORSLEDE at 6 am. The G.O.C. 3rd Cavalry Division will arrange to cover the left flank of the march of the 7th Divn., with one Squadron, until its arrival at YPRES.

   (b) The 7th Division, covered by a strong rearguard, will move to YPRES by any of the roads North of and including the road ROULERS - MOORSLEDE - ZONNEBEKE - YPRES. No portion of the Division to start before 6 a.m.

   (c) One armoured train will be placed at the disposal of the G.O.C. 7th Division, the remainder of the armoured trains and armoured motor cars being placed under the orders of the G.O.C. 3rd Cavalry Division.

   (d) The aeroplanes will be ready to fly off at 6 a.m.

3. The wireless and airline sections of the Signal Company, the Motor Transport of the Royal Flying Corps and Armoured motors, together with the Corps Headquarters transport, will move off at 5 a.m. from the Square, Headquarters transport leading, and will proceed via the DIXMUDE road and turn South west at the crossroads HODGLEDE - POEL CAPPELLE and follow the road to LANGHEMARCQ and remain there for orders.

4. The Cavalry Divisional Ammunition Park and the M.T. Supply Columns of the 3rd Cavalry Divn. and 7th Infantry Divn. will proceed tonight to DUNKIRK.

5. The rendezvous for supplies tomorrow WESTVLETEREN on the FURNES - YPRES road.

6. Headquarters will leave ROULERS at 6 a.m. and proceed to YPRES via MOORSLEDE - ZONNEBEKE - YPRES. Reports to be sent to Headqrs. Cavalry Divn. until reaching YPRES; after that to the Town Hall, YPRES.

R.A.K. MONTGOMERY, Bdr-Genl.
General Staff, 4th Army Corps.

Issued at   p.m.

Copy No. 1 to G.O.C. 3rd Cavalry Division.
 "   "   2 "   " 7th Division.
 "   "   3 "   " O.C. Flying Squadron.
 "   "   4 "   " Officer de liason, Belgian Army H.Q. Staff.

To :-
    Major General the Hon. J.H.G. BYNG, C.B., M.V.O.
        Commanding 3rd Cavalry Division.

                                    Headquarters IV Corps
                                        Le College
                                            POPERINGHE
                                                15th October, 1914.

1.   You will move your Division tomorrow through YPRES to the North of the line POEL CAPELLE - LANGEMARCK, and extend the line of the 7th Divn. to the FORET D'HOUTHULST.

2.   The 7th Divn. is tonight occupying a series of posts from HOLLEBEKE through GHELUVELT and ZONNEBERE.

3.   You will keep touch with the 7th Divn. at ST.JULIEN.

4.   Reports until further orders to Corps Headquarters at POPERINGHE.

5.   Rendezvous for supplies, ELVERDINGHE, the rear will be notified later.

                                    R.A.K. MONTGOMERY,
                                Brigadier-General, General Staff.
                                        IV Corps.

Issued at 4.45 p.m. by hand.

To :-

    Major General T. CAPPER, C.B., D.S.O.

        Commanding 7th Division.

                                    Headquarters IV Corps

                                    Le College

                                    POPERINGHE,

                                    15th October, 1914.

1.   You will establish tonight a series of posts covering the approaches to YPRES from South East and East along the line HOLLEVEKE - ZANDVOORDE - GHELUVELT - ZONNEBEKE - POEL CAPELLE (exclusive).

2.   The 3rd Cavalry Divn. will move from YPRES tomorrow morning and extend the line North, keeping touch with the 3rd Divn. at ST.JULIEN.

3.   Reports until further orders to Corps Headquarters, POPERINGHE.

4.   Rendezvous for supplies ELVERDINGHE, the time will be notified later.

                                    R.A.K. MONTGOMERY

                        Brigadier-General, Gen. Staff,

                                    IV Corps.

<u>Issued at 4.45 p.m. by hand.</u>

TELEPHONE CONVERSATION.

Between :-

G.O.C. IV Corps
    and
Colonel Bridges at FURNES.

Time :-

8.25 a.m. 17th October 1914.

Explained situation of our troops and French Cavalry Divisions.

Asked if it would be any use to ask King to make personal appeal to their Cavalry to move up on our left and occupy trenches already dug N. and E, of Forest of HOUTHULST. Explained would probably have little fighting, but would be very useful.

(Initialled) R.A.K.M.

17/10/14.

TELEPHONE CONVERSATION.

Between :-   Time :-
                                             9.5 a.m. 17th Oct.1914.
   G.O.C. IV Corps.
       and
   General Capper, Commdg. 7th Divn.

You must hold your own line and not move without orders.

If Byng or Gough wants help I will give you orders to move, but you must not give up your line.

Believe large concentration North ROULERS and THOUROUT, and there has been fighting at DIXMUDE.

Then gave dispositions of French and Belgians.

                                  (Initialled)   H.R.

17/10/14.

TELEPHONE CONVERSATION.

Between :-   Time :-
                                                   2.10 p.m. 17/10/14.
   G.O.C. IV Corps
      and
   Belgian Officier de Liaison at POEL CAPELLE.

What is going on ? Are you in touch with General Byng ? You are not ? They are close by on your right.

What are you doing now ? Attacking STADEN ?

How far have you got ?   )
)
) Retiring slightly on Forest.
What is the position now ?)

Are you in the Forest ? The outskirts. If you are retiring, you must retire towards (them) WESTRODESBEKE. The English cavalry is there. That is all I know of them.

There is a French Division of Cavalry (7th) at the Forest, South edge.

I cannot give you any more information.

                                       (Initialled) H.R.

TELEPHONE CONVERSATION.

Between :-   Time :-
                                                   2.25 p.m. 17/10/14.
   G.O.C. IV Corps
      and
   Major Baird at NIEU CAPPELLE.

All right at DIXMUDE, no shooting going on and French and Belgians all right.

                                       (Initialled) H.R.

Copy No........

Operation Order No.2
by
Lieut.General Sir H.Rawlinson Bart.,C.V.O.,C.B.
Commanding IV Corps

IV Corps Headqrs.
LE COLLEGE
POPERINGHE,
18th October 1914.

1. The IV Corps will advance tomorrow to attack the enemy in the neighbourhood of MENIN.

2. The 7th Division will arrange to have its artillery in position by 6.30 a.m., and the infantry will then move forward to the attack.
   The right flank of the 7th Division will be protected by the cavalry of the 2nd Cavalry Division at and about TENBRIELEN and AMERICA, the left flank being protected at and about ST.PIETER by 3rd Cavalry Division.

3. The 3rd Cavalry Division will move forward to the line of the ROULERS - MENIN Road at 6.30 a.m., and will push forward strong reconnaissances to LEDEGHEM, WINKEL ST. ELOI and ISEGHEM. They will occupy ROULERS and maintain touch with the 5th French Cavalry Division at HOOGLEDE.

4. A battery of Horse Artillery will be sent tonight by G.O.C. 7th Division to report to the G.O.C. 3rd Cavalry Division at ZONNEBEKE. This battery will remain with 3rd Cavalry Division until further orders.

5. Two Armoured Trains will proceed to the neighbourhood of HOUTHEM and will from there bring fire to bear on the German batteries which are reported to be in position on the South side of the River LYS at LA BASSEEVILLE and LA BLANDRISSE.

6. Rendezvous for supplies tomorrow the road junction ½ mile S.W. of YPRES on the YPRES - BAILLEUL Road.
   Time for 3rd Cavalry Division ... 1.0 p.m.
   Time for 7th Infantry Division ..5.30 p.m.

7. Corps Headquarters will be established at the Hotel de VILLE, YPRES, from 8 a.m. until 6 p.m. tomorrow.

R.A.K.MONTGOMERY,
Brig.General, G.S.
IV Corps.

Issued at 11 p.m.
By Motor cyclist.
B.G.S ---------------- Copy No 1.
3rd Cavalry Division.. Copy No.2.
7th Division .... Copy No.3.
French Cavalry ----- ... Copy No. 4.
Belgian Officer ---- Copy No 5

Copy No....

Operation Order No.3
by
Lieut.General Sir H.Rawlinson, Bart. C.V.O. C.B.

IV Corps Headqrs.
LIE COLLEGE
POPERINGHE
19th October 1914.

1. The IV Corps will maintain their present position on the line KRUISVIK - BECELAERE - PASSCHENDAELE - WESTROOSBEKE.

2. The 7th Division will push forward tomorrow morning strong reconnaissances in the direction of MENIN with a view to ascertaining the strength and dispositions of the enemy in that neighbourhood.

3. The 3rd Cavalry Division will hold the line WESTROOSBEKE - NIEUWEMOLEN and cover the advance of the 2nd Division which marches at 6.30 a.m. from POPERINGHE in the general direction of THOUROUT via BOESINGHE and YPRES and which will be followed by the 1st Divn.

4. Rendezvous for supplies tomorrow the same as for today.

5. Corps Headquarters will be established at the Hotel de VILLE YPRES from 8 a.m. tomorrow until 6 p.m.

R.A.K.MONTGOMERY
Brig.Genl. G.S.
IV Corps.

Issued at 11.20 p.m.
By Motor cyclist to 3rd Cavalry Division Copy No.2
                     7th Division   Copy No.3

Copy No......

Operation Order No.4
by
Lieut.General Sir H.Rawlinson, Bart. C.V.O., C.B.
Commanding IV Corps.

IV Corps Headqrs.
LE COLLEGE
POPERINGHE
20th October 1914.

1. The 7th Division will maintain the positions they now hold and continue to improve their entrenchments.

2. The 3rd Cavalry Division will concentrate to the South of ZONNEBEKE by 6.30 a.m. tomorrow and will be reponsible for the protection of the right flank of the I Corps as it moves forward from the line ZONNEBEKE - ST.JULIEN - LANGEMARCK at 7 a.m. towards the line OOSTNIEUWKERKE - STADEN. The left flank of the I Corps being protected by the French.

3. Rendezvous for supplies tomorrow the same as for today.

4. IV Corps Headquarters Report Station will be established at the Hotel de VILLE, YPRES at 7.30 a.m. until 6 p.m.

R.A.K.MONTGOMERY,
Brig.Genl. G.S.
IV Corps.

Issued at 10.20 p.m.

By Motor cyclist to:-
3rd Cavalry Division Copy No.2.
7th Division Copy No.3.
I Corps Copy No.4.
Cavalry Corps Copy No.5.

Copy No........

Operation Order No.5
by
Lieut.General Sir H.Rawlinson, Bart, G.V.O., C.B.
Commanding IV Corps.

IV Corps Headqrs.
LE COLLEGE
POPERINGHE
31st October 1914.

1. The IV Corps will maintain its position on the line occupied today, the left resting on ZONNEBEKE STATION (exclusive) in touch with the 2nd Division, the right resting on the CANAL between ZANDVOORDE and HOLLEBEKE in touch with the 2nd Cavalry Division. The point of junction between the 6th Cavalry Bde. and the 7th Division will be the stream which flows S. and E. between ZANDVOORDE and KRUISEIK.

2. The whole of the troops will work during the night in order to improve their trenches, wire entanglements being constructed in front and traverses built against enfilade fire, care being taken to render the trenches as invisible as possible by using straw and leaves to cover the fresh turned earth.

3. The 7th Cavalry Bde. will remain at VOORMEZEELE in general reserve.

4. Rendezvous for supplies as for today, unless further orders are received.

5. Corps Headquarters Report Centre at Hotel de VILLE, YPRES, from 7.30 a.m.

A.A.L. MONTGOMERY,
Brig.Genl. G.S.
IV Corps.

Issued at 3.30 p.m. by Cyclist to:-

   7th Division   ...   Copy No.2.
   3rd Cavalry Divn. ...   Copy No.3.

"A" Form.   Army Form C. 2121.
MESSAGES AND SIGNALS.   No. of Message _____

Prefix Code m.	Words.	Charge.	This message is on a/c of:	Recd. at _____ m.
Office of Origin and Service Instructions.	Sent			Date _____
	At _____ m.		Service.	From _____
	To _____			By _____
	By _____		(Signature of "Franking Officer.")	

TO { GOC 7th Division

Sender's Number	Day of Month	In reply to Number	
HRO 156	24/10/14		A A A

(1) You will retain your present position tomorrow

(2) Be careful to constantly patrol your front during the night and tomorrow push forward reconnaissances towards KOELBERG & TERHAND

(3) The 4th Corps will also be pushing out reconnaissances and a general forward movement the following day

From   GO PAK ? ?
Place   Hill de Ville   YPRES
Time   24/10/14   7.30 pm

The above may be forwarded as now corrected. (Z)   By motor cyclist

SECRET.

Copy No. 1

Operation Order No.6
by
Lieut.General Sir H.Rawlinson, Bart. C.V.O., C.B.
Commanding IV Corps.

Headqrs. IV Corps,
Hotel de VILLE,
YPRES,
25th October 1914.

1. The attack of the I Army Corps and 7th Divn. during the afternoon has progressed favourably. The former captured 2 guns while both took a number of prisoners.

The line held extends from ZANDVOORDE through KRUISTIK, ½ mile W. of BECELAERE, to a point about 1 mile E. of ZONNEBEKE STATION.

On the right flank of the 7th Divn. the 3rd Cav. Divn. holds the line HOLLEBEKE - ZANDVOORDE; on the left flank the French 18th Divn. prolongs the line through NIETWEMOLEN and to the N.W.

2. The advance will be continued on the 26th inst. in accordance with G.H.Q. Operation Order No. 40.

At 7 a.m. the I Corps attacks BECELAERE. The 7th Divn. will advance with its centre on MENIN Road to the 10th Kilometre and KOELBERG, in touch with the right of the I Corps, and will hold KRUISTIK as a pivot, and will dig in on any position gained. The I Corps will have a Reserve in rear of its right to fill up any gap which may occur between its right and the 7th Divn.

3. Special instructions are issued to the Corps Troops.

4. Reports to CHATEAU HOOGE at 4th Kilometre, N, of YPRES - MENIN Road after 7 a.m.

R.A.K.MONTGOMERY,

Brig. Genl. G.S. IV Corps.

Issued at 11.15 p.m. by cyclist

1. Opn Section
2. I A.C.
3. 3 Cavalry Division
4. VIIth Division
5. Corps Cavalry
6. RFC (MW)
7. RFC (NW)
8. DA & QMG

Copy No. 1

Operation Orders No.7
by
Lieut.General Sir H.Rawlinson, C.V.O., C.B.
Commanding 4th Corps.

Headqrs. 4th Corps,
THE CONVENT SCHOOL
MERVILLE
13th November 1914.

1. The 4th Corps will tomorrow at dusk take over the portion of the line from PONTLOGY to BRIDOUX, connecting up with the Indian Corps on the right and the 3rd Corps on the left.

2. The VIII Division will occupy the Section from PONTLOGY to the Road junction immediately South of the R of RUE PATILLON, the road running N.W. through this point forming the junction between the VII and VIII Divisions and being allotted to the former.

3. The billetting areas of the 20th, 21st and 22nd Infantry Brigades at METEREN, BAILLEUL and MERRIS, will be available for the Brigades of the 2nd Corps which will be relieved.

4. Railhead for supplies tomorrow BAS BOULOGNE.

5. H.Q. 4th Corps remains at MERVILLE.

R.A.K.MONTGOMERY, Br.Gen. G.S.

4th Corps.

Issued at 6 p.m.

H.Q. 4th Corps Copies Nos.1 & 2.
By cyclists to :-
    7th Division Copy No.3
    8th   -:-   -:- No.4
    2nd Corps   -:- No.5
    3rd   -:-   -:- No.6
    Indian Corps -:- No.7

SECRET. Copy No..........

ARMY OPERATION ORDER No. 8
BY
LIEUT.-GENERAL Sir H.S. RAWLINSON, BART, C.V.O., C.B.,
COMMANDING IVth CORPS.

Headqrs. IVth Corps.
13th December, 1914.

1. In accordance with orders issued from G.H.Q., the IVth Corps will "carry out active local operations with a view to containing the enemy now in their front, commencing Monday 14th instant at 8 a.m."

These active operations will commence with an increase of artillery fire and with such minor undertakings of an offensive nature as Divisional Commanders may be able to devise, but particularly at night.

During the daytime the infantry units in the fire trenches will establish a superiority of fire over the enemy by increasing the intensity of rifle and machine gun fire all along the front.

The artillery will open at irregular intervals during the day and keep under fire the enemy's trenches and such points in rear as have been already registered. They will also take on any targets that may be located by the aircraft if weather permits.

2. The 21st Infantry Brigade will march to NIEPPE on Monday (14th instant) so as to reach there by 2 p.m. and will report on arrival to G.O.C. 4th Division.

3. The 24th Infantry Brigade will be assembled in billets on the ESTAIRES - SAILLY road by 8 p.m. on Tuesday (15th inst.) and will form a reserve. The Brigade Staff should reconnoitre the road to NIEPPE and make themselves acquainted with the roads in that area.

4. The 1st Bn. South Staffordshire Regiment, from Corps Troops, will from to-day be attached to the 22nd Infantry Bde.

(Sd) R.A.K. MONTGOMERY, Brig.Gen.,
Issued at........ General Staff, IVth Corps.

7th Division copy No.7.   1.30 p.m. by cyclist orderly.
8th   ,,   ,,   8.   ,,   ,,
B.G.R.A.   ,,   6   By hand.
D.A.& Q.M.G.   ,,   5.   ,,
D.D.M.S.   ,,   4.   ,,

SECRET. *Only Office Copy –* Copy No.........

Operation Order No. 9
by
Lieut.-General Sir H. Rawlinson, Bt., C.V.O., C.B.,
Commanding IVth Corps.

Headqrs., IVth Corps,
MERVILLE.
18/12/14.

1. In conjunction with the attacks along the general front of the Allies the IVth Corps will at dusk deliver a vigorous attack against certain portions of the enemy's trenches.

2. Divisional Commanders will select their own points of attack, the objective for the 7th Division being the three lines of German trenches in their front, whilst the objective for the 8th Division will be NEUVE CHAPELLE and the forward trench covering it at one time held by British troops.

3. The units detailed for Corps Reserve are placed at the disposal of Divisional Commanders.

4. The amounts of ammunition which, in accordance with the order of the C.-in-C., may be expended are as follows:-

    13 pr. } as required.
    2.75 }

    18 pr. } 40 rounds per gun.
    4.7 inch)

    4.5 Howitzer - 20 rounds per gun.

but further instructions on this point will be issued later.

5. Reports to MERVILLE.

6. Arrangements are to be made for rapidly strengthening and preparing for defence the enemy trenches when captured, particularly against counter-attacks on the flanks.

R.A.K. MONTGOMERY, Brig.-Gen.,
General Staff, IVth Corps

Issued at

To 7th Division copy No.
To 8th Division copy No.
To 3rd Corps copy No.
To Indian Corps copy No.

WAR DIARY 3rd CAVALRY DIVISION.

17th October to 31st October.

To 22nd Nov 1914

October 17th.
ZONNEBEKE.

1.0 a.m. Troops were ordered to remain in billets on 17th October.

Heavy firing by infantry outposts to S.E. during the night (which was very dark). This was found later to have been caused by an officer (Wilts Regt.) returning by the wrong road from patrolling and resulted in his death. Casualties 3 wounded. This was a quiet day. Several prisoners were captured and 3 or 4 men in the 10th Hussars wounded.

October 18th.
ZONNEBEKE.

The 7th Cavalry Brigade was ordered to keep touch with French Cavalry advancing (i) 2 divisions on CLERCKE and WOEMEN (ii) 2 divisions E. of Foret d'HOUTHULST with right on line POELCAPPELLE - OOSTNIEUWKERKE. Also to send patrols to the ROULERS - STADEN road. The 6th Cavalry Brigade reconnoitred towards the ROULERS - MENIN road.

Casualties during the day 1 killed, 7 wounded, 1 wounded and missing, 1 injured.

October 19th.
ZONNEBEKE.

7.0 a.m. Marched to MOORSLEDE arriving there 7.45 a.m. The division was disposed as follows:- 6th Brigade at St.PEETER, 7th Brigade at 11th kilo ROULERS - MENIN road with one regiment on the line DE RUITER - LE CAVALIER; "C" Battery R.H.A. had joined the Division the previous evening, so a Battery was attached to each Brigade and remains so unless mention is made in this of other arrangements. "C" Battery went with 6th Brigade. Baggage was left at PASSCHENDAELE.

The 7th Division was to have attacked MENIN today and our mission was to protect its left flank.

MOORSLEDE.
10.0 a.m.

The 7th Cavalry Brigade got in touch with troops advancing from ROULERS and had to retire about ¾ mile to a better position. "K" Battery was brought into action N. of MOORSLEDE, but soon changed its position to a more concealed position. It was a lucky move, as the German guns had the range of direction of the first position pretty accurately. With minor changes of position, this Brigade maintained itself here until forced to fall back owing to the severity of gun fire.

Meanwhile the 6th Brigade got into touch at LEDEGHEM with some 150 to 200 of enemy - they soon captured it taking a certain number of bicycles. They suffered a certain number of casualties chiefly from Germans who had concealed themselves in the village.

12.45 p.m.

News is received from 4th Corps of the advance of large columns of the enemy. Some of these obliged the 7th Cavalry Brigade to withdraw to the high ground E. of MOORSLEDE. The 6th Cavalry Brigade were now somewhat isolated, and so General Byng ordered it to withdraw gradually on MOORSLEDE, an operation which its G.O.C. carried out most successfully. The 6th Brigade passed through the 7th and retired on PASSCHENDAELE. The 7th hung on as long as possible but was eventually obliged, owing to the severity of gun fire, to retire.

1.0 p.m.

4.0 p.m.

The Division billeted for the night:- H.Q. and 3rd Signal Squadron at ST. JULIEN; 6th Cavalry Brigade and "C" Battery at POELCAPPELLE; 7th Brigade, "K" Battery and remainder of Divisional troops at ZONNEBEKE. The French held PASSCHENDAELE.

Casualties during the day were:- Officers killed 3, wounded 7; men killed 17; wounded 27, missing 24, injured 5. Total 83.

October 20th.

October 20th.
ST. JULIEN.

5.0 a.m. The Division moved out in order to take up a defensive position in support of the French by 6 a.m. These latter troops were of a very poor description and let us in at least twice during the day. They crowd us out of billets too, so the sooner we say good bye to them the better.

The 7th Brigade was on the right, general line for 2 brigades - Railway ½ mile S. of PASSCHENDAELE to WEST ROOSE BEKE (both exclusive). Very sad to see large crowds of refugees moving back through our lines.

GOUDBERG.
8.0 a.m. Firing could be heard at an early hour from the direction of STADEN and about 8.0 desultory firing took place all along our line from the direction of MOORSLEDE and OOSTNIEUWKERKE.

8.45 a.m. This was succeeded by an artillery duel, which continued until about 12 noon. Reports from both Brigades were quite satisfactory until suddenly without any warning the French on the right and left of the 6th Cavalry Brigade retired, leaving its flanks and the left flank of the 7th exposed. This obliged the Division to withdraw to the line ZONNEBEKE - ST. JULIEN - POELCAPPELLE.

ST. JULIEN.
3.0 p.m. The fight appeared to die away and a move into billets was made. Suddenly it broke out again with great violence on
4.0 p.m. on both flanks. Enquiries showed that the French had retreated from POELCAPPELLE again exposing the flank of the 6th Cavalry Brigade. Somewhat heavy shell fire against this flank obliged us to swing it back to near LANGEMARCK. On our right it was found that a determined attack was being made on ZONNEBEKE. The O.C. there was consequently obliged to push out our transport and send it down the YPRES road for safety.

7.0 p.m. The H.Q. were established at ST. JULIEN and the arrival of the 2nd Coldstreamers helped to make us more secure in the centre.

Casualties:- Captain Cherrington, Royals, killed; Duke of Roxburghe, R.H.G., wounded; other ranks, killed 4, wounded 11, missing 3, injured 1. Total 21.

October 21st.
HOOGE.

After a disturbed night the H.Q. moved at 5.0 a.m. to HOOGE where the 6th Cavalry Brigade and Divisional troops were to rendezvous - the 7th Brigade to be at EKSTERNEST. The intention was that the 1st Corps was to push on towards ROULERS via PASSCHENDAELE and POELCAPPELLE and that the 3rd Cavalry Division was to protect its right flank, the 7th Division maintaining its position about ZONNEBEKE.

The enemy, however, were in considerably greater numbers than the G.O.C. 1st Corps appears to have imagined and we were forced to adopt an almost defensive role for the whole day.

7.30 a.m. The engagement commenced from the direction of GHELUVELT and soon spread along the whole front, the enemy bringing a large number of guns into action.

12 noon. G.O.C. 22nd Infantry Brigade asked for assistance as a portion of his line was reported hard pressed. This was furnished by 1 regiment of 7th Cavalry Brigade, the whole Brigade subsequently moving across to ZONNEBEKE.

1.30 p.m. Later as H.Q. were returning from a visit to H.Q. 22nd Infantry Brigade, news was received that the 2nd Cavalry Division was having a hard time to the south and so 6th Bde. was sent off as rapidly as possible to assist on their left flank, and occupied the two canal crossings N. of HOLLEBEKE.

5.0 p.m. Later an order to connect up with the 7th Division it was found necessary to move this Brigade to the line CHATEAU (½ mile E. of HOLLEBEKE) to ZANDVOORDE (both inclusive), the 3rd Cavalry Brigade taking over the crossings. H.Q. stayed at the CHATEAU on the YPRES - KEMMEL road and Divisional troops at VOURMEZEELE. A quiet night.

Casualties

Casualties were Capt. J. Montgomerie wounded, 1 man killed, 4 wounded and 1 missing.

October 22nd.
HOOGE.

The 7th Brigade and H.Q. moved here at 6:30 a.m., Divnl. Troops staying at VOURMEZEELE. After a quiet morning, 7th Brigade moved to KLEIN ZILLEBEKE and H.Q. and Divnl. Troops to ZILLEBEKE - a filthy village.

5 p.m.

In consequence of an intercepted message, it was thought possible that a strong German attack might be made against ZANDVOORDE. Accordingly 2 battalions 6th Infantry Brigade and a battery were sent up under General Fanshawe as a reserve.

8 p.m.

Heavy firing commenced about 8 p.m. but soon died away. Another short outburst took place about 12:30 a.m., otherwise the night was a quiet one.

The position was to be maintained by the 3rd Cavalry Division, i.e., one brigade on the front CHATEAU (near railway east of HOLLEBEKE) to ZANDVOORDE (both inclusive), one brigade at KLEIN ZILLEBEKE, each battery in action right and left of road behind front brigade; H.Q. and remainder Divnl. Troops ZILLEBEKE.

Casualties during the day were 5 men wounded.

October 23rd.
ZANDVOORDE.

H.Q. motored out at 6 a.m. A quiet morning until 8 a.m. The 129th Baluchis had partially relieved the 3rd Cavalry Brigade in their trenches. The infantry of 6th Inf. Brigade which came up last night rejoined its division this morning.

8 a.m.

Heavy firing commenced which hindred the relief of the 6th Cavalry Brigade by the 7th and necessitated keeping some of the 6th in the trenches until the evening.

Several aeroplanes and a captive balloon in view today - very difficult to distinguish hostile craft from friendly.

9:30 p.m.

A comparatively quiet day. Orders issued for 24th.

Casualties were 4 killed and 23 wounded.

October 24th.
ZILLEBEKE.

Enemy tried, apparently, to shell H.Q. last night but were always a little short. They succeeded in getting into the transport of the 7th Cavalry Brigade and killed some 15 - 20 horses.

The battle continued during the day in bursts of heavy firing followed by lulls.

9 a.m.

Reports received stated the Germans had broken through 7th Division; caused a certain amount of consternation in ZILLEBEKE, but troops from 1st Corps were moved up to deal with these, and there was no necessity for any of our Divn. to move. No move on 25th.

Division was placed under orders of Cavalry Corps Commander.

Night passed quietly. A few shells were fired at H.Q. at 3 a.m. and again at 5 a.m.

Casualties were 1 man killed and 19 men wounded.

October 25th.
ZILLEBEKE.

7th Brigade remained in trenches. 6th Brigade ready to move at 7 a.m. should the Corps Commander desire it.

The Division came under orders of Cavalry Corps from today. As soon as it was light there was a certain amount of firing from the direction of HOUTHEM and the trenches were shelled at intervals during the day, but nothing of importance occurred.

O.C. 4th Hussars constructed a second line of trenches and this was continued later by the 3rd Cavalry Division.

The task allotted to the division was that of keeping in touch with the right of the 7th Division, but the forward movement which had been anticipated did not take place, as the resistance encountered by the 1st Army Corps proved greater than had been expected.

Orders

Orders were received regarding the shortage of 13 pr. shells. The enemy would appear to have a considerable advantage over us in having plenty of ammunition which enabled them to search out hidden ground, etc.

Casualties during the day were Lieut. Sir R. Livinge killed, other ranks, killed 1, wounded 2, injured 1.

October 26th.
KLEIN ZILLEBEKE.

Considerable annoyance being caused by sniping from houses in ZANDVOORDE necessitates all the inhabitants being cleared out.

Nothing of importance occurred during the morning until orders were received for a general advance.

12:40 p.m. In accordance with this, operation orders were issued. The objective of the 3rd Cavalry Division was KORTEWILDE and the attack was to have been delivered by the 7th Cavalry Brigade supported by fire from 6th Cavalry Brigade, and R.H.A.

1:10 p.m. Unfortunately before the advance had started, a message was received from 7th Division saying that the front of the 20th Inf. Brigade had been broken in 3 or 4 places. G.O.C. saw G.O.C. 7th Cavalry Brigade and instructed him not to advance pending further orders from Cavalry Corps Commander who had been informed of what had happened. In the meantime the 7th Brigade was to assemble at the cross roads in KLEIN ZILLEBEKE.

2:25 p.m. A further message was received from General Capper confirming his first one and stating that his Division could not be counted upon to take any part in the proposed advance, and that the 20th Inf. Brigade was falling back to a line N. and S. through VELDHOEK.

3:20 p.m. Later General Capper asked the division to cover the flank of the retirement as far as possible; this message was not received until 4:10 p.m., and shortly afterwards General Byng sent for General Kavanagh and gave him verbal orders to demonstrate towards KRUISEIK with one regiment in order to draw attention off the retiring brigade.

5:25 p.m. Shortly afterwards a message was received from the Cavalry Corps confirming General Byng's action in support of the 7th Division.

In the meantime the demonstration ordered above had been initiated by the Royal Horse Guards. As the regiment advanced across the N.W. shoulder of the ZANDVOORDE ridge with Capt. Lord Alaiston Innes-Keer's squadron in front, it was met by heavy rifle and shell fire. Instead of turning N.E. towards KRUISEIK after crossing the ridge, as had been the intention, this fire caused the ~~sweds~~ squadron in front to swing towards the trenches occupied by the 6th Brigade. They then dismounted, leaving their horses under the cover of a hedge and farm, and engaged the enemy with rifle fire whilst the remainder of the regiment rapidly extended the line to the right.

The whole operation was carried out smartly and rapidly, and it is due to this that the casualties were comparatively small. At dusk the regiment was withdrawn to KLEIN ZILLEBEKE.

General Kavanagh brought to the G.O.C's. notice the gallantry of Colonel Wilson, Capt. Lord A. Innes-Kerr, and Trooper Nevin in particular, and his report was forwarded on by General Byng under a covering letter to the G.O.C. 4th Army Corps on the 27th instant.

6:15 p.m. Whilst the above operation was taking place, the G.O.C. proceeded to YPRES to see the G.O.C. 4th Army Corps and 7th Division to ascertain what the dispositions on the left of our line were to be for the night, as the withdrawal of the 20th Inf. Brigade had completely exposed our flank, and the information concerning the filling up of the gap which had thus been formed was not quite satisfactory or definite. General Capper assured the G.O.C. that the gap would be filled, but apparently difficulty was experienced in finding the necessary troops, and the linking up with our left had not been accomplished by midnight.

ZILLEBEKE.
7:30 p.m.

News of a possible hostile concentration on the YPRES - MENIN road reported by O.C. 10th Hussars did not lessen our anxiety for the safety of the 6th Brigade, though from subsequent investigation it appears probable that the men who were heard collecting were in reality stragglers from the 20th Inf. Brigade.

8:30 p.m.

In the meantime, the Cavalry Corps had been attempting the forward movement ordered in Operation Order No. 14 by G.O.C. Cavalry Corps, but the lateness of the hour prevented sufficient ground being made to make it worth while advancing the existing line of trenches, and the troops accordingly withdrew to the existing line.

The casualties during the day were :- Capt. Sir. F. Rose and Lieut. Turnor killed; other ranks, 4 killed and 10 wounded.

October 27th.
ZILLEBEKE.
12:30 a.m.

A staff officer from the 6th Cavalry Brigade reported that the gap between our left and the 7th Division had not been filled - in fact it appeared that the Gordons had been withdrawn at dusk from which hour our left was absolutely unprotected. It was accordingly decided to move the 7th Cavalry Brigade by 5 a.m. into a position of readiness N. of ZANDVOORDE and on the reverse slopes, and a staff officer was sent out to make the necessary arrangements and report on the situation from time to time.

2:30 a.m.

On reaching ZANDVOORDE, however, it was found that the gap had been filled about 2:30 a.m. and so the above orders were cancelled.

9: 0 a.m.

Owing to the fact that 3rd Cavalry Brigade were ordered to hold on to ZANDVOORDE and assist the advance of 1st Army Corps it was found impracticable to work in with the 3rd Cavalry Brigade by patrolling towards KORTEWILDE as had been intended.

Meanwhile the 2nd Cavalry Division reported all quiet in its immediate front and concerted measures with us for the linking up of a 2nd line of trenches in case of the necessity for firing up ZANDVOORDE arising.

General Byng informed 2nd Cavalry Division that there was no idea at present of withdrawing from ZANDVOORDE, and gave G.O.C. an outline of our dispositions.

The reconnaissances made by the 3rd Cavalry Brigade yesterday showed the country east of the canal, from the N.E. of KORTEWILDE to the CHATEAU to be clear of the enemy, and a quiet morning was passed.

12:15 p.m.

Our outposts were able to detect a maxim being brought up within 600 or 700 yards of the trenches and the construction of new trenches further to the south.

The offensive intended by the 1st Army Corps and 7th Division proceeded but slowly, considerable opposition being met with.

12:30 p.m.

The Cavalry Corps had now 1 regt. cavalry, 2 Battns. Infantry, and 1 battery R.H.A. in hand as a reserve.

2:20 p.m.

Considering the importance of ZANDVOORDE, G.O.C. did not consider the force at his disposal altogether adequate in case of a night attack, and so suggested that a small reserve of infantry should be placed in rear of our trenches.

At.

At the same time a rough sketch of our outposts was sent to the 3rd Cavalry Brigade in the hopes that they might be able to effect something against the enemy's trenches by enfilade.- direct fire producing no results against what was probably overhead cover. A section of howitzers would prove invaluable.

Nothing of importance occurred during the afternoon. During the evening a certain amount of re-organization of part of the troops took place - the 7th Division had been severely shaken and needed reforming. It was therefore decided to do away with the IVth Army Corps for the time being; the 7th Division to come under the 1st Army Corps and the 3rd Cavalry Division to remain with Cavalry Corps. At the same time a more contracted front was allotted to the 7th Division. This necessitated the extension of our line towards the left and this was effected during the night, our front being extended almost up to the Chateau E. of ZANDVOORDE.

No further developments occurred and at dusk our H.Q. moved back into ZILLEBEKE as usual.

The improvement of existing trenches and the construction of new ones (2nd and 3rd lines) was pushed on, civilian labour being employed to assist. It would seem that trenches must be on reverse slopes - field of fire giving way to protection against hostile shell fire. This was not the case with our trenches, but as any alteration would largely affect (and endanger) those of the 7th Division on our left, the idea of moving them back had to be given up for the time. The need for telephone communication, especially from Brigade H.Q. to the firing line, was acutely felt. It was most difficult to get back timely information in case of attack, any movement, especially by day, being fraught with considerable danger.

8.45 p.m. A report was received during the evening of a possible hostile concentration, but nothing came of it. The role allotted to this Division remained practically unchanged.

October 28th
ZILLEBEKE.

The usual night attack was made on our trenches but soon ceased and a quiet night was passed. The trenches were again shelled in the morning and at intervals during the day but nothing further of interest occurred until the afternoon when a pretty general bombardment of our lines took place.

Further attempts were made by the artillery of the 3rd Cavalry Brigade to enfilade enemy's trenches in our front but difficulty in observing and forwarding notes from the firing line impeded the value of this fire. The C.R.A. assisted very largely with the use of his telephones.

Touch was maintained during the day with the troops on our right and left, and 2nd and 3rd line trenches were pushed on. Arrangements were made for an Infantry Brigade to be at hand in case of serious night attack.

The trenches were shelled somewhat more steadily than usual, the 7th Cavalry Brigade reporting 118 howitzers as having fallen in and round the village of ZANDVOORDE. Otherwise the situation along ours and Cavalry Corps front remained unchanged.

11.15 p.m. G.H.Q. reported that reliable information of an attack at 5.30 a.m. had been received. Brigades (and 22nd Infantry Brigade) were informed of this.

October 29th.
KLEIN ZILLEBEKE.

Heavy firing commenced along the line at an early

hour

9.20 a.m. hour - later it was ascertained that this was probably an attack which was launched at 4.30 a.m. against the 4th and 5th Infantry Brigades.

7.0 a.m. The G.O.C. proceeded to ZANDVOORDE to discuss with C.R.E. 1st Corps the possibility of withdrawing our front trenches to the rear crest or reverse slopes of the ZANDVOORDE heights. It did not seem possible to accomplish this without considerable alterations being made in the 7th Division line.

10.0 a.m. News was received that the right of the 1st Infantry Brigade on the YPRES - MENIN road had given way slightly, but a determined counter-attack recovered the lost trenches. Later the enemy were successful in driving back the 7th Division and in occupying the high ground near KRUISEIK. Two counter-attacks were launched against this one by the 1st Army Corps and the other by the 7th Division. These two attacks were to converge on KRUISEIK. The 3rd Cavalry Div. was to protect the right flank of this latter attack, and the 6th Cavalry Brigade was detailed for the task. Cavalry Corps reserves of 5th Sqd. and 1 section R.H.A. was moved up to KLEIN ZILLEBEKE.

12 noon. About noon the situation was 7th Division counter-attacking on the line KRUISEIK - cross roads S.E. of GHELUVELT with the 6th Cavalry Brigade advancing to cover 7th Division's right flank, 10th Hussars on the right with their right flank pivoted on the CHATEAU ½ mile E. of ZANDVOORDE and protecting the 7th Division's right; the Royals in reserve. At the same time the 1st Army Corps counter-attacked in the direction of KRUISEIK from the N. of the YPRES - MENIN road. Our artillery covered this advance and was supported by "F" Battery R.H.A. and the 106th Battery R.F.A. It was hoped that this converging advance would round up the Germans who had broken the line S. of the YPRES - MENIN road. Considerable opposition was, however, met with, and the advance was slow and it was not till about 4.30 p.m. that the ZANDVOORDE attack succeeding in regaining the trenches which had been lost in the morning.

A further advance was stopped partly by the approaching dusk and partly owing to the fact that the advancing infantry were coming under the fire of their own guns. The advance had been helped considerably by fire action from 7th Cavalry Brigade and from the whole front of the 2nd Cavalry Division.

5.0 p.m. About this hour the position was:-

6th Cavalry Brigade, 10th Hussars at and in rear of the Chateau ½ mile E. of ZANDVOORDE, Royals in reserve. Our Cavalry in touch with right of 22nd Infantry Brigade, which together with the 21st Infantry Brigade had re-occupied the trenches lost in the morning. The 20th Infantry Brigade not quite up.

5.10 p.m. The 6th Cavalry Brigade were now ordered to retire to their previous billets, the 7th Cavalry Brigade remaining in the trenches and keeping in touch with the right of the infantry.

The enemy who seem to have been part of the XXIV Army Corps from LILLE appeared to have suffered severely. It was also reported that the amount of gun ammunition in the German parks was beginning to run short. Reliable information reported German reinforcements arriving from WARNETON.

October 30th.
ZILLEBEKE.
5.50 a.m. Several reports were received during the night of movements of the enemy towards the ZANDVOORDE position. When the
7.15 a.m. G.O.C. arrived within about ¾ mile from ZANDVOORDE in accordance with his customary visit to the outposts, a terrific fire broke out against the ridge and the ground in rear. This was so heavy that the forward movement up to BDE. Headquarters was abandoned and the G.O.C. returned to Divisional Headquarters at KLEIN ZILLEBEKE.

KLEIN ZILLEBEKE.
7.30 a.m. The 7th Cavalry Brigade were obliged to retire from the ridge to the 2nd line of trenches - the Greys and 3rd Hussars moving up to KLEIN ZILLEBEKE as a reserve. Casualties were
somewhat

somewhat considerable, some of the trenches being almost completely blown in.

8.30 a.m. By the time the 2nd Line had been occupied, the strength of the German advance became apparent and arrangements were made for holding the KLEIN ZILLEBEKE position. Although the latter had not such a good command and field of fire as the former - it was not so much exposed to hostile gun fire and very much more difficult to locate.

9.0 a.m. The enemy's main attack appeared to be directed against the Chateau, which was heavily shelled. This commanded a covered line of approach for the penetration of our line from which both our W. flank and the E. one of the 3rd Cav. Bde. could be assailed, and so became of very considerable importance.

10.0 a.m. By 10.0 a.m. the enemy were in possession of ZANDVOORDE ridge.

In the meantime all efforts to locate the enemy's artillery proved unsuccessful - it appeared to be from an easterly direction, possibly from AMERICA, and was extraordinarily well directed. The method with which areas were swept was most efficacious, though certainly costly in expenditure of ammunition.

10.5 a.m. The G.O.C. Cavalry Corps visited the scene and pointed out the necessity for a resolute defence - in fact the position was to be held at all costs.

The attack gradually spread towards the 3rd Cavalry Brigade and the 7th Cavalry Brigade had to withdraw through the 6th (which had occupied the 2nd line of trenches running from the near the Chateau, in front of KLEIN ZILLEBEKE Farm to about the BASSEVILLE creek) in order to refit and refill with ammunition - this Brigade then formed our reserve.

10.30 a.m. The attack on the Chateau was repulsed - along the rest of the line the enemy appeared to be relying on shell fire, comparatively few of his infantry being seen.

10.50 a.m. The situation to our left at this time was S. Staffords thrown back across the BASSEVILLE stream with the Gordons close behind, their object being to attack ZANDVOORDE from the west. This information was, however, received very late (1.10 p.m.).

11.15 a.m. Little change occurred during the next hour, at which hour it was hoped that the 2 battalions infantry referred to above would begin to make their arrival felt.

The Greys and 3rd Hussars were now despatched through the KLEIN ZILLEBEKE woods to endeavour to operate on our left flank and relieve the pressure on 6th Cavalry Brigade which was now very acute. This was to be in concert with the infantry counter-attack, and, at the same time, the 4th Hussars were to operate along the railway towards the Chateau. The latter was subsequently ordered to rejoin 3rd Cavalry Brigade (with "J" Battery) owing to raported heavy attack there. The 35th Brigade R.F.A. was also up in support, but observation of fire and selection of targets was very difficult owing to misty weather etc.

1.10 p.m. Soon after noon touch was gained with the 2nd Infantry Brigade, but news from the 2nd Cavalry Division did not increase the security of our position - our right flank becoming somewhat isolated and liable to enfilade; the 4th Hussars were accordingly sent to 3rd Cavalry Brigade.

2.30 p.m. With the advance of the Sussex and Gordons, the pressure on our left began to die away, but the enemy continued to shell the Chateau heavily and our detachment there was obliged to withdraw a short distance to the rear - this movement was also largely due to the evacuation of HOLLEBEKE by the 3rd Cavalry Brigade.

4.0 p.m. The pressure against the Chateau continued to be severe and 2 squadrons Life Guards were sent down both sides of of the railway to endeavour to relieve it. At the same time the attack on 2nd Cavalry Division necessitated the withdrawal of the Scots Greys and 3rd Hussars and a slight gap was formed in consequence between the left of our 6th Cav. Bde. and the right of the infantry.

5.15 p.m. General instructions were received from 1st Army Corps stating that the line to be held for the night ran from GHELUVELT past KLEIN ZILLEBEKE Farm to the shoulder of the canal.

That portion held by the 3rd Cavalry Division was to be taken over by 4th Infantry Brigade and the Division formed into a Mobile Reserve. This was accordingly done, the 7th Cavalry Brigade billetting at VERBRANDEN MOLEN, the 6th Cavalry Brigade near KLEIN ZILLEBEKE and H.Q. Division at ZILLEBEKE. B echelon transport remained parked on YPRES - KEMMEL road.

Casualties during the day were severe - a very large number being returned as missing.

October 31st.
KLEIN ZILLEBEKE.

In accordance with Cavalry Corps orders, the 3rd Cavalry Division formed a mobile reserve at KLEIN ZILLEBEKE, the 6th Cavalry Brigade being near the latter place and 7th Brigade at VERBRANDEN MOLEN.

About 8 a.m. the 6th Cavalry Brigade were moved to the vicinity of HOOGE and the 7th Cavalry Brigade to the cross roads 1½ miles E. of ZILLEBEKE. Within a short time of H.Q. leaving the latter place it was heavily shelled by howitzers and considerable damage done.

9.30 a.m.
Cavalry

About this hour General Allenby reported a heavy attack against WYTSCHAETE and the situation to be critical. He ordered as much of the Division as possible to move to his assistance. The 3rd Division, however, had now come under the orders of the G.O.C. 1st Army Corps who did not consider the situation justified this, and ordered the Division to remain as originally ordered. General Kavanagh had, however, seen this message en route and already marched, and he was allowed to proceed.

About noon the attack against our front in the direction of GHELUVELT became very severe and our infantry were forced to withdraw. At this time matters looked somewhat critical, the enemy having captured GHELUVELT, our infantry being reported as falling back.

The 6th Cavalry Brigade were, accordingly, ordered to take up a position along the road running to VELDHOEK, which they accordingly did, with "C" Battery on their left flank.

2.0 p.m. Various contradictory reports were received, the more pessimistic of which were borne out by the steady line of guns and wounded moving towards YPRES, but eventually it was officially notified (verbally) that the Guards Brigade had succeeded in recapturing the position about GHELUVELT.

3.30 p.m. Sir Douglas Haig rode up and ordered the 6th Cavalry Brigade to support the infantry (who were again advancing) on their right flank, and to clear the woods S. of VELDHOEK. This was rapidly carried out with complete success, the Germans retired in considerable disorder and only darkness robbed us of a more decisive success.

6.30 p.m. The two brigades were withdrawn for the night, the 6th Cavalry Brigade billetting near HOOGE and the 7th at VERBRANDEN MOLEN. Divisional H.Q. were at the junction road junction 1 mile N. of Y in YPRES.

From Col. Seeley
GS. (ANTWERP) Force
to CSO. BRUGES   10/10/14

"A" Form.   Army Form C. 2121
MESSAGES AND SIGNALS.   No. of Message _____

Prefix	Code	m.	Words	Charge	This message is on a/c of:	Recd. at 10.48 a.m.
Office of Origin and Service Instructions.						Date 10.10.14
Sent					10-10-14 Service.	From Mstr Comm
At ___ m. To ___ By ___					(Signature of "Franking Officer.")	By Lett army

To C.S.O.
    BRUGES.   ①

| Sender's Number | Day of Month | In reply to Number | AAA |

Following message received by me by telephone while waiting for a call from Head Quarters at Ostend Captain Lathbury Royal Marines found himself in communication with me and begged me to convey the message. There were no signs of the enemy at DEYNZE at 10 A.M. Captain Lathbury had returned to AELTRE from reconnoitring DEYNZE and was now proceeding to THIELT going on from there to BRUGES to report H.Q.

J E B Seely Col
General Staff

H.Q. BRUGES
10.10.14. 10.48 A.M.

From
Place
Time

The above may be forwarded as now corrected.   (Z)

Censor.   Signature of Addressee or person authorised to telegraph in his name.
* This line should be erased if not required.

From 2 L.G.
To 3 Cav. Bde.

10/10/14

"A" Form.   Army Form C. 2121.
MESSAGES AND SIGNALS.   No. of Message

Recd. at 9.45 a.m.
Date 10.10.14.
From (2)

TO { Third Cav. Div. Headquarters
     and Hotel du Commerce,
     BRUGES.

Sender's Number: 3 Day of Month: Oct 10th In reply to Number: BM 4 AAA

The country is clear of enemy as far as the V of RUDDERVOORDE on map. Am now going to V of SNEVEZEELE on map

From: Patrol 2nd LIFE GUARDS
Place: One mile South of name Ruddervoorde on main Road.
Time: 9 A.M.

(Z) J. McClintock Lt.

From 1st L.G.
To 7 Cav Bde

(3)

10/10/14

"A" Form. Army Form C. 2121.

MESSAGES AND SIGNALS.

Prefix ___ Code ___ m.	Words	Charge	This message is on a/c of:	Recd. at 10.43 a.m.
Office of Origin and Service Instructions	Sent			Date 10-10-14
	At ___ m.		Service	From
	To			
	By		(Signature of "Franking Officer.")	By

TO { 7th Cav Bde (2)

* Sender's Number	Day of Month	In reply to Number	AAA
Two	tenth		

Patrol	from	THOUROUT	reports	place
clear	of	enemy	and	occupied
by	BELGIANS	AAA	BELGIAN	officer
reports	following	at	YPRES	25
GERMAN	cyclists	and	cavalry AAA	at
DIKEBUSCH	few	GERMANS	on	road
bridge AAA	at	KEMMELL	and	NEUVE
EGLISE	large	force	of	GERMANS
AAA	LILLE	is	reported	to
be	bivouacked	by	the	enemy

From 1st L.G.
Place LOPHEM CASTLE
Time 9.15 a.m.

The above may be forwarded as now corrected.
(Z) [signature] Lt & Adj 1st L.G.
Censor. Signature of Addressor or person authorised to telegraph in his name
*This line should be erased if not required.

3662 M. & Co. Ltd. Wt. W839/549—100,000. 6/14. Forms C2121/10

Royals
To 3 Cav Dn

10/10/14

(4)

113

From: O.C. Officer's Patrol, sent out by O.C.
Royal Dragoons, 6th Cav. Bde.

To: G.O.C. 3rd Cav. Divn. Hd Qrs
Hôtel de Commerce, BRUGES

Ref: Map N.W. Europe
R.F. Sheet 1.
1/250000

THOUROUT
10/10/14

(4)

Left VARSSENAERE at 6-30 A.M. and have reached THOUROUT without seeing any sign of enemy. This town is quiet and business proceeding as usual. Belgian troops occupy the town. A Belgian officer informs me that the Germans are holding a line from YP YPRES to COURTRAI & that the country N. of this line is held by the Belgians. I am proceeding to ROULERS

W.P. Browne
2/Lt
O.C. Cav. Patrol
The Royal Dragoons

Time 9-40 A.M.

Received 12.30 P.M.

From Royals
To 3 Cav Dn

10/10/14

115

From: O.C. Cav. Patrol, The Royal Dragoons
To: G.O.C. 3RD CAV. DIVN
   HD. QRS
   HOTEL DE COMMERCE
   BRUGES

2.5 P.M.

THOUROUT
2.5 P.M.
10/10/14

Have completed reconnaissance as far as ROULERS. No sign of enemy. ROULERS strongly held by Belgian troops — town is quiet and business as usual. The O.C. Belgian troops in ROULERS informed me that no German troops were N. of LEDEGHEM (7 miles S. of ROULERS) —

W P Browne
Lieut
The Royal Dragoons
O.C. Cav. Patrol.

Time 2.5 P.M.

From 3rd Cav Bde
To IV Corps

10/10/14

"A" Form.   Army Form C. 2121
MESSAGES AND SIGNALS.

TO { Genl Hd. Qrs.
     4th Army.
     OSTEND

AAA

Ca. 8 Oct. 10=
THOUROUT, RUDDERVOORDE
DEYNZE reported clear of
the enemy at 10-0 a.m.
to-day.

Repeated to G.O.C. 7th Division.

Kavanagh
Gen. Staff
3rd Cav. Div.

From Ga. Hotel du Commerce
Place BRUGES.
Time 10-55 am

From Cap Thomas RE
To GOC 3 Cav Bde (?)
17/10/14

"A" Form. Army Form C. 2121
MESSAGES AND SIGNALS.   No. of Message _____

Prefix ___ Code ___ m.	Words	Charge	This message is on a/c of:	Recd. at 4.45 m.
Office of Origin and Service Instructions.		Sent		Date 11.X
	At ___ m.		Service.	From
	To			By
	By	(Signature of "Franking Officer.")		

TO { General Staff.

| Sender's Number | Day of Month | In reply to Number | AAA |

In	communication	with	an	officer
of	the	General	Staff	of
General	Rawlinson	at	Ostend	
delivered	message	that	General	Byng
was	going	round	the	on to O.C.
for	two	hours	and	required
services	of	three	Belgians	for
assistance	in	billeting &	Reply Message	was
acknowledged	and	answer	given	that
it	would	be	alright	for
General	Byng	to	arrange	for
the	three	Belgians	himself	

From Cpl F E Thomas RE
Place Telephone Hotel de Ville
Time 4.22

From RHG
To 3 Cav Bde

11/10/14

11.10.14

"A" Form.
MESSAGES AND SIGNALS.

TO: 3rd Cav. Div.
THOUROUT

Day of Month: October 11th

AAA

COURTRAI clear of all troops. Enemy last seen there October 8th estimated fifteen hundred. The line of the Canal INGELMUNSTER - WIELSBEKE - OLSENE held at all crossings by Belgian troops. No enemy north of the canal in this neighbourhood. From inhabitants a few of the enemy reported to be at AELBEKE. Heavy firing heard from South estimated distance fifteen twenty miles.

From: Captain H. Brassey - R.H.Gds.
Place: INGELMUNSTER
Time: 12.30 p.m.

(Z) H. Brassey, Capt.

From R.M.A
To   3 Cav Bde

11/10/14

11th October 1914   he 1 10 a.m.
O.C. Armed Motors
    POELCAPELLE
To: G.O.C. 3rd Cavalry Division
    THOROUT

I proceeded to ROULERS, and at the Gendarmerie, I was told that the villages, mentioned in Para. 2 of Special Instructions for Armoured Motor Car reconnaissance, were occupied by Belgian Gendarmes.
A Belgian Armoured Car accompanied us from ROULERS
At these villages no Germans have been seen at all.
I propose reconnoitring towards YPRES via BOESINGHE, and ascertaining what force, if any, is at YPRES.

Williams
Captain R.M.A
O.C. Armed Motors

Recd. 12.15.
  11/X/14

From 3rd Cav. Div.
To IV Corps

12/10/14

"A" Form.　　　　　　　　　　　Army Form C. 2121
MESSAGES AND SIGNALS.　　No. of Message

TO { D.A.G.
4th Corps
OSTEND.

9. a. 13　Oct. 12th
Your note received at ROULERS
at 3.15 p.m.
3rd Cav. Div. H.Q. left THOUROUT
at 10.30 a.m. this morning.
I have instructed N.C.O. i/c patrol
to report to Burgomeister THOUROUT.
The Chateau is in the bend of the
road (OSTEND - THOUROUT) about 1½
miles S.E. of the M in ICHTEGHEM
(Ref. to "Map N.W. Europe).
The Burgomeister said he would
make all arrangements when
required.

W.A. Atherstonhaugh
Genl Staff Maj.
3rd Cav Div

From 3rd Cav. Div.
Place ROULERS
Time Oct. 12th - 3-20 p.m.

From 7th Cav. Bde
To 3rd Cav. Div.

12/10/14

"A" Form. Army Form C. 2121.

MESSAGES AND SIGNALS. No. of Message_____

Prefix_____ Code_____ Words_____ Charge_____ W D   Recd. at 4.50 p.m.
Office of Origin and Service Instructions.   This message is on a/c of: Date_____
Sent At_____m.   Service.   From_____
To_____ By_____   (Signature of "Franking Officer.")   By_____

TO { THIRD CAV DIV
     ROULERS

Sender's Number | Day of Month | In reply to Number | AAA
*BM 5 | Twelfth | |

Have been in occupation of line this afternoon AAA Received only negative reports AAA Am withdrawing to billeting area at 6 o'clock and will inform you details.

From SEVENTH CAV BDE
Place DE GOD
Time 4.22

The above may be forwarded as now corrected. (Z) Kerrell Capt.

From 7th Cav Bde
To 3 Cav Bde

(27)

13/10/14

"A" Form. Army Form C. 2121.
MESSAGES AND SIGNALS.

13-10-14

TO: THIRD CAV DIV
GHELUVELT

* BM 9   Thirteenth   AAA

Arrived MENIN all clear intel touts report no Germans here for some time AAA Met patrol seven strong near GHELUVELT which retired towards Werviq AAA Horses have done 27 miles AAA Hope we can go into billets GHELUWE area

Received 5.20

From: SEVENTH CAV BDE
Place: MENIN
Time: 3.16 pm

G. Hull Capt

From 7th Cav Bde
To 3 Cav Bde

13/10/14

Army Form C. 2121.
MESSAGES AND SIGNALS.

TO: THIRD CAV DIV YPRES

Sender's Number: BM7
Day of Month: Thirteenth

My advanced guard reports patrol of twenty enemy at GHELUVELT AAA Right flank guard also reports in touch with enemy's detail ~~reported~~ patrols at ZILLEBEKE AAA proceeding to MENIN

Recd 2pm

From: SEVENTH CAV BDE
Time: 1.20 pm

From 1 L.G.
To 3 Cav Bde

13/10/14

"A" Form.
MESSAGES AND SIGNALS.
Army Form C. 2121.

Prefix	Code	Words	Charge	This message is on a/c of:	Recd. at 12.55 a.m.
Office of Origin and Service Instructions.		Sent At 9.10 a.m. To By		Service. (Signature of "Franking Officer.")	Date From By

TO: III Cav Bde

Sender's Number	Day of Month	In reply to Number	AAA
1	13th		

I have a squadron at
the Railway crossing on main
ROULERS—MENIN Road and sending
out 2 patrols one section
each the one on ROULERS—ISEGHEM
road and the other on
ROULERS—MOORSLEDE road

9.25
Copy forwarded to
our Patrols have met
with R.C. ..... one on
MOORSLEDE ... and one on
.... of Patrols have
....

From: H Goodson Capt 1st Life Guards
Place: Rly Crossing S of ROULERS
Time: 9.5 a.m.

To 3rd Cav. Div.

13/10/14

"A" Form.
MESSAGES AND SIGNALS. W.

Army Form C. 2121.
No of Message 13 X

TO: III Cav Div

Sender's Number	Day of Month	In reply to Number	AAA
3	13th		

3 Sqn received INGLEMUNSTER
and am patrolling roads running
north and east cyclist company
west all clear MEULEBE and
was OOSTROOSEBEKE clear
at 4 P.M.

From: H Gosram
Place: INGLEMUNSTER
Time:

GS/6.

To Headquarters
3rd Cav. Div.

Ref. Map 1/100000

I beg to report that in accordance with your instructions I left WIELTJE about 2.15 pm today with the 2nd Life Guards and Royal Horse Guards in order to verify the report received from inhabitants of the presence of German troops in OOSTNIEUWKERKE. I was accompanied by an armoured Belgian Motor. When I arrived at WESTROOSEBEKE I received a report from Lt Sir P. Brocklehurst that his patrol had been fired at by a machine gun on the WESTROOSEBEKE — HOOGLEDE road about 1½ miles N.E. of WESTROOSEBEKE. It was very foggy and difficult to see. I sent two squadrons to advance South of the road, and subsequently supported them with the third Squadron (2nd Life Gds). Meanwhile I had sent one troop and the armoured motor car up the road, and I was informed that the maxim had retired, but that the road was held. I then sent Col Wilson about 4 oclock with 2 Sqdns of the Blues to work up the road and North of it. About 4.30 I had formed the opinion that the enemy's infantry were holding a line running from NW to SE about ½ mile SW of OOSTNIEUWKERKE. My Squadrons had made progress, killing & wounding about a dozen of the enemy in the farm houses south of the road. But as it was evident that the enemy had more strength than I could deal with alone, and as it was too dark to see, I ordered the troops to withdraw about 4.30 pm. As far My casualties have not yet been reported. Lt Duff 2nd Life Guards is missing and believed to be killed. I have one or two men wounded and three horses killed.

CMKavanagh
B.Gen.

PASSCHENDAELE
10 pm. 16th Oct

Subject:- Report.   WD 16/X   ...16.

From:-   Major-General Hon. J.H.G. Byng, C.B., M.V.O.,
         Commanding 3rd Cavalry Division.

To:-   The General Officer Commanding,
         4th Army Corps.

                                    ZONNEBEKE,
                                        17th October, 1914.

Sir,

I have the honour to report that the 3rd Cavalry Division advanced yesterday from WYTSCHAETE towards the FORET D'HOUTHULST.

On arriving at WESTROOSEBEKE, the General Officer Commanding 7th Cavalry Brigade found a force of the enemy in occupation of a line running from N.E. to S.E. about ½ mile S.W. of OOSTNIEUWKERKE.

A skirmish ensued about 3-30 p.m. between the 2nd Life Guards and Royal Horse Guards (2 squadrons) and the enemy, during which the enemy lost about a dozen in killed and wounded.

Eventually, owing to the lateness of the hour, the General Officer Commanding 7th Cavalry Brigade was obliged to withdraw his troops to billets.

I regret to say that Lieutenant Sir E. Duff, 2nd Life Guards, was killed, and four men were wounded.

                        I have the honour to be,
                              Sir,
                          Your obedient Servant,

                          (Sgd) J. Byng

                                    Major-General,
                    General Officer Commanding 3rd Cavalry Division.

From GOC IV Corps
To Gen. Byng
3rd Cav. Bde

(1) (3)

17/10/14

"A" Form.   Army Form C. 2121.
MESSAGES AND SIGNALS.   No. of Message _____

| Prefix ___ Code ___ m. | Words. | Charge. | This message is on a/c of: | Rec'd. at 9.258 m. |
| Office of Origin and Service Instructions. | Sent At ___ m. To ___ By ___ | | _____ Service. (Signature of "Franking Officer.") | Date ___ From ___ By 9.9. ___ |

TO { Gen Byng

| Sender's Number | Day of Month | In reply to Number | AAA |
| H.R.O. 30 | Oct. 17th | | |

Your message of last night reporting the actions at OOSTNIEUWKERKE received and you must not expect the 1st Belgian Cav. Div. to do much aaa They have been ordered to go forward to the E edge of the Forest of D'HOUTHULST in conjunction with the 7th French Cav. 7 Div. which moves on the West of the Forest to CLERCKEN aaa (2) there movements are carried out successfully it will reestablish the line on your left but you should keep touch with and watch their progress as I am not very confident that they will complete their movements today

From
Place
Time

Cont/
from G.O.C. IV Corps
to Gen. Byng
3 Cav Div

(2)   37

17/10/14

"A" Form. Army Form C. 2121.
MESSAGES AND SIGNALS.

aaa You are force should maintain its present position sending air reconnaissance towards STADEN and ROULERS aaa let me know later what line the enemy is on and whether he is entrenching aaa The Belgians & French successfully defended the passage at DIXMUNDE yesterday aaa Air reconnaissances are going on over ROULERS THOUROUT OSTEND ROUTE to this morning aaa cannot you get a wire through to me

From: A.C. IV AC
Place: POPERINGHE
Time: 8 AM

From 22 I. Bde
To 3 Cav. Dn.

(39)

17/10/14

"A" Form.   Army Form C. 2121
MESSAGES AND SIGNALS.   No. of Message

Reed. at 10.30 a.m.
Date 17.X

TO 3rd. Cav. Div.   (39)

Sender's Number: BM 2   Day of Month: Oct. 17   AAA

The G.O.C Eleventh Div. is very anxious to know what is taking place to the north AAA Can you possibly give me any information.

From: 22nd. Inf. Bde.
Place: ZONNEBEKE
Time: 11.10 a.m.

G W James Capt.
BM.

6. Cav Bde.   17/10/14
3 Cav. Dn

W.D. 1/17.X/   Recd. 6-30 pm
        ZONNEBEKE.
          17. X. 14.

General Staff
   3rd Cavalry Division

   The Squadron 10th Hussars, sent
out this morning to watch the
MENIN - ROULERS Road, has now
returned. They report the country
between MOORSLEDE and this road
as clear. A patrol of 30 Uhlans
was seen at 4 p.m. going north
on this road.
                    B. D. Fisher
                    B.M. 6. C.B.
6.35 p.m.

3rd Cav. Div.   17/10/14   (1)

Reference 1/100,000 sheets OSTEND & TOURNAI.

INTELLIGENCE

The following is the intelligence up to 12 noon to-day:-

__Belgian dispositions__. (1) Belgian cavalry division is holding the line E. of the FORÊT D'HOUTHULST, from WYNSWEGEN incl. to HOUTHULST exclusive, with a detachment of cyclists entrenched at SCHAEP BAILLIE.

A force consisting of cavalry and guns is at STADENBURG from where they have been shelling German columns between STADEN and ZARREN.

The 3rd Division is reported to have repulsed a German attack on DIXMUDE yesterday.

__French dispositions__. (2) The French cavalry corps (4 and 7 Divisions) are on the line HOUTHULST - CLERCKEN, whence they intend to operate against the German columns on the STADEN - ZARREN road. A French Territorial Brigade is at YPRES and POPERINGHE.

17/10/14

The French and Belgian Cavalry are in touch with one another.

British dispositions (3) The 6th Cavalry Brigade is at the cross roads 2 m S. of NIEUWMOLEN. The 7th Cavalry Brigade is at PASSCHENDAELE with a detachment at WESTROOSEBEKE.

Both Brigades have reconnaissance squadrons watching the MENIN ROULERS road.

German dispositions (4) The following information has been obtained from reliable sources:—
MENIN and KORTRYK. Large forces of all arms are reported at and between these places. MENIN is strongly entrenched.
REZELFERE is entrenched and held by German infantry, strength unknown.
VELDHOEK found unoccupied this morning.
ROULERS. Reported to have been occupied by about 300 infantry, who will no doubt have departed totally short of cavalry.
OOST NIEUWKERKE. Held by about 200 German infantry, a few cavalry, machine guns. This force entrenched. This force may have retired by now.

17/10/14

SLAYHAAGE Infantry and guns have been holding this place for the last 24 hours.

Summary:- (1) Large and continuous movement of German troops of all arms have been taking place during the last 36 hours towards the N.W and N. of ROULERS from the direction of MENIN and ISEGHEM.

The troops state they are bound for BRUGES and OSTENDE. They are reported to be Landwehr troops, and to be well clothed and fed; the men are in excellent spirits, and are always preceded by their bands when on the march.

J.M Cardet
J.P.
G.S.

ZONNEBEKE
October 17. 1914
12 noon.

From 7th Dn.
To 3rd Cav. Bn.

18/10/14

"A" Form.   Army Form C. 2121
MESSAGES AND SIGNALS.   No. of Message _____

TO { Third Cav.
      Zonnebeke

Sender's Number: S-52   Day of Month: Eighteenth   In reply to Number: **AAA**

(57)

Has the Armoured Train Commander Robinson. R.N. been seen this morning?

From: Seventh Dv.
Place: 5 Kilos. Ypres-Menin Road.
Time: 9 a.m.

From 7th Cav. Bde
To 3rd Cav. Div

18/10/14

"A" Form.   Army Form C. 2121.
MESSAGES AND SIGNALS.

Prefix	Code	m.	Words	Charge		This message is on a/c of:		Recd. at 10.30 a.m.
Office of Origin and Service Instructions.			Sent					Date
			At ___ m.				Service.	From
			To					By
			By			(Signature of "Franking Officer.")		

TO — THIRD CAV DIV
ZONNEBEKE

Sender's Number	Day of Month	In reply to Number	AAA
BM 3	Eighteenth		

Brigade arrived fourteen & readiness
point eighteen 1½ mile due East
of VELDHOEK AAA No air
of French Horse Arty officers
in VELDHOSEREKE to be with
them AAA First Life Guards
heard on heavy & Bowreau
Cavalry on mile N E of
PASSCHENDAELE 7.30 am this
morning

From SEVENTH CAV BDE
Place P— ZY
Time 10 am

From
OC Squadron
To OC
Royal Dragoons

O.C.
Royal Dragoons   Rec'd 11.20

Find a German Patrol at
about 12 EAST of Moorslede
on my arrival. They fired
five shots about in the direction
of DADIZEELE.

A report from my Patrol at X roads
2 miles S.E. of MOORSLEDE
states that villagers say that
                took road to
16 Germans MENIN
out of at 6 AM and
2 have road to ROUGERS.

Have found 2 Germans wounded
here. One Badly 2 the other
only in the finger. Think the latter
should be brought in. The leading
after a Bayonet
Please
that he wanted one. They are
at present in the convent
MOORSLEDE. Patrol leaving here
8-30 AM

To. 3rd Cav. Bde
From 4th Hussars

19/10/14

"A" Form.   Army Form C. 2121.
MESSAGES AND SIGNALS.

TO: G.O.C. 3rd Cavalry Division

Sender's Number: N.H. 44   Day of Month: 19.X.14   AAA

Can you please let me know your probable dispositions as have been ordered to keep touch with you AAA 22nd Infantry Brigade have been ordered to fall back to line STROOIBOOMHOEK — TERHAND and we have been ordered to protect the northern flank of this movement AAA Am now on road just south of WATERDAMHOEK AAA Orders just received to retire on ZONNEBEKE tonight

From: O.C. N.H.
Place: Farm south of WATERDAMHOEK

From 3rd Cav Div.
To IV Corps.   20/10/14

WD 2/20.10

GOC. IV ad.
Ga 64. Oct 20th
The French have retired from WESTROOSEBEKE and their Territorial Infantry have left their trenches at PASSCHENDALE

They have still one Regt of Cuirassiers one Battery & some cyclists on my line but all the rest have gone.

I think I can still hold on, as my men are well entrenched. But the shelling is at present heavy - and enemy appear to be coming on from the direction of OOSTNIEUWKERKE.

If forced to retire. I intend to take up line LANGEMARCK - ZONNEBEKE.

J Byng
3rd CD

N of G in GOUDBERG
9-50am/20/X/14

From 6 Cav. Bde
To 3 Cav. Div.

22/10/14

11.40

ZANDVOORDE
22. X. 14

General Staff
3rd Cav. Division

The Chateau was taken
by the Royal Dragoons at
9.30 A.M.

B. J. Fisher
B.M. 6 CB

11 A.M.

From 6 Cav Bde
To. 3 Cav Bde

22/10/14

Recd. 11.40 am.
ZANDVOORDE
22.X.14

General Staff
3rd Cav. Div.

Your GA. 73 stop
Am holding Scots Guards trenches
to the S. and W. of ZANDVOORDE.
AAA. Am in possession of CHATEAU,
which is held by one squadron
AAA. There is a certain amount
of shell fire but very little rifle
fire AAA. Under present circumstances
can hold my position, but in
the event of enemy developing a
strong attack, I should find it difficult as
I have only one squadron in reserve,
as all my men are up in the trenches.

Ernest Makins
Brig. Genl.
6 C. B.

11.20 AM

From IV Corps
to 3 Cav. Bde

22/10/14

"A" Form. Army Form C.2121
MESSAGES AND SIGNALS.

TO 3rd Cavalry Division

Sender's Number: AA 89 74
Day of Month: 22nd
AAA

Colonel Huguet announces that a LAISSEZ-PASSER on pink paper bearing the name of M. V. VALTER, Divisional Commissaire of Police and the number 185 has gone astray and may have fallen into the hands of the enemy AAA Anyone presenting this pass should be at once arrested.

Captain G.S.

From: 4th Corps (Intelligence)
Place: YPRES
Time: 12.10 pm

From Cav Corps
To 3rd Cav Div.

25/10/14

"A" Form. Army Form C. 2121.
MESSAGES AND SIGNALS.

TO: 3rd Cav Div Tyke

Sender's Number	Day of Month	In reply to Number	AAA
G.C. 25	twenty fifth	nil	

In view of the recent large expenditure of 13 Pr Q F Ammunition G O C's Divisions must exercise strict supervision that no target is engaged unless its tactical importance warranted AAA The ordinary daily expenditure must not except in the case of an attack at close range exceed 30 (thirty) rounds per gun a day AAA Artillery fire should be reserved for the following targets Lines attacking Bodies of troops in close formation Guns limbered up or visible in action enemy AAA

Cont

From Cav Corps
To. 3rd Cav Bde

25/10/14

"A" Form.   Army Form C. 2121.
MESSAGES AND SIGNALS.   No. of Message_____

Prefix ___ Code ___ m.	Words	Charge	This message is on a/c of:	Recd. at ___ m.
Office of Origin and Service Instructions	Sent			Date
	At ___ m.		Service	From
	To			
	By		(Signature of "Franking Officer.")	By

TO

| * Sender's Number | Day of Month | In reply to Number | AAA |

Trenches	behind	cover	should	be
very	sparingly	resorted	to	while
engaging	areas	and	sniping	at
small	groups	of	men	must
not	be	permitted	AAA	Please
acknowledge				

From Cav Corps
Place
Time   3 5 P M

The above may be forwarded as now corrected.   (Z)
                                        Censor.   Signature of Addressor or person authorised to in his name

*This line should be erased if not required.

From Cav. Corps
To 3rd Cav. Bde

25/10/14

"A" Form. Army Form C. 2121.
MESSAGES AND SIGNALS.

TO: 3rd Cav. Div.

Sender's Number: G.b.60
Day of Month: 25

Following message received from 1st Corps timed 1 p.m. AAA The infantry of the 1st Corps will advance to the attack at 3 p.m. AAA The 7th Division has arranged to keep touch with right of 1st Corps AAA Can you co-operate on the right of the 7th Division message ends AAA You will keep in touch with right of 7th Division AAA

Addressed 3rd Cav Div. repeated 2nd Cav. Div.

From: CAV. CORPS
Time: 2-42 p.m.

A. M. Henley Capt GS

From 4th Hussars
to 3rd Cav. Div.   25/10/14

3 Cav. Div.   WD 2/25 X

② 25/10/14

We are having trenches dug as shown in red on sketch to provide against any possible retirement from Hollebeke or from your Chateau: or to catch Germans should they break through. If you could have some prepared about X and Y this second line would be complete?

K Howells
Maj.
10.20 a.m.   4 Hrs

4th Hussar Billets
and trenches covering Canal Bridge.   12 ↑

Verbranden Molen

H.Q. 6th C.B.

B Sq.

Klein Zillebeke

H.Q. 4th Hrs

X   Y

C Sq.

A Sq.

Foot Bridge

Canal

Chateau HQ 3 C.B.   Hollebeke   Chateau

From 2nd Cav Div.
To. 3rd Cav Div.   26/10/14

G.O.C. 3rd Cav. Divn.   86
                      9.30 pm
W.G. 296 Oct. 26.   26

Our attack this evening did
not succeed in making enough
ground to make it worth while
advancing our present line
and it was consequently ordered
to withdraw at nightfall.

The result of the attack showed that
the ~~Lock~~ eastern side of
the canal was unoccupied as
far South as the Lock & patrols
approached Kortewilde were not
shot at.
~~Patrols up~~
The enemy are believed to be
somewhere about the last
E of KORTEWILDE.
We are reconnoitring tomorrow morning
on both sides of the canal towards
Lock & Kortewilde: will you push
patrols towards last E of
Kortewilde, and let us know
the result?
Kemmel   2nd Cav Divn
7.30 pm.   W H Greenly.

From 6th Cav Bde
To 3rd Cav. Bde
26/10/14

"A" Form. Army Form C.
MESSAGES AND SIGNALS. No. of Message_____

TO: General Staff
3rd Cavalry Division

AAA

1. The Field Squadron R.E. with their tools etc would be very useful to us tonight in repairing the trenches etc, if they could be sent up tonight.

2. O.C. 10th Hussars reports that enemy appear to be massing on MENIN - ZANDVOORDE Road opposite Gordons and 10th Hussar trenches AAA The maxim gun 10th Hussars has been knocked out and Capt ROSE and LIEUT TURNOR killed, and several men killed and wounded AAA O.C. 10th Hussars anticipates attack tonight and I anticipate consider that support is necessary AAA Trenches are already built for supports.

From:
Place:
Time: 7.30 p.m.

Ernest Makins
Brig General

From 6 Cav. Bde
To 3rd Cav. Dn.

26/10/14

"A" Form.
Army Form C. 2121
MESSAGES AND SIGNALS.

TO: General Staff 3rd Cavalry Division

AAA

G.O.C. 7th Division has just left here; he had a short time previously seen Sir D. Haig. The situation is as follows: the 1st Army is attacking in the direction of BECELAERE; the 7th Division (less Gordon Highlanders) is on a line VELDHOEK - E. of R. BASSEVILLE - a point ½ mile N.W. of ZANDVOORDE. AAA The Gordons still remain in their trenches with their left en l'air, but General Capper is temporarily filling up the gap for the night with two companies Welsh Fusiliers.

From: B.J. Probyn B-M. 6 C.B.
Place: ZANDVOORDE
Time: 5.45 pm 26.x.14

From 3rd Cav Dv.
to IV Corps   27/10/14

G.O.C. W.D. 9/26.X   19
IV A.C.

I forward this report of Br. Gen. Kavanagh on
the action of the Royal Horse Guards.

During the afternoon of the 26th Oct., I became
aware that some units of the 7th Div'n in the
neighbourhood of KRUISEIK had been driven
from their trenches, & that the situation in that
part of the field was somewhat critical.

With a view of diverting the fire of the hostile
Artillery from our retiring Infantry — I ordered
Gen'l Kavanagh to send forward one Regiment to
demonstrate towards KRUISEIK.

This they did, as described by Gen'l Kavanagh,
& to judge by the diversion of the fire of the
enemy's guns on to this Regiment, I cannot
help thinking some relief was given.

I consider myself justified in bringing to
notice the gallantry displayed by Col. Wilson,
Lord Alastair Innes Kerr, Tr Nevin, and the whole
Regiment.

(sd) J. Byng, Brig Gen
             3rd Cav Div.

KLEIN ZILLEBENE
27. X. 1914.

From 7th Cav. Bde.
To 3rd Cav Div.

27/10/14

W.D. 8/26 X

To G.O.C.
3rd Cav. Div.

17

KLEIN ZILLEBEKE.
Oct 27" 14.

Sir,

I have the honour to report that in accordance to instructions issued verbally to me by you, I ordered the Royal Horse Guards to make a demonstration yesterday afternoon in the direction of KRUISIK.

At 4.50 p.m. the Regt. advanced, with Capt. Lord Plowster Innes Ker's Squadron in front over the S.W. shoulder of the ZANDVOORDE Ridge, with the object of turning N.E. after crossing it towards KRUISIK.

On arrival on the Ridge the leading Squadron was met by a heavy shell & rifle fire, & swung to its left towards the trenches held by a Squadron 1st Life Guards. They then dismounted, putting their horses under cover of a hedge & farm & returned the fire. Col. Wilson with the remainder of the Regt. quickly extended this line to the right with the two other Squadrons, though under a very heavy shell fire, & with his whole Regiment brought a heavy fire on the enemy's trenches, completely silencing them, & some of their occupants were seen to retire.

They remained there till dusk before retiring.

The whole operation was very well & quickly carried out and came as a complete surprise to the enemy, who evidently expected it to be followed

From 7th Cav Bde.
To. 3rd Cav. Div.

27/10/14

18

up by other troops behind, as their guns began searching the reverse N.W. slopes of the ZANDVOORDE Ridge.

Col. Wilson showed great coolness & gallantry in carrying out the operation, though his cap was blown off by a shrapnel bullet, &, he reports to me, that after Capt Lord Alastair Innes-Ker had had his horse shot under him, that he carried another dismounted & wounded man back into the 1st Life Guards trenches.

Trooper Nevin also assisted another wounded man Trooper Hardy out of action.

I regret to say that owing to some misunderstanding this advance was not supported by Arty fire, only a comparatively few shots being fired, & those too late, by a section of "K" Bty. R.H.A. to whom I appealed & whose mission had been to support the advance of the 2nd Cav Bde.

I have not had the complete casualty Returns yet but I understand that 1 man was killed & 11 men were wounded, & a few missing, who it is thought, when dismounted, took refuge in the 1st Life Gds trenches, & under the circumstances I think the Regt was extremely fortunate in losing so few, & that in a great measure this was due to the speed & suddenness with which Col. Wilson carried out the operation.

I have the honour to be—
Sir
Yr Obdt Servant
(Sd) C.M. Kavanagh, B. Gen
Comdg 7 Cav Bde

True copy
[signature]
Br. Gen.
GS 3rd CD

- From 3rd Cav Dn
To 6 Cav Bde

27/10/14

G.O.C.
7" Cav. Bde,
ZANDVOORDE.
6 Cav. Bde
Ga. 89.   ZILLEBEKE
Oct 27"
Following message received from
1st Corps. Begins "Following from
1st Div. begins Welsh Patrol
reports several hundred of
enemy on road South West
of point 45 South of
KRUISEIK.

3rd Cav Dn
9-5 pm
ZILLEBEKE
                        3CD

From I Corps
To 3rd Cav. Dn.

27/10/14

"C" Form (Duplicate).　　Army Form C. 2123.
MESSAGES AND SIGNALS.　No. of Message ____

Service Instructions.	Charges to Pay.	Office Stamp.

Handed in at the ____ Office, at 7.40 p.m. Received here at 8.40 p.m.

TO: 3rd Cav. Div.

Sender's Number.	Day of Month.	In reply to Number.	AAA
G 455	27th		

Following from 1st Div begins Welsh patrol reports several hundred of enemy on road W of at point 45 S of KRUISEIK ends

FROM: 1st Corps
PLACE:
TIME: 7.40 p.m.

7 am 4th Hussars
To 3rd Cav Bde.   27/10/14

3 Cav Div.   W R B R.R. Sqn
                  21.8
              27/10/14

(8)

Herewith rough sketch of trenches
dug by 4 Hrs today.
They more or less join
up with your proposed third
line which passes through the
Small Chateau.
Trenches are not yet
complete but could be into five
hours work.
If you are short handed
I will finish off Nos 1, 2, and 3
but I understand that my
boundary is South of the Railway.
I will try & pass before on to
7th Cav. Bde. Bde de Maresche

7.10 p.m.   78

Sketch of Trenches
near Canal Crossing
Klein Zillebeke 73

N ↑

Moulin
      27.x.

Chateau

Total manway
here

Small Chateau

Hollebeke

dead ground

Trenches Nos 1, 2, 3
are in 3 Can Div.
area but have been
dug by 4th Hrs.
No. 4 = max in feet
to steep railway.

Not to Scale

From Cav. Corps
To. 3rd Cav. Div.   27/10/14

"C" Form (Original).
MESSAGES AND SIGNALS.
Army Form C. 2123.

Prefix	Code	Words	Received From / By	Sent, or sent out At / To / By	Office Stamp
				7-85 pm	

Charges to collect

Service Instructions.

Handed in at the ___ Office, at 6.12 pm. Received here at 7.3 pm.

TO 3nd Cav Div

Sender's Number.	Day of Month.	In reply to Number.	AAA
GB 76	27	—	

Situation along the front of Cav Corps remains unchanged aaa the left of 3nd Cav Div. connects with the right of the 1st Div of 1st corps aaa the position will continue to be held tomorrow aaa the 57th rifles and 129th BALUCHIS will be in corps reserve under Gen EGERTON and

FROM

PLACE

TIME

From
3rd Cav
Bde
To 3rd
Cav Bde

G/39

3rd Cavalry Brigade

WD 10/27.X

27/10/14

German trenches in front of our at ZANVOORDEN are shown on enclosed sketch. Can your battery enfilade them? Reference to map 1/100,000 would seem to indicate that the hostile trenches are located along the N. edge of the wood immediately S. of ZANVOORDE. If your battery is able to fire on them, our people will endeavour to observe the fire effect. It is suggested that the whole wood should be thoroughly searched. Please return sketch.

Jn. Gage Lt. Col.
p.
3 Car Div.

27/10/14
2.30 pm.

From 3rd Cav. Div.
To 6th Cav. Bde

WD 10/27.X

27/10/14

VI Cavalry Bde

The 3rd Cav. Bde have been requested to endeavour to enfilade the hostile trenches in your front, with artillery fire. According to the sketch made by your B.M. these would appear to be located along the N. edge of the wood immediately S. of ZANVOORDE. The battery of 3rd Bde has therefore been requested to thoroughly search the N. edge & the wood itself. Please report if you are able to observe the effect of the fire.

J.A.Gore
Lt. Col.
fo. 3 C.B.

27/10/14
2.45 pm

82

27.X
WD 10

Windmill
& Kortewilde
1500x

Covered approach

Château
3 Trps. "A"   12 men   2 MG
B   Bilinghis
Trp.   M.G.   8 men

True N.   To Hollebeke

C   C   B   B
2 Troops 2 Trs 12 men 2 Trs.

Regt H.Q.

23

From 3rd Cav. Bde.
To. 3rd Cav Div

27/10/14

"A" Form.   Army Form C. 2121.
MESSAGES AND SIGNALS.

TO 3rd Cav Div

| Sender's Number. | Day of Month | In reply to Number | AAA |
| BM 94. | 27th | G/39 | |

Will shell the north edge of the wood south of ZANDVOORDE for 10 minutes at 4pm. AAA return your sketch

From 3rd Cav Bde
Time 3·10 pm

R/Wheatley May BM

From 3rd Cav Div
To IV Corps   27/10/14

G/40   W.D. 9/27.X

G of IV. A.C.

The woods holding the line N of ZANDVOORDE
are still considerably missed.
My left is in touch with the Warwick
Regt (22nd Bde) who join up with some
troops of the 3rd Bde.
There are also some of the 7th Division near
KRUISIEK
I understand that the 22nd Bde is
being repined at KLEIN ZILLEBEKE
If this is the case it would be the greatest
possible value to my line of one Bn (or ½ Bn)
could be stationed N of the INN ½ mile
W of ZANDVOORDE for tonight —
She would be a long way in rear of my
trenches + out of artillery fire. but
their support, in case ZANDVOORDE
was attacked would be most valuable.
My trenches are very weakly held —
KLEIN ZILLEBEKE   J Byng. MajGen
2-20   3rd CD
27 - X -14

From Cav Corps
To 3rd Cav Bde

27/10/14.

"A" Form.   Army Form C. 2121.
MESSAGES AND SIGNALS.   No. of Message_____

Prefix __ Code __ m.	Words	Charge	This message is on a/c of :	Recd. at 12.30 p.m.
Office of Origin and Service Instructions.	Sent			Date 27"
W.D. 6/6 27	At ___ m. To By		Service _____ (Signature of "Franking Officer.")	From Lt. Bell By

TO	1st Corps
	3rd Cav Div
	2nd Cav Div

| Sender's Number | Day of Month | In reply to Number | AAA |
| G.679 | 27 | | |

In case of attack on
your right I am prepared
to co-operate with one Cav.
Regiment one Battery R.H.A. and
~~two~~ two battalions AAA
Addressed 1st Corps repeated 3rd Cav Div
and 2nd Cav Div.

From CAV CORPS
Place
Time 11-40 a.m.

The above may be forwarded as now corrected.   (Z) R.M. Huley Capt G.S.

From 6 Cav. Bde
To 3rd Cav. Div.   27/10/14

To The C.S.O   W.D. 6/27.X
    3' Cav Div

O.C. 10" HUSSARS reports a maxim brought up by enemy within six or seven hundred yards of his entrenchments; they are digging fresh trenches 2000 yards away from his position; they are still very active shelling our trenches.

            H Boyd-Rochfort
11.50 am
27/X/14   Staff Capt
                 6" Cav. Bde

   12.15 p

From 3rd Cav. Bde
To) 3rd Cav. Dn
27/10/14

Wt. W1154/2240. 7/11. 7,500,000. Sch. 4a. "A" Form. Army Form
MESSAGES AND SIGNALS. No. of Message

Prefix	Code	m.	Words	Charge	This message is on a/c of:	Recd. at 9.20 m.
Office of Origin and Service Instructions.			Sent		Service.	Date 27/10/14
WD 27			At / To / By	m.	(Signature of "Franking Officer.")	From 3 CB By N.H.

TO: 3rd Cav Div — KLEIN ZILLEBEKE

Sender's Number.	Day of Month	In reply to Number	AAA
BM 85	27		

My Indian Troops have been withdrawn from the trenches which I am now holding with dismounted Cavalry in the same positions as before AAA Operations yesterday show that on the West side of the Canal the enemy has entrenchments along the ROOSEBEEK just above the L in Lock but that on the East side of the Canal there are no entrenchments between the N.E. belt of KORTEWILDE and the Chateau occupied by your squadron AAA Please send me your dispositions and intentions for today.

Reply G/38

From 3rd Cav Bde
Place
Time 8.50 am

(Z) R H Keatley Maj BM

From 2nd Cav Div
To 3rd Cav Div.

27/10/

W.D. 3/1X 3rd Cav. Div. Received 9.8 am 92
wg. 300 Oct. 27. Replied to 9.37

Will you please let us know your
present disposition exactly and
what your intentions are for today —
It would of course be of the utmost
importance for us to know at once
if you had any idea of evacuating
Zandvoorde the more notice
we could have the better.
Also we ought to arrange what
readonal measures we should each take
in the event of your leaving
Zandvoorde, in order to still
maintain touch between your right
& our left.
In any case we must not throw
our left further back than the
elbow of the canal N. of Hollebeke
if it can possibly be avoided
& I am sure you will consider
that in any disposition you
may make.
I gather that the 1st Corps intend
to resume the offensive today —
In our own front things are perfectly quiet.

Wytschaete
8.15 am.

2nd Cav Div.
C H Greenly
8.05

From 3rd Cav. Dn
To 2nd Cav. Dn

27/10/14

G/36   W.D. 2/27.X

G.O.C. 2nd Cavalry Division.

Orders for 3rd Cavalry Division to-day
are to assist the attack of the 1 Corps,
and to hold ZANDVOORDE as a pivot.
Until the situation develops therefore,
the G.O.C. is not able to undertake
any reconnaissance towards the
last E of KORTEWILDE, as suggested by you
yesterday.
Situation here at present quiet.

3rd Cavalry Division.

27/10/14   9 a.m.

From I Corps
To 3rd Cav Dn
27/10/14

Army Form C. 2121.
AND SIGNALS.

TO 3rd Cavalry Division

Recd. at 7.0 a.m.
Date 27
From H.Z.

Sender's Number: G.445
Day of Month: 27th
AAA

Owing to withdrawal of a portion of the 7th Division the 3rd Infantry Brigade has been ordered to send up two battalions to connect with your left at ZANVOORDE. Copy of order issued to 1st Division is forwarded for your information.

No orders received
NM

From 1st Corps
Time 6.15 am

N. Malcolm

From I Corps
To 3rd Cav. Bde.

28/10/14

"A" Form. Army Form C. 2121.
MESSAGES AND SIGNALS. No. of Message 190

Prefix Code   Words 54 Charge
Office of Origin and Service Instructions.

1st Army

This message is on a/c of:
11-15 pm
Service.
Z

Recd. at
Date
From A 28.X.14 HÜ
By

TO 3rd Cav Div   1st Div
    ~~Corps Reserve~~   7th Div

Sender's Number Day of Month In reply to Number
G 486 28th   AAA

Following received from GHQ begins
Reliable information state German
27th Reserve Corps will attack
GHELUVELT — OUDE KRUISEIK tomorrow
5.30 am English time and that
the German Cavalry Corps will
cooperate towards ZANDVOORDE to
ascertain if the main or advanced
position is there ends AAA
Acknowledge.

Ga 92 Oct. 25th
Above repeated to 6th & 7th Cav. Bdes. &
22nd Inf. Bde. 11-30 pm
                    W---

From 1st Corps
Place
Time 8.5 pm

From 3rd Cav. Dn
To I Corps

28/10/14

G/34 WD 4/28 8
H'dQrs I AC Chateau E of HOOGE

Situation in front of 3rd Cavalry Division as follows

Heavy shelling on ZANDVOORDE all day. Slight casualties in trenches near village.

Occasional shell fire directed on KLEIN ZILLEBEKE ridge and houses.

Enemy advanced towards ZANDVOORDE last night - but retired on being fired upon.

J. Byng. Maj Genl
3rd Cav Dvn

KLEIN ZILLEBEKE
4-45 pm
28-X-14

From I Corps
To 3rd Cav. Div.

28/10/14

"C" Form (Original).   Army Form C. 2123.
MESSAGES AND SIGNALS.   No. of Message _____

Prefix	Code	Words	Received	Sent, or sent out	Office Stamp.
			From	At 4-30 p.m.	
Charges to collect	£ s. d.		By	To 28	
Service Instructions. Priority 1st C. Msg				By	

Handed in at the _____ Office, at _____ m. Received here at _____ m.

TO 3nd Cav Div

Sender's Number.	Day of Month.	In reply to Number.	AAA
G.480	28		
following	message	from	G H Q
begin	it	is	reported
from	reliable	source	that
the	27th	German	reserve
corps	has	been	ordered
to	take	the	cross
roads	s.e	of	YPRES
today	ends	a.a.a	first
and	seventh	divs	please
report	situation	in	your
front	addressed 1st		and
& 7th	divn	3rd	Cav
div	and	corps	reserve

FROM   1st Corps
PLACE
TIME   3-4 pm

* This line should be erased if not required.
W. 5375—423. 75,000 Pads—12/12—B. & F.— orms/C.2123/1.

From
3rd Cav Dn
To
Cav. Corps
28/10/14

G/31 W.D 2/28 X

G.O.C. Cavalry Corps

Infantry line in trenches was reconnoitred during the night.

I now hold trenches (pointed out by you) between ZANDVOORDE & old Château, to E. of village.

The line is continued Northwards by 21st Bde (7th Division) to a point near G.H. stone on YPRES-MENIN road.

The 22nd Bde are reforming here - one Bn (about 500 strong) near ZANDVOORDE.

Have liaison with 7th Division HdQrs

Enemy advanced towards ZANDVOORDE last night, but retired on being fired at. The village is being shelled again this morning -
J Byng M.Gen
3rd Cav Div
KLEIN ZILLEBEKE
9-35am/28/X/14

W.D 3/27.X

G.O.C. 7th Division

Hd Qrs 22nd Bde are now established near me.

Have arranged with G.O.C. 1st Bde for a Battalion to report each day for reinforcement for ZANDVOORDE.

Please ask G.O.C. 21st Bde to notify me exactly where his Hd Qrs are and I will send him sketch of our trenches -

J Byng M.Gen
3rd Cav Div
KLEIN ZILLEBEKE
11-45
28.X.14

From 3rd Cav. Bde.
To 3rd Cav. Bde.

28/10/14

5.40 am

Wt. W1154/2240. 7/11. 7,500,000. Sch. 4a.	"A" Form.		Army Form C. 2121.

MESSAGES AND SIGNALS. No. of Message _____

Prefix ___ Code ___ m.	Words	Charge	This message is on a/c of:	Recd. at 7:10 a m.
Office of Origin and Service Instructions.				Date 28
	Sent		_____ Service.	From 2
W⁄3	At 28 m.			By
	To			
	By		(Signature of "Franking Officer.")	

TO: 3rd Cav Div — KLEIN ZILLEBEKE

Sender's Number.	Day of Month	In reply to Number	A A A
BM 1	28th		

Please inform me of the situation in your part. Hrs can we assist you by shelling the north edge of the woods south of ZANDVOORDE. Hrs coc Barnes reported air shells 500 – 700 yards short of the trenches opposite him when we were firing at 4 pm yesterday.

From: 3rd Cav Bde
Place:
Time: 5.40 am

(Z) R J Kearsley May BM

From Cav Corps
To 3rd Cav D.
29/10/14

G Form. (Duplicate.)	MESSAGES & SIGNALS.		No. of Message 1	Army Form C 2123.

Office Stamp. WD1 30

Inquiries respecting this Message, or application for repetition of the same, may be made at the Delivering Office; but any complaint as to its delay &c., should be made in writing and addressed to the officer in charge. In either case this form must accompany such inquiries or complaint.

Service Instructions.   Charges to pay £ s. d.

Handed in at the S Office at 10-50 Received here at 12-1 AM

TO   3rd Cav Div

Sender's Number	Day of Month	In reply to Number	A.A.A.
GB 103	29		

First Corps report wire of constant movement of wounded men + vehicles from north to south to the east of their position between 7·30 pm + 9 pm

Rec'd 12 M(id)

men

FROM Cav Corps
PLACE
TIME 11-50 p

From Cav Corps
To. 3rd Cav Dn

29/10/14

(5840 Wt. W 401-1924. 5-11. 10,000 Pads. WY. & S. LTD. Sch. 19.	Army Form C 2123.
C Form. (Duplicate.) **MESSAGES & SIGNALS.**	No. of Message 21

Office Stamp. 10.45 P.M.

Service Instructions.   13/29

Handed in at the S.E.W. Office at 9.30 p.m.   Received here at 10.33 p.m.

TO 3rd Cav Div.

Sender's Number	Day of Month	In reply to Number	A. A. A.
SGB 99.	29.		

Reliable information to the effect that about 3000 German Cavalry crossed the Lys today at WARNETON moving northwards aaa That another force of Cavalry crossed at PONT ROUGE moving towards MESSINES the head of this column was seen at midday at LA POTTERIER farm aaa New trenches were being dug at LES QUATRE ROIS at X roads MESSINES COMINES and WARNETON OOSTAVERNE aaa The 1st Corps successfully repulsed all German attack on their

FROM PLACE TIME

Cont

From Cav Corps
To: 3rd Cav Bde.

29/10/14

(5840 Wt. W 401-1924. 5-11. 10,000 Pads. Wy. & S. Ltd. Sch. 19.	Army Form C 2123.
C Form. (Duplicate.) MESSAGES & SIGNALS.	No. of Message 21

Office Stamp.

PM

Inquiries respecting this Message, or application for repetition of the same, may be made at the Delivering Office; but any complaint as to its delay, &c., should be made in writing and addressed to the officer in charge. In either case this form must accompany such inquiries or complaint.

Service Instructions.   Charges to pay £ s. d.

Handed in at the   Office at   .M.   Received here at   .M.

TO

Sender's Number	Day of Month	In reply to Number	A. A. A.

| front | today | and | took | some |
| ground | about | KRUSEIK | aaa | |

FROM	Cav.	Corps			
PLACE					
TIME		4·30 pm.			

From Cav. Corps
To. 3rd Cav. Div

29/10/14

C Form. (Duplicate.)   MESSAGES & SIGNALS.   Army Form C 2123.

No. of Message ....

Office Stamp. R 12.45 pm

Service Instructions. WD 12/29

Handed in at the SE. Office at 12.20p Received here at 12.23p

TO   3rd Cav. Div.

Sender's Number: JGB 95   Day of Month: 29   A.A.A.

It is reported that enemies losses north of DIXMUDE in last few days have been very heavy also that action of French is proceeding favourably in the North AAA Very reliable information shows that end + 5th German Cav Corps required 5000 rounds of gun ammunition last night AAA They were informed this morning that only 1900 rounds were available

FROM in LILLE AAA Cav. Corps.

TIME 12-20 pm

From 2nd Cav Bde
To 3rd Cav Bde   29/10/14

W.D 10/29   3rd Cav Div   51
bg. 3 & 5 Oct. 29

We are going to open a good
heavy fire now all along our
front just to frighten them
and make them think we
are going to attack —
I tell you in case you thought
we were being heavily attacked
ourselves.

                          D. Carden
Chateau near   W H Greenly.
  Hollebeke   C.S.O.
   4 pm
      Rec'd 4.15 pm
           July

From 3rd Cav. Bde
To 3rd Cav. Dn   29/10/14

"A" Form.
MESSAGES AND SIGNALS.
Army Form C. 2121

TO: 3rd Cav Divn

Sender's Number: BM 22   Day of Month: 29   AAA

To create a diversion and to assist the attack of the 1st Corps I have ordered my men in the trenches to open fire on the nearest objective till dark with as many rifles as possible

From: 3rd Cav Bde
Time: 3.35 pm

Signature: A.D. Beactley (?) Major BM

From 7th Cav Bde
To 3rd Cav Bde   29/10/14

"A" Form.   Army Form C. 2121.
MESSAGES AND SIGNALS.   No. of Message _____

| Prefix___ Code___ m. | Words. | Charge. | This message is on a/c of: | Recd. at 5.55 m. |
| Office of Origin and Service Instructions. | Sent At___ m. To___ By___ | | _____Service. (Signature of "Franking Officer.") | Date 29/10/14 From 7CB By ___ |

TO { Third Cav Bde

Sender's Number	Day of Month	In reply to Number	AAA

We are full up. We have the KRUISTR[?] ... road running to CHATEAU AAA Bde HQrs ... still ...

From
Place ZANVOORDE
Time   4.55 pm

The above may be forwarded as now corrected. (Z) C Kavanagh Capt
                Censor.   Signature of Addressor or person authorised to telegraph in his name
* This line should be erased if not required.
(24473). M.R.Co., Ltd. Wt.W4843/511. 50,000. 9/14. Forms C2121/10.

From C.R.A. 7th Div.
To 3rd Cav. Dn.

29/10/14

"A" Form.
MESSAGES AND SIGNALS.

TO 3rd Cav. Div.

Sender's Number	Day of Month	In reply to Number	AAA
BM 95	29		

Shells from our artillery falling among our infantry attacking KRUISEIK AAA cannot trace this to our divl. artillery AAA if you have any guns firing towards KRUISEIK please inform them of above.

From 7th Divl Arty.
Place 5th Kilo
Time 3.30 pm

From 3rd Cav Div
To I. Corps

29/10/14

W.D. 6/24

G/41

1st Army Corps
repeated 7th Division.

Following from 7° Cav. Bde. ZANDVOORT begins AAA Slopes just N of KRUSEIK are full of British troops AAA also we have a brigade just S. of the white road running E from ZANVOORDE past chateau AAA Officer from this Brigade reports further advance of our troops is being stopped owing to shell fire from our batteries AAA 3rd C message ends AAA. Our guns have been warned AAA.

3rd Cav. Division
29/10/14
5.12pm

From 3rd Cav Bde
To Cav. Corps

29/10/14

G/37

To: Cav Corps W.D. 6/29.X

Counter stroke on the YPRES-MENIN
road has not been able to make any
progress.

I have been ordered to push all my reserve
from ZANDVOORDE in the direction of
KRUISEECKE

My 6th Bde are carrying this out
in conjunction with the 2nd Inf Bde

I think it would be advisable if your
reserves could be directed on this
place.

J. Byng. M.Gen
3rd Cav Div

KLEIN ZILLEBEKE
12-5
29.X.14

From 3rd Cav Dn.   29/10/14
To I. Corps

G/41 I.a.C   W.D. 2/29

As far as we can see at present
the 22nd left Bde & the 6 (or 13)th
have retaken the KRUISEECKE
heights

J. Byng. M.Gen.

KLEIN ZILLEBEKE 3rd Cav Divn

4.30pm
29.X.14

From C. R.H.A.
To 3rd Cav. Bde.
29/10/14

W.D. 5/29.X

G.S. 3rd Cav. Divn

1. I have established my
HQrs at farm on the road
KLEIN ZILLEBEKE – ZANDVOORDE
about 400x N W of HQrs 7th Cav. Bde.
Lt D'Arcy will find it out.
K Battery RHA is in action quite
close to above farm.

2. I understand that the 106th Bty
RFA is in action near 2nd L of
KLEIN ZILLEBEKE

3. The observing stations of C and
K are close together on the ridge
at a spot due N of letter E in
ZANDVOORDE and due E of
1st letter E in BASSEVILLE R.

4. I can communicate with O.C.
C & K by the battery telephone

5. Communication from you to me
could be sent by telephone to HQ 7th Cav. Bde.
where I have an orderly. B de Rougemont
29.X.14. 11.50 pm Lt Col RHA

From 3rd Cav Div.
To 7th Div.

29/10/14

C/39
G.O.C. 7th Division
Your T 95.
My 6 Cavalry Bde has moved in support of the 22nd Bde in the direction of KRUISEECKE

J Byng. M.Gen
3rd Cav Div.

W D 4/29

KLEIN ZILLEBEKE
1-20
29.X.14.

From 7th Div.
To 3rd Cav Div
29/10/14

"C" Form (Original).
MESSAGES AND SIGNALS.
Army Form C. 2123.

TO: 3 Cav Div

Sender's Number.	Day of Month.	In reply to Number.	AAA
95	29 October		

I have sent forward all my troops to counter attack on line KRUISIK — Cross roads SE of GHELUVELT AAA Are you joining in this movement or is your front not clear. AAA If you need any infantry apply to 22 Bde who ~~messages are sending~~

(Reply G 39.)

FROM: 7 Div
PLACE: 5 kils
TIME: 12.45 PM

From 6th Cav Bde
To 3rd Cav Div

29/10/14

Army Form C. 2121
MESSAGES AND SIGNALS.

WD 4/19

Recd. at 2h m.
Date 29/10/14
From 6 C.B.
By Orly

TO G.O.C. 3rd Cav Division

AAA

Am pushing forward one Regiment with its right on CHATEAU ½ mile E. of ZANDVOORDE to guard right flank of the advance of 22nd Brigade, which is advancing in the direction of X Roads S.E. GHELUVELT (Kilo 9) — KRUISTIK AAA Am holding other Regiment in Reserve with a view to mounted action. AAA.

From Place ½ Mile N. of 7th Cav Bde H.Q.
From O C 6th Cav Bde
Time 29 . X . 14 1.50 pm

(Z) Ernest Makins Brig

From 3rd Cav. Dn
To. 7th Dn.

29/10/14

G/ 3rd Division   WD 4/24

I have ordered the 6th Cav Bde to move forward in the direction of KRUISEECKE in support of your 22nd Bde moving from the neighbourhood of ZANDVOORDE.

J Byng. M.Gen

KLEIN ZILLEBEKE 3rd Cav Divn
12-30
29. X. 14

From 7th Div.
To 3rd Cav Div

29/10/14

Army Form C. 2123.

SIGNALS.

Received From 7 Div
By NH
1.25 pm

TO 3 Cav Div

Sender's Number	Day of Month	In reply to Number	AAA
T 97	29 Oct	-	

My countermovement will tend to close to left where enemy is pressing North of YPRES – MENIN Road AAA Thanks for your Cooperation

M 120

FROM 7 Div
PLACE 5 kilo,
TIME 12.55 PM

From 6th Cav. Bde
To 3rd Cav Dn.

29/10/14

MESSAGES AND SIGNALS.

No. of Message _____

Prefix _____ Code _____ m. | Words | Charge
Office of Origin and Service Instructions.

WD/29

Sent At _____ m. To _____ By _____

This message is on a/c of:
_____ Service.
(Signature of "Franking Officer.")

Recd. at 9 p.m.
Date 29/10/14
From 6CB
By _____

TO { General Staff
     3rd Cavalry Division. }

Sender's Number | Day of Month | In reply to Number | AAA

1. The 6th Cavalry Brigade arrived back in KLEINZILLEBEKE at 6.15 p.m.

2. On arrival at H.Q. 7th Cavalry Bde. I obtained touch with G.O.C. 22nd Inf. Bde, who stated that he was advancing on the line Cross Roads S.E. GHELUVELT (Kib g) – KREISIK AAA. I arranged to cover his right flank, and ordered the 10th Hussars to advance on their right on the CHATEAU, ½ mile E of ZANDVOORDE, retaining the Royals in Reserve with a view to using for mounted action if the opportunity occurred AAA The Infantry advance was not opposed in any strength, and eventually two Brigades of the 7th Division regained their line of this morning AAA In accomplishing this, the 22nd Brigade brought their left shoulders up and masked the advance of the 10th, who were thus

From _____
Place _____
Time _____

The above may be forwarded as now corrected. (Z)

Censor. | Signature of Addressor or person authorised to telegraph in his name.
This line should be erased if not required.

Cont
From 6 Cav Bde
to 3rd Cav Dn

29/10/14

MESSAGES AND SIGNALS.

placed between the right flank of the 22nd Brigade and the left flank of the outposts of the 7th Cavalry Brigade AAA The 10th supported the advance of the right flank of the 22nd Brigade until 5.45 p.m. when I received orders for the Brigade to return to KLEIN ZILLEBEKE. AAA My casualties were 2 men 10th Hussars wounded.

From: G.O.C. 6th Cav Bde
Place: KLEIN ZILLEBEKE
Time: 8.35 p.m. 29 x 14.

Ernest Makins Brig Genl

From 3rd Cav Bde
To 3rd Cav Dn.
29/10/14

"A" Form.   Army Form C. 2121.
MESSAGES AND SIGNALS.   No. of Message_____

Prefix	Code	m.	Words	Charge	This message is on a/c of:	Recd. at 10.35 a.m.
Office of Origin and Service Instructions			Sent		_____Service.	Date 29/10/14
			At ___ m.			From 3 Cav Bde
W D 3/A			To ___		(Signature of "Franking Officer.")	By M'Ly
			By ___			

TO: 3rd Cav Div

Sender's Number	Day of Month	In reply to Number	AAA

3rd Cav Bde has been ordered to be prepared to support you. There are 5 Sqns + 1 Bt. H.battie available. It is not proposed to move guns which can support you from existing position. The 5th & 16th N Lancers have been ordered to be ready to turn out and the Regt (4 bd) will be concentrated by the canal bridge 1 m. N of HOLLEBEKE on the HOLLEBEKE – VERBRANDEN MOLEN road. The 5 Sqns can be moved to KLEIN ZILLEBEKE or any where you wish but in view of info given me by Lt BROCKLEHURST I do not propose to move them at present.

From C H Qu
Place North of H in HOLLEBEKE
Time 0-50

The above may be forwarded as now corrected.   (Z) _Vaughan B-hurst_
     Censor.   Signature of Addressor or person authorised to telegraph in his name.

* This line should be erased if not required.

From 3rd Cav. Div.
To   Cav. Corps   29/10/14

W.D. 2/4

G.H.Q. & 3rd D. repeated to 1 & 2 Cav. D.

Have received a very hot message. Have just seen G.O.C. I Army Corps as follows:—
2. Left flank of the 4th Inf. Bde. is at ZILLEBEKE and has been very heavily attacked & has given way slightly.
2nd & 4th I.G.C. are apparently getting along with the 3rd and 20 Bdes. in the direction of KRUISEIR
He suggests a reconnaissance on towards OTTENBRIE(?)
Forcenburn if a large force be necessary prepared to attack during LANDVOORDS
I am unable to do this as the enemy's trenches are close up to ours.
Both our batteries are now engaged with KRUISEECKE supporting 1st Corps attack which may be able to push or move in that direction if they can be ——— of any use to ensure a success.

                    J. Byng, Lt. Gen.
KLEIN ZILLEBEKE   3rd Cav. Div.
  10 am
  29.X.14
                                    26

From 2nd Cav Bde
To 3rd Cav Bde   29/10/14

"C" Form (Duplicate).
MESSAGES AND SIGNALS.
Army Form C. 2123.

SM RB 45
9.40 am   VB
Service Instructions. VB 29 M.m

Handed in at the _____ Office, at 9·10 a.m. Received here at 9·20 a.m.

TO WD/an + 3rd Cav Div

Sender's Number: Ja 38   Day of Month: Twenty ninth   In reply to Number: AAA

1. Fourth and fifth Brigades report attack on our right and centre about 4·30 am this morning not serious aaa
2. No report yet received from 3rd Bde

FROM: 2 Cav Div
PLACE: WYTSCHAETE
TIME: 9-15 am

From 2nd Cav. Div.
To 3rd Cav. Dv.   30/10/14

(end missing)
N.F.

WD 3/30   R'd 9.40 a — 70
~~CAV. CORPS.~~
~~1. CAV. DIV.~~
3. CAV. DIV.

G.a. 43. Thirtieth.

1. Movement of troops heard during the night apparently going S.E. along the HOUTHEM and GAPAARD roads leading to COMINES aaa.

2. At 6.30 A.M. some of the enemy's trenches nearest to our left (HOLLEBEKE) were reported vacated aaa

3. About 200 enemy infantry were seen moving from the wood just beyond farm on stream ½ mile N.E of 9 Kilo on WARNETON Road moving along dead ground in a S.W. direction aaa

4. There was a great deal of movement in the enemy's trenches during the night. aaa

From 7th Cav. Bde
To 3rd Cav. Dn
30/10/14

"A" Form.　　　　　　　　　　　Army Form C. 2121.
MESSAGES AND SIGNALS.　　No. of Message ___

TO　Third Cav Div

Sender's Number: BM 3　Day of Month: 30th　　　AAA

reports from trenches are that sounds of wheels and enemy singing were heard during night and direction of movement seems to be from west to east.

From 7th Cav Bde
Place Zandvoorde
Time 6.50 am

From 7th Cav Bde
To 3rd Cav Div

30/10/14

"A" Form.   Army Form C. 2121.
MESSAGES AND SIGNALS.   No. of Message _____

| Prefix ___ Code ___ m. | Words | Charge | This message is on a/c of: | Recd. at 7.30 a.m. |
| Office of Origin and Service Instructions. | Sent At ___ m. To ___ By ___ | | W- 4/30 Service (Signature of "Franking Officer.") | Date 30th From K.2 By M. |

TO { G.S. Third Cav Div

| Sender's Number | Day of Month | In reply to Number | AAA |
| BM 4 | 30th | | |

Very heavy bombardment now going on principally from long range howitzers against ridge and low ground west of it

From 7th Cav Bde
Place ZANDVOORDE
Time

A Kearsey Capt
BM 7 Cav Bde

From 7th Cav. Bde
To 3rd Cav. Div

30/10/14

"A" Form.   Army Form C. 2121.
MESSAGES AND SIGNALS.

| Prefix | Code | m. | Words | Charge | | This message is on a/c of: | | Recd. at | m. |

Sent At ___ m.   W⁴/₄₁   Service.   Date 7·45 a
To   (Signature of "Franking Officer.")   From
By   By

TO — GS Third Cav Div

Sender's Number   Day of Month   In reply to Number   AAA
BM 5   Thirtieth

Blues 12 Centre trenches have
been blown in men
retired AAA enemy advancing in
force

From 7th Cav Bde
Place ZANDVOORDE
Time

A Kearsey Capt
acting BM 7th Cav Bde

From 3rd Cav. Bde
To I Corps

30/10/14

"A" Form.   Army Form C. 2121.
MESSAGES AND SIGNALS.

TO: 1st Army Corps, Wheeled Corps, 2nd Cavalry Division, 7th Division, Cavalry

AAA

C/43 Night Germans are now on ZANDVOORDE Ridge and hostile infantry advancing towards HOLLEBEKE CHATEAU AAA 7th Cavalry Brigade retiring to entrenched position just N of B on BASSEVILLE River westwards to Canal AAA 6 Cav Bde in support in trenches in rear of this line AAA 4 Hussars just gone as further support AAA Greys and 3rd Hussars in reserve KLEIN ZILLEBEKE AAA

From 3rd Cav. Div.
Place
Time 7.30 a.m.

From 3rd Cav. Div.
To I Corps

30/10/14

"A" Form. Army Form C. 2121.
MESSAGES AND SIGNALS.

Prefix	Code	m.	Words	Charge			
Office of Origin and Service Instructions.			Sent		This message is on a/c of:	Recd. at ___ m.	
Army Corps - 7th Div			At ___ m.			Date	
Cav. Corps			To		___ Service.	From	
2. Cav. Div.			By		(Signature of "Franking Officer.")	By	
3. Cav. Div.							

TO { 7. Cav Corps
     I Army

Sender's Number	Day of Month	In reply to Number	AAA
Ga 97	30		

The shelling is so heavy on the
Zandvoorde trenches that my
troops may have to retire.
Some of the trenches have been
blown in — There appears
to be a decided attack on
my line as the enemy
are advancing in force.

(Sd) J. Byng

From
Place H.C. Tille
Time   7-50 am

The above may be forwarded as now corrected.   (Z)

From 7th Cav Bde
To 3rd Cav Div.

30/10/14

MESSAGES AND SIGNALS.

Prefix	Code	Words	Charge	This message is on a/c of:	Recd. at 8.30 m.
Office of Origin and Service Instructions		Sent At m. To By		W⁵/30 Service (Signature of "Franking Officer.")	Date 30/10/14 From 7.15 By

TO — GOC Third Cav Div

Sender's Number	Day of Month	In reply to Number	AAA
BM 6	30th		

Have occupied with Reserve second line of trenches

Kavanagh
A/Capt
a/o BM
7 Cav Bde

From
Place
Time 8.20 am

From 3rd Cav. Div.
To Cav. Corps   30/10/14

GOC Cav Corps   WD 5/30
repeated GOC I AC
90/100
My first line of trenches have been blown in — and the 13th in centre is retiring.

I am trying to hold on to the KLEIN ZILLEBEKE ridge as long as possible. with both Bdes.

There is a reserve for the I A C (3 Regts) at my HQrs.

Byng
3 Cav Div

KLEIN ZILLEBEKE

8.30
30.X.14

From 3rd Cav. Div
To I Corps

30/10/14

"A" Form.   Army Form C. 2121.
MESSAGES AND SIGNALS.

TO 1st Army Corps
repeated 7' Division & 7 Cav Bde

AAA

6/42 enemy's infantry advancing on
W of ZANDVOORDE ridge in
direction of HOLLEBEKE AAA
AAA 7th Cav Bde falling back from
ZANDVOORDE ridge

From 3" Cav. Division
Place Klein Zillebeke
Time 9.6 [?]

From
To. O.C. Royals
KLEIN ZILLBEKE

30/10/14

O C Royals W.D 6/30
I am being shelled out
of the chateau garden.
And Germans massing
at from on my front
this side of the railway
line
T Boringten
CHATEAU
8.20 am

From 7th Cav. Bde
To 3rd Cav. Div.
30/10/14

"A" Form.

MESSAGES AND SIGNALS.

TO: Third Cav Div

Sender's Number: BM 5 Day of Month: 30th AAA

Enemy's infantry advancing in
our [?] in the direction
of [?] CROZAY - all
now falling back
3rd [?] please pass on
to 3rd Cav Bde

From: 7th Cav Bde
Place: ZANDVOORDE
Time:

A Kearsey Capt
BM 7th Cav Bde

From 7th Cav. Bde
To. 3rd Cav. Bde

30/10/14

MESSAGES.

Prefix	Code	Words	Charge	This message is on a/c of:	Recd. at 9.50 m.
Office of Origin and Service Instructions.		Sent At m. To By		W.O. Service (Signature of "Franking Officer.")	Date 30/10/14 From 7/B By

TO { **GOC 3rd Cav Div**

Sender's Number	Day of Month	In reply to Number	AAA
BM 9	30th		

[message text illegible — approximately: "... centre ... has been ... ... troops ... ... right"]

From 7th Cav Bde
Place LANDINCK?
Time

The above may be forwarded as now corrected.

From 7th Cav. Bde
To I Corps
" 7th Dn
" Cav. Corps.

G.O.C. I A.C. WD 7/30
9a. 10 I. Oct 30 Repeated 7 Div
The enemy is in possession + Cav Corps
of ZANDVOORDE Ridge

[signature]

Fr. G.O.C. 3rd Cav Div.
KLEIN ZILLEBEKE
10-0 am.

30/10/14

- From 3rd Cav. Bde.
  To 1st Div.

30/10/14

B/43 1st Division WD 8/30 your T.102

We have been unable to locate position of hostile forces, but direction appears to be from E generally AAA ZANVOORDE Ridge from the village westwards is in hands of hostile infantry AAA.

M.F. Gage S. Cl.
&.

30/10/14 9-45 a.m.

From 1st Dn
To 3rd Cav. Dn

30/10/14

"C" Form (Original). Army Form C. 2123.
MESSAGES AND SIGNALS. No. of Message _____

Office Stamp. Rd 9.40 am

TO: 3 Cav Div

Sender's Number.	Day of Month.	In reply to Number.	AAA
T 102	30 Oct	—	

Our Heavy Artillery want
to know direction of
guns troubling you besides those
in AMERICA which they
know about AAA Major Stewart
7. Div Staff has already gone
to see you & arrange ~~about~~ Infantry
support

M42

FROM: 1st Div
PLACE: 5 mls
TIME: 9.15 pm

From 3rd Cav Bde.
To 3rd Cav. Bde.

30/10/14

"A" Form. Army Form C. 2121
MESSAGES AND SIGNALS.

| TO | 3rd Cav Bde |

Sender's Number	Day of Month	In reply to Number	AAA
BM 41	30	G.92	

We are receiving a heavy bombardment and are holding our positions AAA. There is no infantry advance of the enemy in my front AAA. They located their most forward trenches this morning AAA. Please instruct your right to maintain touch with the left of the 129th Baluchis in HOLLEBEKE village.

From: 3rd Cav BC
Time: 9.25 am

R H Crawley Maj BM.

From 3rd Cav. Bde
To   I Corps
"   Cav. Corps
"   7th Div

30/10/14

C/46
G.O.C. I A.C. repeated   WD 11/30
G.O.C. Cavalry Corps & 7th Division.

The attack on the Chateau of HOLLEBEKE has been repulsed by the Royal Dragoons.

The enemy's main attack seems directed across the ZANDVOORDE ridge in a N.W direction

Am holding the KLEIN ZILLEBEKE ridge at present with all troops

J. Byng. M.G.C.

KLEIN ZILLEBEKE 3rd Cav Bde
10.30
30.X.14.

From 3rd Cav. Bde
To 2nd Cav Bde

30/10/14

"A" Form. Army Form C. 2121.
MESSAGES AND SIGNALS.

TO: 2nd British 2nd Cav Division

B/4d The attack on the château
4 HOLLEBEKE has been repulsed
by the Royal Dragoons AAA the
enemy's main attack seems directed
towards the ZANDVOORDE RIDGE in a
NW direction AAA am holding
the KLEINEZILLEBEKE RIDGE at present
with all troops and putting
in counter attack with the
remnants from the woods E of
KLEINEZILLEBEKE towards HOLLEBEKE
AAA

From 3rd Cav Brigade
Time 11.15 am

From I Corps
To 3rd Cav. Div.

30/10/14

"C" Form (Duplicate).   Army Form C. 2123.
MESSAGES AND SIGNALS.   No. of Message

SM /MD 69

Service Instructions.   Received 1.10 pm

Handed in at the RCA Office, at ___ m. Received here at 1 ___ m.

TO: 3rd Cav Div

Sender's Number.	Day of Month.	In reply to Number.	AAA
G 550	30		

Situation	7th	Division	10-50 am
was	South	Stafford	thrown
back	across	the	stream
through	first	E	in
BASSEVILLE	river	AAA	Gordon
Highlanders	moving	behind	AAA
when	ready	these	two
battalions	were	to	attack
ZANDVOORDE	from	the	west
Hd Qrs	7th		Divn
to	Chateau	east	of
ZILLEBEKE	aaa	are	you

FROM: in touch
PLACE: 1st Corps
TIME: 12.20 pm

From
To. 3rd Cav. Div

30/10/14

3 Cav. Div. W⁰/2.40 p.m.
⑨ 20/10/14   14/30

My regt is now on right of 6th Bde in canal valley N. of Chateau. I expected 3rd & preys to come this way also but have not seen them.

From 2nd Cav. Div. I got orders to join preys in counter-stroke upon Zandvoorde but do not now know where preys are or where counterstroke starts from. Gen. Makins asked me to watch his right & be ready to support Chateau. Shall I do this or move off N. to look for preys? So far little more than heavy shelling here but Chateau has had two or three infy attacks — ffooooo may

12.15 noon

From 3rd Cav Bde
To 2nd Cav Bde

30/10/14

2nd Cav Divn G/52 WD 14/30

A counter attack of 3 Bns 2nd Inf Bde and two Cavalry Regts (3rd Hrs & 4ths) is being directed on ZANDVOORDE ridge.

The is one Cavalry Regt (4th Hrs) ordered back here.

Do you require this Regt to be sent in support of y[our] line.

GOC Cavalry Corps is here

J Byng M-Genl
3rd Cav Divn

KLEIN ZILLIBEKE
12.30
30/X/14

From 3rd Cav Div
To. 7th Div

30/10/14

"A" Form.　　　　　Army Form C. 2121.
MESSAGES AND SIGNALS.

TO: 7th Division

Sender's Number: G/54
In reply to Number: G/550
AAA

Your G/550 AAA in touch
with 9nd infantry Brigade near
the BASSEVILL Stream AAA.

From 3 Cav Div
Place Klein ?illebeke
Time 1.10 pm

- From 2nd Cav Div
To 3rd Cav Div

30/10/14

Cav Corps.
3rd Cav Div.   WD 15/30
                FB 159 Oct 30   33

The left of the line held by the 2nd Cav Div is being heavily attacked. The Germans have been driven out of the salient S.E. of HOLLEBECKE. The Division is falling back slowly before the Germans attack. Div H.Q. moved to WIT INN about the 6 kilo stone on ST ELOI - OOSTAVERNE road.

Chateau N of H   2 Cav Div
u HOLLEBEKE   Sgd Brig-Gen CGS ?

12.45 pm

From 2nd Cav. Dn
To 3rd Cav Dn

30/10/14

WD 15/31 Third Cav. Div.

G.a. 47 Thirtieth. 6/52

Your 6/52 received ...
The Third Cav. D^n has been
forced back from the Salient
held by 5th Lancers & is retiring
slowly ...

Please send 1st Sqn to report
to G. of 7th B^de at CHATEAU
N of HOLLEBEKE at once ...

Second Cav. Div. J. Allenby Maj Gen
                  G.O.C. 2 Cav Div
X roads at INN
½ mile N.W. of OOSTTAVERNE

From Cav. Corps
To 3rd Cav Bde   30/10/14

"C" Form (Duplicate).		Army Form C. 2123.	
MESSAGES AND SIGNALS.		No. of Message	

Service Instructions: WD 15/30

Handed in at S.E.   Office 1.49 p.m.   Received ___ m.

TO: 3rd Cav. Div.

Sender's Number	Day of Month	In reply to Number	AAA
GB118	30		

Following received from 2nd Cav.
Div. timed 12-45 pm AAA
JB259 The left of the
line held by 2nd Cav.
Div. is being heavily attacked
AAA 5th Lancers have been
driven out of the Salient
SE of Zollebeke AAA The
Div is falling back slowly
before the enemy attack AAA
Divisional hdqrs moved to Windsor
Inn about sixth kilo stone
on ststoi ST. ELOI OOSTTAVERNE
road AAA Message ends

FROM: Cav Corps
PLACE & TIME: 1-49.

From O.C. 4th Hussars
To   6 Cav. Bde

30/10/14

"A" Form.   Army Form C. 2121.
MESSAGES AND SIGNALS.

Prefix	Code	Words	Charge	This message is on a/c of:	Recd. at 3/- m.
Office of Origin and Service Instructions: 1b. WO/30		Sent At To By		Service. (Signature of "Franking Officer.")	Date 30/10/14 From By

TO — OC 6th Cav Bde (Thro 3rd Cav Divn)

Sender's Number	Day of Month	In reply to Number	AAA
(13)	30/10		

3rd Cav Bde inform me that HOLLEBEKE is being vacated by BALUCHIS and whole 3rd Cav Bde is falling back to its 2nd position which runs from railway near Canal Bridge (just N. of HOLLEBEKE) along N. of Canal and on to St ELOI. I have sent up to inform CHATEAU Garrison which will presumably also have to retire to your 2nd position. Will you duplicate information to Chateau Garrison. I am leaving one Squn Dn East of Railway to help your withdrawal AAA Enemy Heavy Shell fire but enemy do not appear to be pressing very vigorously with infantry

From — OC 4th Hrs
Place
Time

From 2nd Cav. Div.
To 3rd Cav. Div.

30/10/14

4-0 p.m.   WD 17/30   8°
Third Cav. Div.

G.a. 48. Thirtieth G.a 102.

1. The Third Dⁿ and BALUCHIS have been driven out of trenches at HOLLEBEKE aaa

2. This necessitates the withdrawal of my line to my second position. aaa

3. I shall hold line from MESSINES — WYTSCHAETE — INN ½ mile S.S.E of ST ELOI — broken bridge over canal due N of H in² HOLLEBEKE aaa My left will then extend along canal facing S. as far as sharp bend in canal N of HOLLEBEKE village. aaa

J. Allenby Maj.
G. 2nd Cav Div.

Second Cav. Div.
INN ½ mile S S.S.E. of ST ELOI
3.45 pm.

From 3rd Cav. Dvn
To I. Corps   30/10/14

GOC. I a C repeated WD 16/30
    God. Cav Corps.
Ga 103. Oct 30th
The 3rd Cav Bde in the trenches near
HOLLEBEKE have retired.
I shall have to evacuate Chateau near
Camal in consequence

Am taking up position in rear of
Chateau but a strong infantry attack
is being developed against it

        J Byng MajGen

KLEIN ZILLEBEKE 3rd Cav Divn
    2-30
    30/x/14

From 3rd Cav Bde
To 2nd Cav. Bde

30/10/14

O.C. 2nd Cav Bde   W.D. 16/30

9a.10z. Oct 30th
I am told that the troops holding
the trenches round HOLLEBEKE
have left their trenches.
This will render the Chateau of
HOLLEBEKE untenable.

J. Byng M.Gen
3rd Cav Div

KLEIN ZILLEBEKE
3pm
30/X/14

From 3rd Cav. Div.
To I. Corps.   30/10/14

"A" Form.   Army Form C. 2121.
MESSAGES AND SIGNALS.

TO { GOC I Army Corps
      Repeated Cavalry Corps

Sender's Number: Ga 104   Day of Month: 30th   AAA

The attack on the Chateau of HOLLEBEKE is being pressed very strongly. I have used up all my reserve in holding onto the KLEIN ZELLIBEKE plateau. There is a slight gap between my left and the infantry (2nd Bde) but I have no troops to fill it.

J. Byng.
M. Gen.
3rd Cav Div

From: 3rd Cav Div
Place: KLEINE ZILLEBEKE
Time: 4-0 p.m.

From 7th Cav. Bde
To 3rd Cav Div

31/10/14

"A" Form. Army Form C. 2121.

MESSAGES AND SIGNALS.

No. of Message _____

Prefix ___ Code ___ m. | Words | Charge
Office of Origin and Service Instructions.

Sent At ___ m. To ___ By ___

This message is on a/c of:
WD/30 Service.
(Signature of "Franking Officer.")

Recd. at ___ m.
Date 5.50 a
From 3/2
By

TO { THIRD CAV DIV
     ZILLEBEKE }

Sender's Number	Day of Month	In reply to Number	AAA
BM 1	Thirtyfirst		

Casualties yesterday reported First Life Guards 2/Lt Visct Althorp and 35 men missing also Lord Hugh Grosvenors Sqdns which however is believed to have retired AAA Second Life Guards Capt CUNNINGHAME wounded 28 rank and file killed wounded missing also three troops believed to have retired from trenches in company with Welch Fusiliers AAA Blues killed 2/Lieut Hon F.E Lambton 3 rank & file Wounded Captain Harrison Lieut Mackintosh 23 rank and file also 25 rank and file missing

From SEVENTH CAV BDE
Place VERBRANDENMOLEN
Time 4.40 am

The above may be forwarded as now corrected. (Z)

Censor.   F Hull Capt BM
Signature of Addressor or person authorised to telegraph in his name

From Cav. Corps
To 3rd Cav. Div.   31/10/14

"C" Form (Duplicate).
MESSAGES AND SIGNALS.

Army Form C. 2123.

AK 71

Received 2.30 WD 3/31

Received 1.20 m

TO: 3rd Cav Div & 1st Corps

Sender's Number	Day of Month	In reply to Number	AAA
GB152	31		

7th Cavalry Brigade has been ordered to move at once to reinforce 4th Hussars who are holding the line of the canal from railway one mile north east of third E of HOLLEBEKE to the broken bridge 3/4 mile north of H in HOLLEBEKE connect with French on their right and left addressed 7th Cav Bde repeated 3rd Cav Div and 1st Corps

FROM PLACE & TIME: Cav Corps 1.14 pm

From 3rd Cav. Bde
To I Corps
3rd Cav Div

31/10/14

"A" Form.
MESSAGES AND SIGNALS.

Prefix	Code		Words	Charge	This message is on a/s of:	Recd. at _____ m.
Office of Origin and Service Instructions.						Date _____
			Sent		W D ⅔ Service.	From _____
			At _____ m.			
			To			
			By	(Signature of "Franking Officer.")	By _____

TO { 1st Corps
     3rd Cav Div

Sender's Number	Day of Month	In reply to Number		AAA
V-30	31			

A considerable body of Germans debouched about HOLLEBEKE. They are intrenching on the ridge to N & E of the village and have given heavy fire at (this evening) at 7 or 8 on 4th Hussars even when we are holding North side of canal. I have no support available for 4th Hussars and have to communicate with them by the main ST ELOI - YPRES road and not again by via VERBRANDEN MOLEN. The bridge over the canal cutting due S of VERBRANDEN MOLEN was destroyed by a landslide 2 years ago. Civilian labour has constructed deviations i.e. a causeway over the canal but it is boggy & only available for infantry or patrols in single file. The enemy were also shelling it this evening. Consequently it is necessary for 4th H rs to be supported by 3rd Cav Div.

The best support however would be to shell the bridges ridge N of HOLLEBEKE from the E of HOLLEBEKE north east wards. This position could be enfiladed from N.E. & S.W.

From 3rd Cav Bde
Place ST ELOI
Time 12-30 a.m.

The above may be forwarded as now corrected.   (Z) Kavanagh B Genl

Censor.   Signature of Addresser or person authorised to telegraph in

* This line should be erased if not required.

Op. order
From I Corps
To 3rd Cav Dn.

31/10/14

"A" Form.   Army Form C. 2121.
MESSAGES AND SIGNALS.

TO 3rd Cavalry Division

Sender's Number: G.541   Day of Month: 31st   AAA

As soon as the French battalions have moved forward to the attack of the HOLLEBEKE CHATEAU I will be glad if you would move one ~~two~~ brigade of cavalry midway between HOOGE and VELDHOEK south of that road aaa the troop should keep well under cover and would be available as a mobile reserve. Addressed 3rd Cavalry Division repeated Cavalry Corps

Your other brigade shall concentrate at road junctions about midway between KLEIN ZILLEBEKE and kilometre 5 on YPRES — MENIN road.

From: 1st Corps
Time: 6.55 A.M.

WAR DIARY - 3rd CAVALRY DIVISION.

1st - 22nd November, 1914.

1st November.
HOOGE
The Bdes. billeted for night of 31st Oct./1st Nov. at HOOGE. From a report of the day's operations received it appears that the enemy's assaults have been everywhere successfully repulsed.

1-0 a.m.
During the night the General Scheme of operations for 1st was received. The French were to attack at 6-30 a.m. from ST. ELOI towards HOUTHEM, and General Moussy was to co-operate, and General Bulfin was to assist the latter, whilst the 7th Division was to move forward with General Bulfin's left.

The enemy with whom we are fighting appeared to be from the 15th Corps, 2nd Bav. C. and 26th Divs. and the cavalry operating against ZANDVOORDE have apparently been replaced by infantry.

6-0 a.m.
The 3rd Cav. Div. concentrated near HOOGE as Corps Reserve; the troops in hand were 11 squadrons, and a quiet morning was spent.

News of the reported arrival of the German Emperor was received.

At 11-30 a.m. orders were received for 1 Bde. to move at once to the assistance of General Bulfin. The 6th was accordingly sent forward and took up a position near his left. In the meantime a hostile aeroplane had passed over us comparatively low down. It was heavily fired at without result, but it was considered advisable to change the position of the troops. This left a reserve of 5 squadrons 7th Cav. Bde., but these were shortly increased by the arrival of the 2 squadrons which had been left overnight with the 4th Hussars.

2-0 p.m.
News was received that the Irish Guards were being driven in; the 7th Cav. Bde. accordingly moved up in support of them; the enemy appeared to be massing in the woods S. of HOOGE.

The fight gradually died down and the Bdes. were withdrawn to the neighbourhood of HOOGE for the night.

Orders were received for the move of the Div. on the 2nd.

2nd November.
YPRES
Instructions were received at 10-30 p.m. on the 1st concerning to-day's operations. The French attacked towards GHELUVELT with eight battalions supported by their own artillery.

S. of HOOGE
5-45 a.m.
The 3rd Cav. Div. moved to the woods S. of HOOGE as a Reserve.

In the meantime there had been heavy fighting in the direction of WYTSCHAETE.

1-30 p.m.
Reports that the line about VELDHOEK was giving way resulted in the 7th Cav. Bde. being sent off to strengthen the 1st Div. along the YPRES - MENIN Rd. The Bde. galloped up under a severe shell fire and occupied the
line

line of the road N. & S. through VELDHOEK.

About the same time news was received that considerable pressure was being brought to bear at the point of junction of 7th Div. and 2nd Bde.

A regiment was accordingly held in readiness to move up if required by Lord Cavan.

Near HOOGE
2-5 p.m.

It was found, however, that the French attack towards GHELUVELT relieved the pressure in that quarter, and about 4-0 p.m. the 7th Cav. Bde. moved back to its original rendezvous.

5-35 p.m.   Similarly, the 7th Div. and 2nd Bde. were able to maintain their line, and as darkness fell the 6th Cav. Bde. moved into bivouac near HOOGE and the 7th Cav. Bde. into some farms about 1 mile E. of ZILLEBEKE. Hd. Qrs. returned to the Rd. junction of MENIN and ZONNEBEKE roads at YPRES.

9-0 p.m.   The general situation in the evening was that we had maintained our line against very severe attacks throughout the day, whilst on our right the French had made some progress and taken over 100 prisoners. On our left the 9th (French) Corps had maintained its position; in short, the state of affairs was considered satisfactory.

3rd November.   In accordance with instructions received overnight, the 3rd Cav. Div. rendezvoused as on the 2nd, the Hd. Qrs. being established near the 3rd Kil. YPRES - MENIN Rd.

A certain amount of shelling took place, but otherwise the day passed without anything of interest occurring.

A report was received from Hd. Qrs. 1st A.C. warning all ranks that the 1st Cav. Div. had been attacked at night by Germans dressed in British uniforms.

The Div. was ordered to be in reserve on the 4th. Situation generally appeared to have improved. French attack on our right progressed satisfactorily, and Belgians also had marked success N. of DIXMUDE.

4th November
YPRES 6-30 a.m.
The Bdes. rendezvoused, the 6th at a farm near Ry. 1 m. N. of YPRES - MENIN Rd., the 7th in woods near cross-roads 1 m. E. of ZILLEBEKE. Both brigades had been turned out during the night and warned to assist 2nd Bde., but alarm proved unfounded and only 1 sqd. of 7th Cav. Bde. was actually employed.

9-15 a.m.   The 3rd Fd. Sq. R.E. was lent for the day to the 1st Div. to assist in strengthening their position. The G.O.C. forwarded a short report on the operations of the 3rd Cav. Div. from 30th Oct. to 3rd Nov.

Warning was received and passed on to Bdes. that a

Staff

staff officer who was unknown and might be a German had been alarming troops as to the situation.

The Div. was not called upon during the day and at dusk moved into bivouacs and billets, the 6th Bde. at its rendezvous and the 7th at VERBRANDEN MOLEN. The latter supplied two dismounted squadrons to assist the 2nd Inf. Bde. (Lord Cavan) during the night if necessary; they were to bivouac in rear of KLEIN ZILLEBEKE. The fighting throughout the whole area appeared to have been satisfactory during the day and a steady improvement on the last few days. Some German guns were captured N. of DIXMUDE, and the French attack on WYTSCHAETE - MESSINES had progressed favourably.

The Div. was to rendezvous as for to-day and to be in reserve. Hd. Qrs. for the night moved down some 200 yards towards YPRES (main road) owing to last night's Hd. Qrs. having been partially destroyed by shell fire.

5th November
6-30 a.m.

Bdes. rendezvoused as for the 4th. The 3rd D.Gs. had joined the division the previous evening. A very quiet day was spent, no call being made on the troops.

8-30 p.m.

The 6th Cav. Bde. was lent to the 1st Div. in the evening to relieve the 3rd Inf. Bde. in the trenches south of VELDHOEK. They took them over at 8-30 p.m. The 7th Cav. Bde. billeted at VERBRANDEN MOLEN and were at Lord Cavan's disposal if required. Hd. Qrs. remained as for last night, 200 yards S.W. of the YPRES - MENIN, YPRES - ZONNEBEKE road junction.

The 7th Bde. was ordered to be in Corps Reserve on the 6th.

6th November
3rd Kil. YPRES-
Menin Rd.

4-0 p.m.

Up to the forenoon, little of interest occurred and arrangements were on train for the relief of the 6th Cav. Bde. It was understood that the 7th Cav. Bde. would probably have to take over part of the 1st Inf. Bde's. trenches; the 7th Cav. Bde's. numbers had been so depleted that only 600 rifles could be counted upon for this duty. About 4 p.m. a verbal message (which was followed later by a written one) was received stating that the French were falling back rapidly on Lord Cavan's right. The 7th Cav. Bde. at once advanced to his support. General Kavanagh deployed the 1st and 2nd Life Guards N. of the ZILLEBEKE - KLEIN ZILLEBEKE Rd. with the Blues in reserve behind the centre. His advance encouraged the French to re-assume the offensive and all went well until near ZWARTELEEN when General Kavanagh halted his Bde. to allow the French to re-occupy their line (running) along the road N.E. from that place. Suddenly the French returned at the run, reporting a strong advance of the Germans. General Kavanagh doubled a couple of squadrons across the road to endeavour to stem the rush, and suffered a certain number of casualties in so doing. Considerable confusion ensued and there was a melee of English, French and Germans, and the 7th Cav. Bde. was obliged to retire some 150 yards to the reserve trenches before it could extricate itself. It succeeded in establishing itself there and in protecting Lord Cavan's right flank until he was able, with the assistance of the 22nd Inf. Bde. to re-establish his line - indeed the 1st Life Guards did not leave their position until about 2 a.m.

Lord Cavan reported that the Bde. behaved in a most

gallant

gallant manner, was most ably and bravely led, and saved what threatened to be a critical situation.

Unfortunately it suffered severely, 17 officers and some 60 men being killed or wounded. Amongst the officers killed were both the Commanding Officers of the Blues and 2nd Life Guards, Colonels Wilson and Dawnay, both of whom received special mention in General Kavanagh's report of the engagement. The gallantry of Major Hon. A. Stanley, 1st Life Guards, and Lt. S. Menzies, 2nd Life Guards, was also brought to the notice of the G.O.C., 3rd Cav. Div. who forwarded a report concerning the matter to the 1st Corps.

Both Sir Douglas Haig and Sir John French thanked Gen. Kavanagh for the way he carried out the above operation.

7th November
YPRES-MENIN Rd.
5-30 a.m.

Owing to the attack on Lord Cavan's right and also partly to one which took place against the 2nd Div. N. of the YPRES-MENIN Road, it was not till 5-0 a.m. that the 6th Cav. Bde. were relieved from the trenches, when they fell back to their previous bivouacs N. of WITTE POORT. It was also found necessary to move the 7th Cav. Bde. up to Lord Cavan's assistance at 5-30 a.m., when he initiated a counter attack in order to regain the road running N.E. from KLEIN ZILLEBEKE through the woods.

On the latter operation proving successful, the 7th Cav. Bde. was allowed to withdraw to VERBRANDEN MOLEN and remain in a position of readiness. Lord Cavan in his advance captured 3 machine guns, but a strong counter-attack by the Germans obliged him to withdraw to the line occupied overnight, and it was not until well on into the afternoon that the line was regained. About 2 p.m. the 6th Cav. Bde. became the 'Bde. for Duty' in case of Lord Cavan needing assistance, and moved to a position of readiness near the 3rd Kil. YPRES - MENIN Rd., the 7th Cav. Bde. moving into the area formerly occupied by the 6th.

The usual afternoon scare caused the 10th Hussars to be sent to ZILLEBEKE about 4-0 p.m., but it was soon found possible to withdraw the regiment again to its former position.

8th November
YPRES.

The 3rd Cav. Div. was again in Corps Reserve. The day passed uneventfully. The line on our right had practically been re-established. During the afternoon the 10th Hussars were sent up to prepare support trenches in rear of Lord Cavan; this was to save having to turn the Bde., or portions of it, out in case of alarm during the night, and to give Lord Cavan a more easily accessible reserve.

General Vidal entrenched a line from HOOGE, through ZILLEBEKE to VOORMEZEELE as a base for a fresh French advance which may take place.

Casualties amongst officers of the 2nd Life Guards have been particularly severe. They have now only four officers for duty, 2 of whom are Indian Army, and 1 a Reserve Officer who has not been with the Regiment for some time. During the afternoon orders, confirmed later by wire, were received for 500 rifles to take over a portion of Lord Cavan's line. This duty fell to the 6th Cav. Bde., who passed a quiet

night

5.

night in the trenches.

9th November
YPRES

Nothing of interest occurred. Reliefs were carried out in the evening, 520 men of the 7th Cav. Bde. taking over the trenches occupied by the 6th Cav. Bde. for the previous 24 hours.

Col. David Campbell, 9th Lancers, took over command of the 6th Cav. Bde., vice Br. Gen. Makins - ill.

10th November
YPRES

No change took place in the situation in our immediate front during the previous 24 hours. The 7th Cav. Bde. had a quiet night and morning.

3-0 p.m.

Arrangements were made to try and make the men's bivouacs more comfortable; the O.C., 3rd Field Sqdn. R.E. brought up some hurdles and men to show how shelters could be improvised. Lord Cavan reported that the enemy appeared to be massing along his front and also along the front of the 3rd Div.; the 6th Cav. Bde. therefore moved up to the vicinity of ZILLEBEKE to be ready to support him if required; the 3rd D.Gs. were posted immediately north of the Farm 1 m. due E. of that place, the remainder of the Bde. (whose tour of duty it was in the trenches) being held in readiness a little further in rear.

11th November
YPRES

The 6th Cav. Bde. passed a quiet night in the trenches, but soon after dawn were heavily shelled and continued to be so during most of the day. The situation appeared to be satisfactory in spite of reported reverses by French about BIXSCHOETE and DIXMUDE.

9-30 a.m.

The rumour that the Germans were transferring troops to the East was not borne out by the strong attacks which were made by fresh troops (1st Guards Regt. of Guards Corps) on our front during the day. As early as 9-37 a.m. the

10-0 a.m.

1st Div. reported an attack in large numbers up the MENIN road, and shortly afterwards that the enemy had broken through the 1st Bde. in the vicinity of the S.W. corner of the POLYGONE Wood.

10-25 a.m.

Our R.H.A. was ordered to co-operate in repelling this attack, and the 7th Cav. Bde. was sent towards the wood S.E. of WESTHOEK so as to be in readiness. Shortly afterwards, however, the Brig. Gen., Gen. Staff, 1st Corps, arrived, and after consultation with General Byng and

11 a.m.

G.O.C., 1st Div. decided to recall the 7th Cav. Bde. to original rendezvous and the situation along the MENIN road appeared to have improved, and it was feared that possibly reinforcements might be required for Lord CAVAN'S right.

3.30 p.m.

In spite of heavy shelling throughout the day, no call was made upon the division until Lord CAVAN asked for a regiment to support the London Scottish who had had a bad time. The 3rd Dragoon Guards were accordingly sent up for the night. The situation in this quarter however, was so

5.45 p.m.

much improved by 5.45 p.m. (the London Scottish having successfully charged the trenches from which the enemy had been harassing them) that Lord CAVAN was able to send the 3rd Dragoon Guards back to their bivouac.

Meanwhile, in spite of a report that the line
across

across the MENIN road had been regained, the 1st Division found it necessary to ask for the assistance of the 7th Cavalry Brigade to assist them to recover ground lost near the S.W. corner of the POLYGON wood.

The Composite Regiment of Household Cavalry joined the Division during the afternoon - a welcome reinforcement for the 7th Cavalry Brigade.

12th November.
YPRES.

News was received during the night that a counter-attack was to be initiated at 1 a.m. to endeavour to regain the trenches between POLYGON wood and VELDHOEK. From reports received verbally it does not seem that this was very well organized and little result was obtained, and a new line was formed from the above wood along S.E. edge of NONNEBOSCHEN wood to join up with the left of the 3rd Division near MENIN road.

The 7th Cavalry Brigade which had been detailed to support the above counter-attack, was not engaged, and joined the portion of the 6th Cavalry Brigade not employed in the trenches as part of the Corps Reserve about 11 a.m.

From statements made by prisoners captured yesterday it seems certain that a great effort had been made by means of the German Guard regiments to break through our line to YPRES.

9.40 a.m.

Meanwhile, a report was received that the left of our line (held by the 6th Infantry Brigade) and the right of the French was being heavily attacked, but the assistance of the 3rd Cavalry Division was not required to reinforce our line in that quarter. The troops of the 6th Cavalry Brigade in the trenches (520 rifles) under Lord CAVAN experienced the usual shelling, but otherwise were not attacked, and in the evening their place was taken by the 3rd Dragoon Guards who had been held in close support near Lord CAVAN'S headquarters, the 2nd Life Guards taking the place of the latter regiment, as Lord CAVAN anticipated a night attack.

3.35 p.m.

On the whole, the situation at the end of the day appeared to have improved. Large numbers of Germans were reported to have been killed in front of various portions of the line.

A complimentary telegram was received from SIR DOUGLAS HAIG on behalf of the C-in-C thanking the troops for their conduct in yesterday's fight.

The North Somerset and Leicestershire Yeomanry joined the division during the day.

13th November.
YPRES.
9.40 a.m.

A quiet night was passed by the troops in the trenches, but early information was received of a possible attack on KLEIN ZILLEBEKE; accordingly the 7th Cavalry Brigade was held in readiness to move at a moment's notice in support.

10-40 a.m.

The general situation appeared to have improved a certain amount; the French on our right had been reinforced and had recovered some ground E. of ZONNEBEKE which they lost in the fighting on the 12th. The enemy's losses are stated on reliable information to have been very heavy, the total casualties to the end of September being put down at 507,000, whilst it is estimated that 250,000 more have been killed or wounded.

The

7.

The 7th Cavalry Brigade were to take over the trenches for 48 hours from the 6th in the evening, the latter brigade having held them for 72 hours.

2.35 p.m.   Later in the day reports were again received of a possible attack against Lord CAVAN, and at 3.40 p.m. that officer asked for the 7th Cavalry Brigade to move up in support, the 2nd Life Guards having already been called upon by him. As, however, the 7th Cavalry Brigade were ordered to take over the trenches, it was thought better to send up the 6th.

6 p.m.   The anticipated attack did not take place, and as the situation appeared normal, the 6th Cavalry Brigade was withdrawn to its original bivouac by the 2½ kilo, MENIN road. The position of the Brigade had been somehow or other ascertained by the enemy during the afternoon, and a sudden burst of shell fire caused a few casualties amongst the men and some 60 amongst the horses.

14th November.
YPRES.
8 a.m.   The night passed without incident. The 3rd Field Squadron R.E. put in some excellent work (their third consecutive night out) digging an advanced trench with a communicating one trench back to the original one, and blowing up some houses from which snipers had been annoying the men in our section of the trenches,

The whole front was heavily shelled yesterday, but everywhere the enemy's attacks were repulsed with loss. The 3rd Cavalry Division was again in Corps Reserve, but the position of the 6th Cavalry Brigade having apparently been ascertained by the enemy and heavily shelled (68 horses were hit), it was found necessary to move this brigade.

It was decided, therefore, to have one brigade on duty, finding 500 rifles for the trenches, 300 for Lord CAVAN'S immediate support and 400 as Corps Reserve, the latter in dug-outs in railway cutting near HALTE (2nd kilo, MENIN road). All the horses of the brigade to be kept west of YPRES. The other Brigade was to be held in readiness somewhere W. of YPRES, one regiment being kept saddled up.

2 p.m.   The 6th Cavalry Brigade was moved during the day to billets near Divisional Headquarters, and positions for the 7th were reconnoitred.

An attack by the enemy on the 13th and 9th Brigades was reported, but nothing more came of it.

3 p.m.   News was received that the French were to take over the positions E. of YPRES from to-morrow night,

15th November.
YPRES.   The casualties in the Guards Division appear to have been heavier than was at first thought, only 5% of its original serving soldiers being left. Little change has taken place in our own front in spite of a series of attacks against Lord CAVAN'S trenches,

12.45 a.m.   During the night information was received that the 3rd Division expected the attack along their front to be renewed, one regiment (10th Hussars) was accordingly ordered to be near BELLEWARDE Farm by 6:30 a.m. and the remainder of the 6th Cavalry Brigade to be in readiness.

9 a.m.

9:0 a.m.	The situation appeared normal, the withdrawal of the 10th Hussars was sanctioned
1:30 p.m.	The relief of the I.C. and 3rd Cavalry Division line is/to commence from the left tonight - to facilitate the reliefs which will take place, the 3rd Cavalry Division have taken over the trenches occupied last night by the 1st Cavalry Division.
6-30 p.m.	This, together with the normal 500 rifles in the trenches, requires the whole of the 6th Cavalry Brigade; the Corps Reserve of 400 rifles has, therefore, been found by the 7th Cavalry Brigade. Lord Cavan reports a successful day and able artillery co-operation which kept down annoyance by snipers.

NOVEMBER 16th.
YPRES.

Another quiet day. The general situation continued satisfactory and strong French reinforcements arrived to relieve our much tried troops.

The heavy rain of the last few days has turned the 7th Cavalry Brigade area into a quagmire. Efforts were again made to find them a more suitable area W. of YPRES but without success.

The 6th Cavalry Brigade continued to occupy part of the trenches in Lord Cavan's line with 1,000 rifles and a local reserve of 200, the 7th Cavalry Brigade finding the Corps Reserve of 400 rifles, which, during the afternoon, was moved from the farm by 2½ kil. MENIN road to dug-outs prepared in the railway cutting 200 yards south of HALTE, 2nd kil. MENIN road.

3:30 p.m.	Lord Cavan reported all quiet during the afternoon.
7:20 p.m.	The situation continues satisfactory. Considerable execution is reported by prisoners to have been done by our H.E. shell yesterday. The French continued to take over part of our line of trenches.

NOVEMBER 17th.
YPRES.

From early morning heavy artillery fire was opened against our whole front, it appeared to be particularly severe in the direction of KLEIN ZILLEBEKE. It was succeeded by a lull and then by a certain amount of musketry fire, but as no reserves were called up from the division, it was not thought that any serious attack was being made; Lord Cavan had reported the concentration of considerable numbers in his front to the 3rd Division, but this information was not received by us till 4:45 p.m.

1:35 p.m.

During the morning, Lord Cavan's H.Q. had been so persistently shelled that he had been obliged to move them further back. Information was also received that part of our trenches (500 rifles) was to be taken over by the Hertfordshire T.F.

8:0 p.m.

It was not until the evening that we learned how determined an attack had been made during the day, and how it had been repulsed everywhere with considerable loss to the enemy. The general situation appeared most satisfactory.

The 7th Cavalry Brigade relieved the 6th in the trenches.

NOVEMBER 18th.
YPRES.
9:20 a.m.

The full gravity of yesterday's attack only became apparent this morning. After a severe bombardment, during which the trenches held by the 3rd D.G's had been blown in, two distinct attacks were made, one at 1 p.m. and one at 4 p.m. Our casualties were severe, amounting to some 130 odd killed and wounded, including 6 officers killed. It

is

is satisfactory to know that the enemy's losses were very severe, some 370 dead being counted in front of our own trenches, whilst according to I.C. at least 800 in all were killed.

During the morning an aeroplane passed over the dug-outs occupied by Divisional H.Q. and the Corps Reserve of 400 rifles; it was shortly followed by some fairly accurate shrapnel fire, but, as in the meantime, all horses had been moved away, only one casualty was the result.

Verbal reports were received that our trenches were again being shelled, and that the 2nd Life Guards had had a certain amount of casualties.

A congratulatory telegram was received from Sir Douglas Haig on the work of the 6th Cavalry Brigade during the previous day.

The G.O.C. subsequently forwarded a report from the Brigadier and commanders of sections of the trenches on the attack on the 6th Cavalry Brigade November 17th. He drew particular attention to the conduct of the North Somerset Yeomanry which had behaved most staunchly. He also mentioned the good work done by Lieut. Hon. J. Grenfell, No. 5241 Sergt. MacLellan, and No.231 Corpl. Kelman all of the Royal Dragoons on 16th and 17th. Also of Captain Wright and Lieut. Chapman (both killed) 3rd D.G's, in the recapture of some buildings in the possession of the Germans.

NOVEMBER 19th. YPRES.

The trenches were again shelled during the night of the 18th/19th, and it was reported that the 7th Cavalry Brigade had suffered some further casualties amounting to about 32. The right trench appears open to a certain amount of enfilade fire and in spite of repeated work by the 3rd Field Squadron R.E. it is here that the heaviest casualties occur.

Orders for the relief of our trenches were received during the day, and in accordance with them the 6th Cavalry Brigade and the divisional troops were ordered to move to the concentration area on the 20th; the 7th Cavalry Brigade to follow them on the 21st. No. 1125 Corpl. of Horse Warren, R.H.G's distinguished himself during the day's fighting.

NOVEMBER 20th. YPRES.

In accordance with orders of 19th the 3rd Cavalry Division moved to the concentration area which had been allotted it. The formation of the 8th Cavalry Brigade was to take place as soon as this was reached, and so the 10th Hussars and R.H.G's were to move direct into an area set apart for that brigade. The concentration area was in the vicinity of HAZEBROUCK, the 7th Cavalry Brigade was to be in the area HONDEGHEM - ST. SYLVESTRA - EECKE - CAESTRE; the 6th and 8th Cavalry Brigades and divisional troops in the area HAZEBROUCK - VIEUX BERQUIN - VIERHOUEK - THIENNES. The G.O.C. and one S.O. proceeded to 7th Cavalry Brigade H.Q., the remainder of the staff to LA MOTTE where it had been intended to establish divisional H.Q. En route information was received that this place was not available, and so other quarters had to be found. These were eventually procured in HAZEBROUCK.

NOVEMBER 21st. HAZEBROUCK.

The 6th Cavalry Brigade did not arrive until very late last night owing to the slippery nature of the roads. For the same reason, although the 7th Cavalry Brigade marched

at

at 9 a.m., it was dark before they reached their new billets, and the bulk of their transport did not arrive before the following day.

NOVEMBER 22nd - 30th.
HAZEBROUCK.

For the remainder of the month there was no material change in the situation and the division remained in reserve and was again incorporated in the Cavalry Corps.

The formation of the 8th Cavalry Brigade was proceeded with.

HAZEBROUCK.   General Staff.

December, 1914.   3rd Cavalry Division.

Report on Operations p. 12 noon.
Oct. 26th

O.1

12.40 p.m. Orders were issued for 7. C. Bde. to advance against KORTEWILDE at 3-0 p.m. This advance was to be supported by 6. C. Bde., who were to remain in their trenches, and by both Bys. R.H.A., which came under orders of C.R.A.

1.10 p.m. The above orders had only just been issued when a report was received from 7. Div. stating that 20. Inf. Bde. front had been broken in 3 or 4 places near KRUISEIK and that it might be necessary to fall back after dark.

Brigadiers were informed & advance postponed pending instructions from G.O.C. Cav. & Corps.

2-40 p.m. A Staff Officer fr. IV A.C. (Col. Dallas) asks if 3. C. Div. could assist in extricating 20. Inf. Bde. At this hour the position was:— 6. Cav. Bde. and 1 Sqd. 7. Cav. Bde. in trenches from Chateau near Railway about 1 mile E. of HOLLEBEKE to ZANDVOORDE - WERVICQ Rd. (both incl.); 7. Cav. Bde. assembling at X Rds. in KLEIN ZILLEBEKE; "C" & "K" Bys. in action in original positions in rear of 6. C. Bde, but preparing to take up new positions under C.R.A. to cover advance on KORTEWILDE.

After seeing Brigadiers, G.O.C. ordered Genl. Kavanagh to make a demonstration towards KRUISEIK with the idea of relieving the pressure against the 20. Inf. Bde.

4-30 p.m. About this time the above demonstration was carried out most successfully by the Royal Horse Guards. Unfortunately this was not adequately supported by the Artillery owing to the fact that they had commenced to move to their new positions.

5.30 pm. About this hour G.O.C. motored in to H.Q. to ascertain the dispositions of the Inf. on the left of 6" C. Bde. as a rumour had reached him that the line was only prolonged by the Gordon Hgrs. whose left flank was completely en l'air. 7" C. Bde. were to move into billets at KLEIN ZILLEBEKE, 6" C. Bde. to remain in the trenches & both Bys. to move to ZILLEBEKE.

8.45 pm. It was understood that line was being re-occupied by G.O.C. 7" Div.

27.X.14

WAR DIARY - 3rd CAVALRY DIVISION.

1st - 22nd November, 1914.

1st November. The Bdes. billeted for night of 31st Oct./1st Nov. at
HOOGE   HOOGE. From a report of the day's operations received it
               appears that the enemy's assaults have been everywhere
               successfully repulsed.

1-0 a.m.   During the night the General Scheme of operations for
               1st was received. The French were to attack at 6-30 a.m.
               from ST. ELOI towards HOUTHEM, and General Moussy was to
               co-operate, and General Bulfin was to assist the latter,
               whilst the 7th Division was to move forward with General
               Bulfin's left.

               The enemy with whom we are fighting appeared to be from
               the 15th Corps, 2nd Bav. C. and 26th Divs. and the cavalry
               operating against ZANDVOORDE have apparently been replaced
               by infantry.

6-0 a.m.   The 3rd Cav. Div. concentrated near HOOGE as Corps
               Reserve; the troops in hand were 11 squadrons, and a quiet
               morning was spent.

               News of the reported arrival of the German Emperor was
               received.

               At 11-30 a.m. orders were received for 1 Bde. to move
               at once to the assistance of General Bulfin. The 6th was
               accordingly sent forward and took up a position near his
               left. In the meantime a hostile aeroplane had passed over
               us comparatively low down. It was heavily fired at without
               result, but it was considered advisable to change the
               position of the troops. This left a reserve of 5 squadrons
               7th Cav. Bde., but these were shortly increased by the
               arrival of the 2 squadrons which had been left overnight with
               the 4th Hussars.

2-0 p.m.   News was received that the Irish Guards were being
               driven in; the 7th Cav. Bde. accordingly moved up in support
               of them; the enemy appeared to be massing in the woods S.
               of HOOGE.

               The fight gradually died down and the Bdes. were with-
               drawn to the neighbourhood of HOOGE for the night.

               Orders were received for the move of the Div. on the 2nd.

2nd November. Instructions were received at 10-30 p.m. on the 1st
YPRES   concerning to-day's operations. The French attacked towards
               GHELUVELT with eight battalions supported by their own
               artillery.

S. of HOOGE   The 3rd Cav. Div. moved to the woods S. of HOOGE as a
5-45 a.m.   Reserve.

               In the meantime there had been heavy fighting in the
               direction of WYTSCHAETE.

1-30 p.m.   Reports that the line about VELDHOEK was giving way
               resulted in the 7th Cav. Bde. being sent off to strengthen
               the 1st Div. along the YPRES - MENIN Rd. The Bde.
               galloped up under a severe shell fire and occupied the
                                                                    line

line of the road N. & S. through VELDHOEK.

About the same time news was received that considerable pressure was being brought to bear at the point of junction of 7th Div. and 2nd Bde.

A regiment was accordingly held in readiness to move up if required by Lord Cavan.

Near HOOGE
2-5 p.m.

It was found, however, that the French attack towards GHELUVELT relieved the pressure in that quarter, and about 4-0 p.m. the 7th Cav. Bde. moved back to its original rendezvous.

5-35 p.m.

Similarly, the 7th Div. and 2nd Bde. were able to maintain their line, and as darkness fell the 6th Cav. Bde. moved into bivouac near HOOGE and the 7th Cav. Bde. into some farms about 1 mile E. of ZILLEBEKE. Hd. Qrs. returned to the Rd. junction of MENIN and ZONNEBEKE roads at YPRES.

9-0 p.m.

The general situation in the evening was that we had maintained our line against very severe attacks throughout the day, whilst on our right the French had made some progress and taken over 100 prisoners. On our left the 9th (French) Corps had maintained its position; in short, the state of affairs was considered satisfactory.

3rd November.

In accordance with instructions received overnight, the 3rd Cav. Div. rendezvoused as on the 2nd, the Hd. Qrs. being established near the 3rd Kil. YPRES - MENIN Rd.

A certain amount of shelling took place, but otherwise the day passed without anything of interest occurring.

A report was received from Hd. Qrs. 1st A.C. warning all ranks that the 1st Cav. Div. had been attacked at night by Germans dressed in British uniforms.

The Div. was ordered to be in reserve on the 4th. Situation generally appeared to have improved. French attack on our right progressed satisfactorily, and Belgians also had marked success N. of DIXMUDE.

4th November
YPRES 6-30 a.m.

The Bdes. rendezvoused, the 6th at a farm near Ry. 1 m. N. of YPRES - MENIN Rd., the 7th in woods near cross-roads 1 m. E. of ZILLEBEKE. Both brigades had been turned out during the night and warned to assist 2nd Bde., but alarm proved unfounded and only 1 sqd. of 7th Cav. Bde. was actually employed.

9-15 a.m.

The 3rd Fd. Sq. R.E. was lent for the day to the 1st Div. to assist in strengthening their position. The G.O.C. forwarded a short report on the operations of the 3rd Cav. Div. from 30th Oct. to 3rd Nov.

Warning was received and passed on to Bdes. that a

Staff

staff officer who was unknown and might be a German had been alarming troops as to the situation.

The Div. was not called upon during the day and at dusk moved into bivouacs and billets, the 6th Bde. at its rendezvous and the 7th at VERBRANDEN MOLEN. The latter supplied two dismounted squadrons to assist the 2nd Inf. Bde. (Lord Cavan) during the night if necessary; they were to bivouac in rear of KLEIN ZILLEBEKE. The fighting throughout the whole area appeared to have been satisfactory during the day and a steady improvement on the last few days. Some German guns were captured N. of DIXMUDE, and the French attack on WYTSCHAETE - MESSINES had progressed favourably.

The Div. was to rendezvous as for to-day and to be in reserve. Hd. Qrs. for the night moved down some 200 yards towards YPRES (main road) owing to last night's Hd. Qrs. having been partially destroyed by shell fire.

5th November
6-30 a.m.

Bdes. rendezvoused as for the 4th. The 3rd D.Gs. had joined the division the previous evening. A very quiet day was spent, no call being made on the troops.

8-30 p.m.

The 6th Cav. Bde. was lent to the 1st Div. in the evening to relieve the 3rd Inf. Bde. in the trenches south of VELDHOEK. They took them over at 8-30 p.m. The 7th Cav. Bde. billeted at VERBRANDEN MOLEN and were at Lord Cavan's disposal if required. Hd. Qrs. remained as for last night, 200 yards S.W. of the YPRES - MENIN, YPRES - ZONNEBEKE road junction.

The 7th Bde. was ordered to be in Corps Reserve on the 6th.

6th November
3rd Kil. YPRES-
Menin Rd.

4-0 p.m.

Up to the forenoon, little of interest occurred and arrangements were on train for the relief of the 6th Cav. Bde. It was understood that the 7th Cav. Bde. would probably have to take over part of the 1st Inf. Bde's. trenches; the 7th Cav. Bde's. numbers had been so depleted that only 600 rifles could be counted upon for this duty. About 4 p.m. a verbal message (which was followed later by a written one) was received stating that the French were falling back rapidly on Lord Cavan's right. The 7th Cav. Bde. at once advanced to his support. General Kavanagh deployed the 1st and 2nd Life Guards N. of the ZILLEBEKE - KLEIN ZILLEBEKE Rd. with the Blues in reserve behind the centre. His advance encouraged the French to re-assume the offensive and all went well until near ZWARTELEEN when General Kavanagh halted his Bde. to allow the French to re-occupy their line (running) along the road N.E. from that place. Suddenly the French returned at the run, reporting a strong advance of the Germans. General Kavanagh doubled a couple of squadrons across the road to endeavour to stem the rush, and suffered a certain number of casualties in so doing. Considerable confusion ensued and there was a melee of English, French and Germans, and the 7th Cav. Bde. was obliged to retire some 150 yards to the reserve trenches before it could extricate itself. It succeeded in establishing itself there and in protecting Lord Cavan's right flank until he was able, with the assistance of the 22nd Inf. Bde. to re-establish his line - indeed the 1st Life Guards did not leave their position until about 2 a.m.

Lord Cavan reported that the Bde. behaved in a most

gallant

gallant manner, was most ably and bravely led, and saved what threatened to be a critical situation.

Unfortunately it suffered severely, 17 officers and some 60 men being killed or wounded. Amongst the officers killed were both the Commanding Officers of the Blues and 2nd Life Guards, Colonels Wilson and Dawnay, both of whom received special mention in General Kavanagh's report of the engagement. The gallantry of Major Hon. A. Stanley, 1st Life Guards, and Lt. S. Menzies, 2nd Life Guards, was also brought to the notice of the G.O.C., 3rd Cav. Div. who forwarded a report concerning the matter to the 1st Corps.

Both Sir Douglas Haig and Sir John French thanked Gen. Kavanagh for the way he carried out the above operation.

7th November
YPRES-MENIN Rd.
5-30 a.m.

Owing to the attack on Lord Cavan's right and also partly to one which took place against the 2nd Div. N. of the YPRES-MENIN Road, it was not till 5-0 a.m. that the 6th Cav. Bde. were relieved from the trenches, when they fell back to their previous bivouacs N. of WITTE POORT. It was also found necessary to move the 7th Cav. Bde. up to Lord Cavan's assistance at 5-30 a.m., when he initiated a counter attack in order to regain the road running N.E. from KLEIN ZILLEBEKE through the woods.

On the latter operation proving successful, the 7th Cav. Bde. was allowed to withdraw to VERBRANDEN MOLEN and remain in a position of readiness. Lord Cavan in his advance captured 3 machine guns, but a strong counter-attack by the Germans obliged him to withdraw to the line occupied overnight, and it was not until well on into the afternoon that the line was regained. About 2 p.m. the 6th Cav. Bde. became the 'Bde. for Duty' in case of Lord Cavan needing assistance, and moved to a position of readiness near the 3rd Kil. YPRES - MENIN Rd., the 7th Cav. Bde. moving into the area formerly occupied by the 6th.

The usual afternoon scare caused the 10th Hussars to be sent to ZILLEBEKE about 4-0 p.m., but it was soon found possible to withdraw the regiment again to its former position.

8th November
YPRES.

The 3rd Cav. Div. was again in Corps Reserve. The day passed uneventfully. The line on our right had practically been re-established. During the afternoon the 10th Hussars were sent up to prepare support trenches in rear of Lord Cavan; this was to save having to turn the Bde., or portions of it, out in case of alarm during the night, and to give Lord Cavan a more easily accessible reserve.

General Vidal entrenched a line from HOOGE, through ZILLEBEKE to VOORMEZEELE as a base for a fresh French advance which may take place.

Casualties amongst officers of the 2nd Life Guards have been particularly severe. They have now only four officers for duty, 2 of whom are Indian Army, and 1 a Reserve Officer who has not been with the Regiment for some time. During the afternoon orders, confirmed later by wire, were received for 500 rifles to take over a portion of Lord Cavan's line. This duty fell to the 6th Cav. Bde., who passed a quiet

night

night in the trenches.

9th November YPRES	Nothing of interest occurred. Reliefs were carried out in the evening, 520 men of the 7th Cav. Bde. taking over the trenches occupied by the 6th Cav. Bde. for the previous 24 hours. Col. David Campbell, 9th Lancers, took over command of the 6th Cav. Bde., vice Br. Gen. Makins - ill.
10th November YPRES	No change took place in the situation in our immediate front during the previous 24 hours. The 7th Cav. Bde. had a quiet night and morning.
3-0 p.m.	Arrangements were made to try and make the men's bivouacs more comfortable; the O.C., 3rd Field Sqdn. R.E. brought up some hurdles and men to show how shelters could be improvised. Lord Cavan reported that the enemy appeared to be massing along his front and also along the front of the 3rd Div.; the 6th Cav. Bde. therefore moved up to the vicinity of ZILLEBEKE to be ready to support him if required; the 3rd D.Gs. were posted immediately north of the Farm 1 m. due E. of that place, the remainder of the Bde. (whose tour of duty it was in the trenches) being held in readiness a little further in rear.
11th November YPRES	The 6th Cav. Bde. passed a quiet night in the trenches, but soon after dawn were heavily shelled and continued to be so during most of the day. The situation appeared to be satisfactory in spite of reported reverses by French about BIXSCHOETE and DIXMUDE.
9-30 a.m. 10-0 a.m.	The rumour that the Germans were transferring troops to the East was not borne out by the strong attacks which were made by fresh troops (1st Guards Regt. of Guards Corps) on our front during the day. As early as 9-37 a.m. the 1st Div. reported an attack in large numbers up the MENIN road, and shortly afterwards that the enemy had broken through the 1st Bde. in the vicinity of the S.W. corner of the POLYGONE Wood.
10-25 a.m. 11 a.m.	Our R.H.A. was ordered to co-operate in repelling this attack, and the 7th Cav. Bde. was sent towards the wood S.E. of WESTHOEK so as to be in readiness. Shortly afterwards, however, the Brig. Gen. Gen. Staff, 1st Corps, arrived, and after consultation with General Byng and G.O.C., 1st Div. decided to recall the 7th Cav. Bde. to original rendezvous and the situation along the MENIN road appeared to have improved, and it was feared that possibly reinforcements might be required for Lord CAVAN'S right.
3.30 p.m. 5.45 p.m.	In spite of heavy shelling throughout the day, no call was made upon the division until Lord CAVAN asked for a regiment to support the London Scottish who had had a bad time. The 3rd Dragoon Guards were accordingly sent up for the night. The situation in this quarter however, was so much improved by 5.45 p.m. (the London Scottish having successfully charged the trenches from which the enemy had been harassing them) that Lord CAVAN was able to send the 3rd Dragoon Guards back to their bivouac.

Meanwhile, in spite of a report that the line
across

6.

across the MENIN road had been regained, the 1st Division found it necessary to ask for the assistance of the 7th Cavalry Brigade to assist them to recover ground lost near the S.W. corner of the POLYGON wood.

The Composite Regiment of Household Cavalry joined the Division during the afternoon -- a welcome reinforcement for the 7th Cavalry Brigade.

12th November.
YPRES.

News was received during the night that a counter-attack was to be initiated at 1 a.m. to endeavour to regain the trenches between POLYGON wood and VELDHOEK. From reports received verbally it does not seem that this was very well organized and little result was obtained, and a new line was formed from the above wood along S.E. edge of NONNEBOSCHEN wood to join up with the left of the 3rd Division near MENIN road.

The 7th Cavalry Brigade which had been detailed to support the above counter-attack, was not engaged, and joined the portion of the 6th Cavalry Brigade not employed in the trenches as part of the Corps Reserve about 11 a.m.

From statements made by prisoners captured yesterday it seems certain that a great effort had been made by means of the German Guard regiments to break through our line to YPRES.

9.40 a.m.

Meanwhile, a report was received that the left of our line (held by the 6th Infantry Brigade) and the right of the French was being heavily attacked, but the assistance of the 3rd Cavalry Division was not required to reinforce our line in that quarter. The troops of the 6th Cavalry Brigade in the trenches (520 rifles) under Lord CAVAN experienced the usual shelling, but otherwise were not attacked, and in the evening their place was taken by the 3rd Dragoon Guards who had been held in close support near Lord CAVAN'S headquarters, the 2nd Life Guards taking the place of the latter regiment, as Lord CAVAN anticipated a night attack.

3.35 p.m.

On the whole, the situation at the end of the day appeared to have improved. Large numbers of Germans were reported to have been killed in front of various portions of the line.

A complimentary telegram was received from SIR DOUGLAS HAIG on behalf of the C-in-C thanking the troops for their conduct in yesterday's fight.

The North Somerset and Leicestershire Yeomanry joined the division during the day.

13th November.
YPRES.
9.40 a.m.

A quiet night was passed by the troops in the trenches, but early information was received of a possible attack on KLEIN ZILLEBEKE; accordingly the 7th Cavalry Brigade was held in readiness to move at a moment's notice in support.

10-40 a.m.

The general situation appeared to have improved a certain amount; the French on our right had been reinforced and had recovered some ground E. of ZONNEBEKE which they lost in the fighting on the 12th. The enemy's losses are stated on reliable information to have been very heavy, the total casualties to the end of September being put down at 507,000, whilst it is estimated that 250,000 more have been killed or wounded.

The

7.

The 7th Cavalry Brigade were to take over the trenches for 48 hours from the 6th in the evening, the latter brigade having held them for 72 hours.

2.35 p.m. Later in the day reports were again received of a possible attack against Lord CAVAN, and at 3.40 p.m. that officer asked for the 7th Cavalry Brigade to move up in support, the 2nd Life Guards having already been called upon by him. As, however, the 7th Cavalry Brigade were ordered to take over the trenches, it was thought better to send up the 6th.

6 p.m. The anticipated attack did not take place, and as the situation appeared normal, the 6th Cavalry Brigade was withdrawn to its original bivouac by the 2½ kilo, MENIN road. The position of the Brigade had been somehow or other ascertained by the enemy during the afternoon, and a sudden burst of shell fire caused a few casualties amongst the men and some 60 amongst the horses.

14th November.
YPRES.
8 a.m.
The night passed without incident. The 3rd Field Squadron R.E. put in some excellent work (their third consecutive night out) digging an advanced trench with a communicating one trench back to the original one, and blowing up some houses from which snipers had been annoying the men in our section of the trenches.

The whole front was heavily shelled yesterday, but everywhere the enemy's attacks were repulsed with loss. The 3rd Cavalry Division was again in Corps Reserve, but the position of the 6th Cavalry Brigade having apparently been ascertained by the enemy and heavily shelled (68 horses were hit), it was found necessary to move this brigade.

It was decided, therefore, to have one brigade on duty, finding 500 rifles for the trenches, 300 for Lord CAVAN'S immediate support and 400 as Corps Reserve, the latter in dug-outs in railway cutting near HALTE (2nd kilo, MENIN road) All the horses of the brigade to be kept west of YPRES. The other Brigade was to be held in readiness somewhere W. of YPRES, one regiment being kept saddled up.

2 p.m. The 6th Cavalry Brigade was moved during the day to billets near Divisional Headquarters, and positions for the 7th were reconnoitred.

An attack by the enemy on the 13th and 9th Brigades was reported, but nothing more came of it.

3 p.m. News was received that the French were to take over the positions E. of YPRES from to-morrow night.

15th November.
YPRES.
The casualties in the Guards Division appear to have been heavier than was at first thought, only 5% of its original serving soldiers being left. Little change has taken place in our own front in spite of a series of attacks against Lord CAVAN'S trenches.

12.45 a.m. During the night information was received that the 3rd Division expected the attack along their front to be renewed, one regiment (10th Hussars) was accordingly ordered to be near BELLEWARDE Farm by 6:30 a.m. and the remainder of the 6th Cavalry Brigade to be in readiness.

9 a.m.

9:0 a.m.	The situation appeared normal, the withdrawal of the 10th Hussars was sanctioned
1:30 p.m.	The relief of the I.C. and 3rd Cavalry Division line/to commence from the left tonight - to facilitate the reliefs which will take place, the 3rd Cavalry Division have taken over the trenches occupied last night by the 1st Cavalry Division.
6-30 p.m.	This, together with the normal 500 rifles in the trenches, requires the whole of the 6th Cavalry Brigade; the Corps Reserve of 400 rifles has, therefore, been found by the 7th Cavalry Brigade.
	Lord Cavan reports a successful day and able artillery co-operation which kept down annoyance by snipers.

NOVEMBER 16th.
YPRES.

Another quiet day. The general situation continued satisfactory and strong French reinforcements arrived to relieve our much tried troops.

The heavy rain of the last few days has turned the 7th Cavalry Brigade area into a quagmire. Efforts were again made to find them a more suitable area W. of YPRES but without success.

The 6th Cavalry Brigade continued to occupy part of the trenches in Lord Cavan's line with 1,000 rifles and a local reserve of 200, the 7th Cavalry Brigade finding the Corps Reserve of 400 rifles, which, during the afternoon, was moved from the farm by 2½ kil. MENIN road to dug-outs prepared in the railway cutting 200 yards south of HALTE, 2nd kil. MENIN road.

3:30 p.m. Lord Cavan reported all quiet during the afternoon.

7:20 p.m. The situation continues satisfactory. Considerable execution is reported by prisoners to have been done by our H.E. shell yesterday. The French continued to take over part of our line of trenches.

NOVEMBER 17th.
YPRES.

From early morning heavy artillery fire was opened against our whole front, it appeared to be particularly severe in the direction of KLEIN ZILLEBEKE. It was succeeded by a lull and then by a certain amount of musketry fire, but as no reserves were called up from the division, it was not thought that any serious attack was being made; Lord Cavan had reported the concentration of considerable numbers in his front to the 3rd Division, but this information was not received by us till 4:45 p.m.

1:35 p.m.

During the morning, Lord Cavan's H.Q. had been so persistently shelled that he had been obliged to move them further back. Information was also received that part of our trenches (500 rifles) was to be taken over by the Hertfordshire T.F.

8:0 p.m. It was not until the evening that we learned how determined an attack had been made during the day, and how it had been repulsed everywhere with considerable loss to the enemy. The general situation appeared most satisfactory.

The 7th Cavalry Brigade relieved the 6th in the trenches.

NOVEMBER 18th.
YPRES.
9:20 a.m.

The full gravity of yesterday's attack only became apparent this morning. After a severe bombardment, during which the trenches held by the 3rd D.G's had been blown in, two distinct attacks were made, one at 1 p.m. and one at 4 p.m. Our casualties were severe, amounting to some 130 odd killed and wounded, including 6 officers killed. It is satisfactory to know that the enemy's losses were very severe, some 370 dead being counted in front of our own trenches, whilst according to I.C. at least 800 in all were killed.

During the morning an aeroplane passed over the dug-outs occupied by Divisional H.Q. and the Corps Reserve of 400 rifles; it was shortly followed by some fairly accurate shrapnel fire, but, as in the meantime, all horses had been moved away, only one casualty was the result.

Verbal reports were received that our trenches were again being shelled, and that the 2nd Life Guards had had a certain amount of casualties.

A congratulatory telegram was received from Sir Douglas Haig on the work of the 6th Cavalry Brigade during the previous day.

The G.O.C. subsequently forwarded a report from the Brigadier and commanders of sections of the trenches on the attack on the 6th Cavalry Brigade November 17th. He drew particular attention to the conduct of the North Somerset Yeomanry which had behaved most staunchly. He also mentioned the good work done by Lieut. Hon. J. Grenfell, No. 5241 Sergt. MacLellan, and No.231 Corpl. Kelman all of the Royal Dragoons on 16th and 17th. Also of Captain Wright and Lieut. Chapman (both killed) 3rd D.G's, in the recapture of some buildings in the possession of the Germans.

NOVEMBER 19th. YPRES.

The trenches were again shelled during the night of the 18th /19th, and it was reported that the 7th Cavalry Brigade had suffered some further casualties amounting to about 52. The right trench appears open to a certain amount of enfilade fire and in spite of repeated work by the 3rd Field Squadron R.E. it is here that the heaviest casualties occur.

Orders for the relief of our trenches were received during the day, and in accordance with them the 6th Cavalry Brigade and the divisional troops were ordered to move to the concentration area on the 20th; the 7th Cavalry Brigade to follow them on the 21st. No. 1125 Corpl. of Horse Warren, R.H.G's distinguished himself during the day's fighting.

NOVEMBER 20th. YPRES.

In accordance with orders of 19th the 3rd Cavalry Division moved to the concentration area which had been allotted it. The formation of the 8th Cavalry Brigade was to take place as soon as this was reached, and so the 10th Hussars and R.H.G's were to move direct into an area set apart for that brigade. The concentration area was in the vicinity of HAZEBROUCK, the 7th Cavalry Brigade was to be in the area HONDEGHEM - ST. SYLVESTRA - EECKE - CAESTRE; the 6th and 8th Cavalry Brigades and divisional troops in the area HAZEBROUCK - VIEUX BERQUIN - VIERHOUEK - THIENNES. The G.O.C. and one S.O. proceeded to 7th Cavalry Brigade H.Q., the remainder of the staff to LA MOTTE where it had been intended to establish divisional H.Q. En route information was received that this place was not available, and so other quarters had to be found. These were eventually procured in HAZEBROUCK.

NOVEMBER 21st. HAZEBROUCK.

The 6th Cavalry Brigade did not arrive until very late last night owing to the slippery nature of the roads. For the same reason, although the 7th Cavalry Brigade marched

at

at 9 a.m., it was dark before they reached their new billets, and the bulk of their transport did not arrive before the following day.

NOVEMBER 22nd - 30th.
HAZEBROUCK.

For the remainder of the month there was no material change in the situation and the division remained in reserve and was again incorporated in the Cavalry Corps.

The formation of the 8th Cavalry Brigade was proceeded with.

HAZEBROUCK.   General Staff.

December, 1914.   3rd Cavalry Division.

My dear General
 Herewith report you asked for re operations of the 3rd Can. Div. during the last 4 days.

Yrs sincerely
[signature]

4/11/19
11.40 a.m.

G/77

YPRES
November 4th 1914

Report on operations 3rd Cavalry Division
October 30th – November 3rd 1914

On October 30th, after a severe artillery bombardment, the 7th Cavalry Brigade of the 3rd Cavalry Division was driven from its entrenchments in and around ZANDVOORDE with heavy loss by a superior force of hostile infantry. With the aid of 2 regiments from the Cavalry Corps, the Division then held a position on the KLEIN ZILLEBEKE RIDGE (parallel to the BASSEVILLE RIVER) until nightfall, when it was relieved by the 4th Brigade.

From October 31st to November 4th, the Division has acted as Corps Reserve to the 1st Army Corps, and has been called upon seven times to re-inforce the infantry line which had been reported broken. The whole Division was so employed on the 31st October, and on the 1st November, one Brigade on the 2nd November, and two squadrons on the 3rd November. On each occasion the troops have counter-attacked successfully on foot, and the infantry line has been restored.

I regret to report the loss of 2 squadrons on 30th October. The officers and men remained in the trenches at ZANVOORDE until the

2.

enemy's infantry exterminated them in practically hand to hand fighting.

Lord Hugh Grosvenor, 1st Life Guards, and Captain Vandeleur, 2nd Life Guards, the two squadron leaders, and their men, as far as one can gather, met their deaths with the finest gallantry.

Since that date our loss has been less severe, casualties occurring mostly amongst horses, from shell fire.

The Division is now located in close support to the infantry line from GHELUVELT to KLEIN ZILLEBEKE.

Byng
Major General
Commanding 4th Cavalry Division

The G.O.C.
Cavalry Corps.

"C" Form (Duplicate). Army Form C. 2123.
MESSAGES AND SIGNALS. No. of Message

AB K
          SE
              R
Service Instructions.
        Priority SE
                        W.D 2/1

Handed in at the _____ Office, at _____ m. Received here at 11 p.m.

TO   ~~1st~~ ~~3rd~~ & 3rd Cav Divn

Sender's Number.	Day of Month.	In reply to Number.	AAA
GB 161	31		
The	Germans	attacked	along
the	whole	line	held
by	the	cav	Corps
and	first	corps	and
were	repulsed	aaa	They
did	not	attack	3rd
~~con~~ Corps aaa		The	cavalry
Corps	with	the	units
attached	to	divs	as
today	will	retain	and
strengthen	its	position	aaa
The	north	umberland	Fus
and	Lincolns	are	placed

FROM   under the command of
PLACE 2nd Cav Div aaa
TIME   Reports to chateau at

		£	s.	d.
Service Instructions.				

Handed in at the .... Office, at .... .m. Received here at .... .m.

TO	(2)
Sender's Number.	Day of Month.	In reply to Number.	AAA
T	of	MONT	NOIR
till	6-am and	after
to	GROOTVIERSTAAT	aaa
ACKNOWLEDGE		

Rec'd 12 mid
3/11/14

FROM	Cav Corps.
PLACE	
TIME	10-pm

Service Instructions.

Handed in at the _____ Office, at _____ .m. Received here at _____ .m.

TO (2)

Sender's Number. | Day of Month. | In reply to Number. | AAA

The Germans are massing in the NE corner of MESSINES aaa On the the right the KOSB made considerable progress

FROM Cav Corps
PLACE
TIME 11.56 pm

"A" Form. Army Form C. 2121.
MESSAGES AND SIGNALS.   No of Message _____

Prefix ___ Code ___ m.	Words	Charge		Recd. at ___ m.
Office of Origin and Service Instructions.	Sent		*This message is on a/c of:	Date ___
	At ___ m.		WD 3/1	From ___
	To		Service.	By ___
	By		(Signature of "Franking Officer.")	

TO ~~1st Division~~ ~~General Bulfin~~
~~2nd Division~~ ~~Lord Cavan~~
~~7th Division~~   3rd Cav. Dvn.

| Sender's Number | Day of Month | In reply to Number | AAA |
| G.585 | 3P. | | |

1/ The French are attacking tomorrow morning at 6-30 a.m. from ST. ELOI in the direction of HOUTHEM in co-operation with our Cavalry Corps.

2/ As the attack goes forward Genl. Moussy will co-operate. Genl. Bulfin will then move forward in co-operation with Genl. Moussy. 7th Dvn. will move forward with Genl. Bulfin's left.

3/ Another attack will be made by the French from our left flank directed on MOLENHOEK and BECELAERE starting at 6-30 a.m. 2nd Dvn. will attack on REUTEL and NOORDWEST HOEK under direction of Genl. Munro in co-operation with the French.

4/ The French troops will assemble W. of ZONNEBEKE at 5 a.m. & will pass through our lines about 6-30 a.m. Report to WHITE HOUSE near level crossing

From 1st Corps
Place
Time 11-15 p.m.

The above may be forwarded as now corrected.

Sgd. J.E. Gough B.G.

Censor. Signature of Addressor or person authorized to telegraph in his name

3662 M. & Co. Ltd. Wt. W929/549—100,000. 6/14. Forms C2121/10.

FRO___
PLACE
TIME

W. 5375—423. 75,000 Pads—12/12—B. & F.—Forms/C.2123/1.

1st November 1914
9.40 p.m.

"C" Form (Duplicate). Army Form C. 2123.
MESSAGES AND SIGNALS. No. of Message _____

	Charges to Pay.	Office Stamp.
WD2/Jeff	£ s. d.	
	5.25 a.m.	
Service Instructions.	1/-	
oaado		

Handed in at the ____ Priory ____ Office, at 4.0 a.m. Received here at 5.24 a.m.

TO: GHQ 3rd Corps 1st Corps 1st Cav Dn 3rd Cav Div

Sender's Number.	Day of Month.	In reply to Number.	AAA
9A131	1st.		

MESSINES–WYTSCHAETE ridge has
been heavily attacked all
night aaa Enemy reported
to have broken through
at one point N.
of MESSINES aaa also
reported some of the
enemy to have got
into WYTSCHAETE aaa two
battalions of infantry are
now moving on WYTSCHAETE
to restore the situation

FROM: 2nd Corps
PLACE:
TIME: 4 a.m.

1st November 1914
9.40 p.m.

O.170   German maps scale W.D. 1/1

Information   (a) German attacks against our line have
               everywhere been unsuccessful. The 29th
               Indian Inf Bde has now been definitely
               located against the enemy.
               (b) The French attacks are progressing
               favorably.

Intention   2. The 3rd Cavalry Division will be in reserve
               between Reninghelst and Ypres.

Distribution   3. (a) That portion of the 7th Cavalry Brigade
                  now covering the 4 Brigade will
                  withdraw to Dickebusch when the 4 Brigade
                  arrives.
                  (b) On relief, the 7 Cavalry Brigade
                  will move back to Westoutre.
                  (c) The other two brigades will be
                  billeted in the villages as heretofore
                  as far as possible.
                  (d) Reports until I am informed
                  to the road junction immediately
                  S.E. of the Y in YPRES, after that
                  time at WESTB.

1 November 1914   M.Gough Lieut Col.
9.45 p.m.   B.

"A" Form. Army Form C. 2121.

MESSAGES AND SIGNALS.   No of Message_____

Prefix	Code	m.	Words	Charge	This message is on a/c of:	Recd. at	m.
Office of Origin and Service Instructions.			Sent			Date	
			At		Service.	From	
			To			By	
			By		(Signature of "Franking Officer.")		

TO ~~1st Division~~ ~~7th Division~~
   ~~2nd Division~~   3rd Cavalry Division

Sender's Number	Day of Month	In reply to Number	AAA
G.596	First		

3rd Cavalry Division is in Corps
Reserve but in case of great
emergency may be called
upon by ~~~~ Commander of
1st Division

Received
8.50 a.m.
1/11/14

From 1st Corps
Place
Time 8 am.
The above may be forwarded as now corrected. (Z) [signature]
                                                 Censor. Signature of Addressor or person authorised to telegraph in his name

*This line should be erased if not required
3662 M.&Co. Ltd. Wt. W929/549—100,000. 6/14. Forms C2121/10.

Time 7.20 a.m.
The above may be forwarded as now corrected. (Z)

TIME 1.12 am

"A" Form.   Army Form C. 2121.

MESSAGES AND SIGNALS.   No. of Message____

Prefix____Code____m.	Words	Charge	This message is on a/c of :	Reed. at____m.
Office of Origin and Service Instructions.				Date____
W.D.	Sent At____m.		____Service.	From____
	To____			
	By____		(Signature of "Franking Officer.")	By____

TO { 1st Army Corps

Sender's Number	Day of Month	In reply to Number	AAA
G66	1/11/14	G591	

I	have	in	hand	11
Squadrons	AAA	viz	6	Squadrons
of	the	6th Brigade	and	5
Squadrons	of	the	7th Brigade	
together	with	2 batteries	R.H.A.	
AAA	These		troops	are
concentrated	at	HOOGE	South	of
the	road	AAA.		

From 3rd Cav Division
Place HOOGE
Time 7.20 a.m.

The above may be forwarded as now corrected.   (Z)

Censor.   Signature of Addressor or person authorised to telegraph in his name
*This line should be erased if not required.
3662 M. & Co. Ltd.   Wt. W929/519—100,000.   6/14.   Forms C2121/10.

Place
Time
The above may be forwarded as now corrected.   (Z)

Censor.   Signature of Addressor or person authorised to telegraph in his name
*This line should be erased if not required.
3662 M. & Co. Ltd.   Wt. W929/549—100,000.   6/14.   Forms C2121/10.

TIME | 1.12 a.m.

W. 5975—423.   75,000 Pads—12/12—B. & F.—Forms/C.2123/1.

"A" Form.   Army Form C.

MESSAGES AND SIGNALS.   No. of Message____

Prefix ____ Code ____ m.	"Words	Charge			Recd. at ____ m.
Office of Origin and Service Instructions.			This message is on a/c of:		Date
	Sent At m.	W/		Service.	From
	To				By
	By		(Signature of "Franking Officer.")		

TO { THIRD | CAV | DIV | | }

* Sender's Number	Day of Month	In reply to Number		AAA
BM 4	First			
Second	Life	Guards	and	Royals
have	occupied	Eastern	Edge	of
Wood	pointed	out	to	you
a	few	Irish	Guards	in
trenches	there	which	have	been
filled	up	by	Cavalry	AAA
Understand	the	original	trenches	from
which	Irish	Guards	were	driven
back	are	about	400 x	
front	half	way	between	the
two	woods	AAA	Irish	Guards
are	now	reforming	on	Eastern
Edge	of	Wood	near	main
road	AAA	Do	you	want
us	to	push	forward	to
original	trenches	AAA	Adjutant	Irish
Guards	says	they	have	not

From
Place
Time

The above may be forwarded as now corrected.   (Z)

TIME   1-12 am

sufficient	strength	to	hold	them
and	that	it	would	take
considerable	force	to	reach	them

From SEVENTH CAV BDE
Place
Time 4.35

PLACE
TIME 1-2 pm

"C" Form (Duplicate). Army Form C. 2123.
MESSAGES AND SIGNALS.
No. of Message

SM AF 73
WDY Jff
SG

| Service Instructions. | Charges to Pay. £ s. d. 5.25 am 1m | Office Stamp. |

Handed in at the _____Sto_____ Office, at __1-12 a__.m. Received here at __1-30 a__.m.

TO 1st 2nd 3rd Cav Div.
G.O.C. 9th Inf Bde Genl Durtel G.ll Rouge

| Sender's Number. | Day of Month. | In reply to Number. | |
| GC | 1st | | AAA |

The following sent by 1st Corps aaa
begins on a captured german officer
states 15th Corps 2nd Bavarian Corps
+ 26th Wurtenburg division are to
to attack the English at ZANDVOORDE
+ eastwards of that place aaa
Prisoners stated German Cav. were
withdrawing from the trenches on
night 28/29 to replaced by infy

FROM	Cav. Corps
PLACE	
TIME	1-12 am

"A" Form.   Army Form C. 2121.

MESSAGES AND SIGNALS.

TO: 3rd Cavy. Divn.

Sender's Number: 4002   Day of Month: 1st   AAA

Send a brigade at once to reinforce Genl Bulfin in the woods ~~[struck through]~~ about a mile east of KLEIN ZILLEBEKE

From: 1st Corps
Time: 11.30 a.

TIME: 12.40 p

Time: 1.50

TIME: 2.50 pm

"C" Form (Duplicate).　　Army Form C. 2123.
MESSAGES AND SIGNALS.　No. of Message _____

MK 2?

Service Instructions. RLA　　Randlw

Charges to Pay. £ s. d.　　Received 1/11/14

Office Stamp. 1.55?

Handed in at the _____ Office, at _____ m. Received here at 1-23 m.

TO　3rd Cav Div　WJQ

Sender's Number. G607　Day of Month 1st　In reply to Number.　AAA

Re your request for return of 2 squadrons detained near HOLLEBEKE aaa Cavalry corps has been asked to return

FROM　1st Corps
PLACE
TIME　12.40 pm

Time 1.50
The above may be forwarded as now corrected. (Z)
Censor.　Signature of Addresser or person authorised to telegraph in his name.
* This line should be erased if not required.

PLACE
TIME　2.50 pm

"A" Form. Army Form C. 2121
MESSAGES AND SIGNALS. No. of Message 221

Prefix	Code	m.	Words	Charge	This message is on a/c of:	Recd. at 2-0 .m.
Office of Origin and Service Instructions.			Sent			Date
Private			At	WD m.		From Hooge
			To		Service	
			By		(Signature of "Franking Officer.")	By

TO { Cav. Bde. HOOGE

Sender's Number	Day of Month	In reply to Number	A A A
AD.10			

Irish Guards driven from trenches near KLEIN ZILLEBEKE at 1.15. Holding line of woods AA. Move at once in support with whole Bde

From 1st C(?)
Place
Time 1.50

R Stollins Capt
C S

The above may be forwarded as now corrected. (Z)

PLACE	
TIME	2.50 pm

"C" Form (Duplicate).   Army Form C. 2123.
MESSAGES AND SIGNALS,   No. of Message _____

Bt 56   Lairdlaw

Service Instructions.

Handed in at the 1st Div Office, at ___ m. Received here at 3.20 m.

TO   3rd Cav Div

Sender's Number: GR5   Day of Month: 1st   In reply to Number: AAA

Enemy reported massing in the Lange woods south of HOOGE and east of KLEIN ZILLEBEKE cavans bde is believed to be counterattacking with grenadier battalion

FROM: 1st Div
PLACE:
TIME: 2:50 pm

"A" Form. Army Form C. 2121.
MESSAGES AND SIGNALS.   No. of Message____

Prefix____ Code____ m.	Words	Charge	The message is on a/c of:	Recd. at____ m.
Office of Origin and Service Instructions.		Sent		Date____
	At	m.	Service.	From____
	To			
	By		(Signature of "Franking Officer.")	By

TO { 7th Cavalry Bde
      KLEINEZILLEBEKE

| Sender's Number | Day of Month | In reply to Number | AAA |
| 6177 | 1/11/14 | | |

If all is quiet it is hoped to withdraw the whole or a portion of your brigade to-night to HOOGE AAA G.O.C. now awaits communication from General Cavan as to whether he can do without you aaa The Supply Column is being brought to HALTE on YPRES-MENIN road do you wish to have any of your B echelon brought there? No orders have been issued as to your A echelon by D.H.Q. aaa
The French division advancing S of the Canal has reached a N & S line through OOSTAVERNE with advanced troops about ½ mile in advance. French troops N of CANAL have advanced S.E. along canal

From
Place

                    McGage Lt Col
                         for

From 3 Cav. Div.
Place House & side of road about E of HOOGE.
Time 6.35 p.m.

"A" Form.   Army Form C. 2121.
MESSAGES AND SIGNALS.   No. of Message _____

Prefix ___ Code ___ m.	Words	Charge	This message is on a/c of:	Recd. at ___ m.
Office of Origin and Service Instructions.				
	Sent			Date
	At ___ m.		Service.	From
	To			
	By		(Signature of "Franking Officer.")	By

TO {

| Sender's Number | Day of Month | In reply to Number | A A A |

Left now about KLEINZILLEBEKE
FARM aaa.
          Your B.M.4 has been received
G.O.C is at present at 1st Army Corps HQ,
but it would appear undesirable
to push forward to proposed rendez
in the dark aaa
3rd Divisional HQ are at present
at HOOGE but may be moved,
in which case a motorcyclist will
be left here until 8.30 pm to
receive communications from you aaa

                    Mulgage Lt Col
                              f.

From 3 Cav. Bde.
Place House & side of road about E of HOOGE.
Time 6.35 p.m.

The above may be forwarded as now corrected.   (Z)

Censor. | Signature of Addressor or person authorised to telegraph in his name

Copy No.

1st ARMY CORPS OPERATION ORDERS, No. 30.

~~1st Division.~~
~~2nd Division.~~
~~7th Division.~~
~~Cavalry Corps.~~
3rd Cavalry Division.
~~Br.-Gen. Lord Cavan.~~

G.B.23.   1st.

On our right the French have maintained their position from about KLEIN ZILLEBEKE along the North bank of the Canal to the West AAA The French 32nd Division which is attacking in an easterly direction has pushed as far as the line INN West of WYTSCHAETE - HOLLEBEKE - Canal Bridge just North of HOLLEBEKE and is supported by a cavalry division on its left AAA The enemy made today several violent attacks on our line south of the MENIN - YPRES Road but have been everywhere unsuccessful in breaking through and have suffered heavy loss AAA The 3rd Cavalry Division will be in Corps Reserve about HOOGE with headquarters at the most Westerly house on South side of road at HOOGE AAA The Worcesters are in reserve in rear of the left of 7th Division AAA Tomorrow the French will continue their attack towards HOLLEBEKE on our right and will also attack from the North-West towards GHELUVELT AAA The 1st Corps will maintain its position which will be strengthened in every possible way AAA Reports to WHITE HOUSE just West of HALTE on MENIN Road. *Acknowledge.*

(signed) H.S. JEUDWINE, Colonel,
for Senior General Staff Officer,
6.45 p.m.   1st Corps.

334
3rd Cav Div

"A" Form.   Army Form C. 2121.

MESSAGES AND SIGNALS

Prefix	Code	m.	Words	Charge		Recd. at 10.30 p.m.
Office of Origin and Service Instructions.					This message is on a/c of:	Date 1st
	WP/a		Sent			From
		At	m.		Service.	
		To				By
		By		(Signature of "Franking Officer.")		

TO —
1st Divn.   Lord Cavan
2nd Divn.   3rd Cav. Divn.
7th Divn   Cavy. Corps.

Sender's Number	Day of Month	In reply to Number	AAA
G623.	1st		

The French attack on our left will be made by eight battalions supported by its own artillery aaa General direction of attack from S.W. corner of big wood north of VELDHOEK on GHELUVELT aaa The attack will be prepared by the French artillery commencing at about 9 a.m. aaa The French Infantry advance will pass through our lines at about 10 a.m. aaa

In order to strengthen up our right and to ensure that the enemy do not penetrate our lines during the early morning, the following moves will be made by 5.45. am.

(a) The Corps Reserve (3rd Cavalry Division) will move to neighbourhood of road

From
Place
Time

The above may be forwarded as now corrected. (Z)

Censor.   Signature of Addressor or person authorised to telegraph in his name

This line should be erased if not required.

3662 M. & Co. Ltd. Wt. W929/549—100,000. 6/14. Forms C2121/10.

Place
Time 10.15 p.m.

The above may be forwarded as now corrected. (Z)

Censor.   Signature of Addressor or person authorised to telegraph in his name

This line should be erased if not required.

3662 M. & Co. Ltd. Wt. W929/549—100,000. 6/14. Forms C2121/10.

Position of 3rd Cav. Divn
10.0 am NOV. 2nd 1914.   Frklin
                     Wn Zillebeke.

"A" Form. Army Form C. 2121.
MESSAGES AND SIGNALS.

| Sender's Number | Day of Month | In reply to Number | AAA |

Y623

junction 1 mile S. of HOOGE.
(b) Divisional reserves of 1st Division will be South of YPRES - MENIN road
(c) 7th Division reserve will be in rear of right flank of their line.

From 1st Corps
Place
Time 10.15 p.m.

Position of 3rd Cav. Divn Fr. Klein
10.0 am NOV. 2nd 1914.   W. Zillebeke.

W.O. 2

G.O.C. 6th Cav. Bde
" 7th Cav. Bde

Ga. III. Nov 1st

The 6th & 7th Cavy Bdes. will
rendezvous tomorrow morning
in the vicinity of the road
junction 1 mile south of
HOOGE by 5-45 a.m.

W.A. Kennedy?
Major
2. 3rd C. Div.
X Rds. N. of YPRES.   GS 3CD
10-45 p.m.

Position of 3rd Cav. Div'n
10.0 am NOV. 2nd 1914.   F. KLEIN
                          WN Zillebeke.

W.D. 2/2

To YPRES.

33

H.Q.
3. C.D.

To Zillebeke.

"C"

6. Bty.

7. Bty.

About 3" 61 m.

Position of 3rd Cav. Div'n
10.0 am NOV. 2nd 1914.

To Klein
W. Zillebeke.

WO ?/?

"C" Form (Duplicate).   Army Form C. 2123.
MESSAGES AND SIGNALS.   No. of Message _____

An JHR 515

                    Laidlaw   Charges to Pay.   Office Stamp.
                                   £   s.   d.
Service Instructions.   Received 10.30
                                            p.m.
                                   1. 11. 14.

Handed in at the SE Sadds Office, at ___m. Received here at 10h ___m.

TO 1st 2nd and 3rd Cavalry Divns
    1st and 3rd Corps

Sender's Number.   Day of Month.   In reply to Number.   AAA
GB179 First

3rd Corps were not
attacked today 1st Corps
were repeatedly attacked and
each time repulsed the
enemy with great losses
The cavalry corps (Less 3rd
Cavalry Division) will maintain
and strengthen in every
way possible the positions
now occupied aaa Should
the french troops now
holding WYTSCHAETE evacuate that
place in the course ~~corps~~

FROM ~~of the operations and~~
PLACE
TIME

TIME   9/35½

From
Place   S.E. K.W.
Time   12.55 p.m.

The above may be forwarded as now corrected.   (Z)

Censor.   Signature of Addressor or person authorised to telegraph in his name.
* This line should be erased if not required.

"C" Form (Duplicate). Army Form C. 2123.
MESSAGES AND SIGNALS. No. of Message _____

			AAA
of	the	operations	2nd
Cavalry	Division	will	occupy
and	hold	it	at
all	costs	aaa	3rd
Cavalry	division	operates	to-
morrow	under	orders	of
1st	Corps	aaa	Reports
to	chateau	at	f
of	MONT	NOIR	till
6 am	and	after	that
hour	to	WESTOUTRE	

FROM: Cavalry Corps
PLACE:
TIME: 9-35 a

"A" Form.   Army Form C. 2121.

MESSAGES AND SIGNALS.   No. of Message_____

Prefix	Code _____ m.	Words	Charge	This message is on a/c of:	Recd. at _____ m.
Office of Origin and Service Instructions.		Sent			Date 2/11/__
W O 4/2		At _____ m.		_____ Service.	From_____
		To			By_____
		By		(Signature of "Franking Officer.")	

TO { 1st Div.   6 Cav Bde.
     3rd Cav. Div.   7th Cav Bde.

| Sender's Number | Day of Month | In reply to Number | AAA |
| T 121. | 2 Nov. | | |

Enemy reported to have broken line at point of junction between 7 Div right and 2nd Brigade left AAA. I have sent my Reserves to that point.

From 7 Div.
Place 5 Kilo.
Time 12.55 pm

The above may be forwarded as now corrected.   (Z)
_____   _____
Censor.   Signature of Addressor or person authorised to telegraph in his name.

* This line should be erased if not required.

MESSAGES AND SIGNALS.   Army Form C. 2121.

Prefix	Code	m.	Words	Charge	This message is on a/c of:	Recd. at 2 h m.
Office of Origin and Service Instructions.			Sent			Date 2·10·14
W.O 3/2			At	m.	Service.	From
			To			By
			By		(Signature of "Franking Officer.")	

TO — 1st Division   Cavalry Corps
     2nd Division   3rd Cavalry Div
     4th Div

Sender's Number	Day of Month	In reply to Number	A A A
G 040	2nd		

At 11·20 am there was considerable pressure against the 1st Division along the MENIN - YPRES road. About that hour the enemy attack on our left seem to make itself felt and pressed in our retired.

From	
Place	
Time	

The above may be forwarded as now corrected.   (Z) R.H. Collins, Capt. B

Censor. Signature of Addressor or person authorised to telegraph in his name
*This line should be erased if not required.

2662 M. & Co. Ltd. Wt. W929/319 —100,000. 6/14. Forms C2121/10.

"A" Form.
Army Form C. 2121.

MESSAGES AND SIGNALS.

Prefix	Code	Words	Charge		
		63		This message is on a/c of	
Office of Origin and Service Instructions.		Sent			
AHQ		At	5-35 AM		
		To			
		By	(Signature of "Franking Officer.")	By	

TO ~~1st Divn~~
~~2nd Divn~~
3rd Cavy. Divn.

~~Br. Gen. Lord Cavan~~

Sender's Number	Day of Month	In reply to Number	AAA
G 648	2nd		

Reports sent at about 3 o'clock indicate that attack on the junction between 7th Divn & 2nd Bde. has been repulsed and that the original line held by these troops is intact. About the MENIN Road 1st Bde. reports that it does not require reinforcements aaa French have gone forward towards GHELUVELT.

From 1st Corps
Place
Time 4.25 pm

(sd) H.S. Gudwin

Issued at 10.30 pm.

"A" Form.   Army Form C. 2121.
MESSAGES AND SIGNALS

TO 1st Division   General Cavan.
    2nd Division
    7th Division

G654   2nd   AAA

We have maintained our line against very severe attacks throughout the whole day. aaa On our right the French after a series of attacks and counter attacks made some progress and reported having taken over 100 prisoners aaa. On our left the 9th French Corps has maintained its line aaa. Our 3rd Corps was also attacked unsuccessfully by the enemy aaa. General FOCH commanding the French armies in Belgium is satisfied with the general situation aaa. The line will be maintained tomorrow at all costs, every effort will be made to organize local reserves which will be employed for immediate counter-attack in the event of the enemy penetrating our line aaa. The Cavalry Division will be in Corps Reserve and will be at the road junction one mile south of HOOGE

Issued at 10.30 p.m.

"A" Form.   Army Form C. 2121.

MESSAGES AND SIGNALS   No of Message____

Prefix____ Code____ m.	Words	Charge	This message is on a/c of :	Recd. at____ m.
Office of Origin and Service Instructions				Date____
	Sent			From____
	At____ m.		Service.	
	To			
	By		(Signature of " Franking Officer.")	By____

TO ─

Sender's Number | Day of Month | In reply to Number | AAA
5

by 1·45 AM. as today. The London Scottish will be in Corps Reserve near YPRES on the MENIN road, arriving about noon aaa. A French battalion will probably arrive in the morning and will also go into Corps Reserve near HOOGE aaa. Arrangements will be made to pull out one or two battalions of the 2nd Division which will also go into Corps Reserve near HOOGE aaa. Further orders will be issued when the French plan of operations for tomorrow has been decided.

From 1st Corps
Place
Time 8.30 pm.

The above may be forwarded as now corrected.   (Z)

Issued at 10.30 pm.

Copy No. 54

W.D/3 3rd Cav. Div. Operation ~~Routine~~ Order No. 18

YPRES

Reference 1/100,000   Nov. 2nd 1914.

1. <u>Information</u>. We have maintained our line against very severe attack throughout the whole day.

2. <u>Intention</u>. The line will be maintained ~~held~~ tomorrow at all costs.

3. <u>Distribution</u>. The 3rd Cav. Div. will be in Corps Reserve tomorrow and will ~~embus~~ rendezvous under Bde. arrangements by 6-30 a.m. ~~East of~~ in the covers east of the farm where Div. H.Q. were situated today.

4. <u>Entrenching Tools</u>. A motor lorry with entrenching tools is now attached to the 3rd Fd. Sqdn. which is with the Amm. Col.; these can be drawn upon by Bdes. as required.

5. <u>Reports</u>. Reports to the same farm as today after 6.30 a.m.
A Staff Officer from each Brigade will meet the G.O.C. there at 6.30 a.m. tomorrow.

Issued at 10.30 p.m.

M.H. Gage
G.S.

"A" Form.   Army Form C. 2121.
MESSAGES AND SIGNALS.   No. of Message____

Prefix	Code	m.	Words	Charge			Recd. at 1.30 m.
Office of Origin and Service Instructions.			Sent		This message is on a/c of:		Date 3/4/14
			At / m.			Service.	From
	W.D		To				
			By		(Signature of "Franking Officer.")		By

TO { 1st Divn   3rd Cav. Divn
     2nd Divn   Ld. Cavan. 4 Bde
     3rd Divn   Corps Troops

Sender's Number	Day of Month	In reply to Number	
IG 249	3rd		AAA

1st Cav Divn report that
in attacks on them Germans wore
British uniforms especially kilts +
when approaching our trenches shout
don't fire we are short of ammunition
and similar expressions aaa all
troops in trenches are to be warned
of this practice by the enemy.

Repeated to 6th & 7th
                        Cav B.

From 1st CORPS
Place
Time 11.45 am

                                        J. Charteris
                                              Capt.

The above may be forwarded as now corrected.   (Z)

Censor.   Signature of Addressee or person authorised to telegraph in his name

(Sd) H. Gough B.G

---

position to Div. H.Q.
6. Report to A Staff Office from each Bde.
will meet the G.O.C. on the YPRES-MENIN
Rd. about the N. of HOOGE at 6.30 a.m.
Issued at 9.45 pm.   M. Gough B.G. p.

From	1st Corps		
Place	8.40 a.m.		H. Gough B.G
Time			

"A" Form.

MESSAGES AND SIGNALS.   No of Message____

	m.	Words	Charge	This message is on a/c of:	Recd. at 8.0 p m.
Instructions.					Date____
		Sent		WO 3/3 Service.	From____
copy	At		m.		
	To				
	By			(Signature of "Franking Officer.")	By____

TO { 1st Divn.   3rd Cav. Divn.
     2nd Divn.   Lord Cavan.
     7th Divn.

| Sender's Number | Day of Month | In reply to Number | AAA |
| G.679 | 3rd | | |

The French attack on our right progressed satisfactorily and further large reinforcements are expected at once aaa The Belgians also have had a marked success north of DIXMUDE aaa

The position we now hold will be further strengthened aaa

The Corps Reserve will consist of the 3rd Cav. Divn. south of HOOGE and two battns. of ZOUAVES in the neighbourhood of HOOGE aaa

Reports to CHATEAU DE TROIS TOURGE (2½ miles N.W. of YPRES) from 8.0 pm. to 6.0 am. aaa After 6.0 am. to junction of MENIN-ZONNEBEKE road at YPRES

From	1st Corps
Place	YPRES
Time	6.30 pm.

The above may be forwarded as now corrected.   (Z) (Sd) J.E. Gough A.G

---

position to Div. H.Q.

6. Reports A Staff officer from each Bde. will meet the G.O.C. on the YPRES-MENIN Rd. about the N. of HOOGE at 6.30 a.m.

Issued at 9.45 pm.   M.Gas. 1st Corps.

From	1st Corps.
Place	8.40 a.m.
Time	

The above may be forwarded as now corrected.   (Z)

Copy No. 55

3rd Cav. Div. Operation Order No. 19
~~Routine~~

WO 1/4

YPRES.
Reference 1/100,000   Nov. 3rd 1914.

1. **Information.** The French attack on our right has progressed satisfactorily & further large reinforcements are expected very shortly.
The Belgians have had a marked success N. of DIXMUDE.
The positions we now hold are to be further strengthened tomorrow.

2. **Intention.** The 3rd Cav. Div. & 2 Bns. Zouaves are to form the Corps Reserve tomorrow.

3. **Distribution.** The 6th & 7th Cav. Bdes. will rendezvous tomorrow at 6·30 a.m. in the same place as today.

4. **Maps.** From tomorrow (inclusive) the maps which will be normally referred to in orders & messages will be the 1/40,000 YPRES, which will be issued to-night.

5. **Ammunition** Coln. & 3rd Fd. Sqd. will rendezvous under arrangements to be made by the C.R.A. who will report their position to Div. H.Q.

6. **Report** A Staff officer from each Bde. will meet the G.O.C. on the YPRES-MENIN Rd. about the N. of HOOGE at 6·30 a.m.

Issued at 9·45 p.m.   M. Gore Lt. Col. ps.

From	Corps.	
Place	8·40 a.m.	
Time		

The above may be forwarded as now corrected. (Z)

Signature of Addressor or person authorised to telegraph in his name

"A" Form. Army Form C. 2121.
MESSAGES AND SIGNALS.

TO: 3rd Cav. Div.

Recd. at 9.15 a.m.
From 4th

Sender's Number: G.D. 12
Day of Month: 4th

Sir Douglas Haig would be very glad to have the services of your Field Squadron if possible to help in strengthening the line to-day.

From 1st Corps.
Time 8.40 a.m.

G/77

W.D 3/u YPRES
November 4th 1914

Report on Operations 3rd Cavalry Division
October 30th – November 3rd 1914

On October 30th, after a severe artillery bombardment the 7th Cavalry Brigade of the 3rd Cavalry Division was driven from its entrenchments in and around ZANDVOORDE with heavy loss by a superior force of hostile infantry. With the aid of 2 regiments from the Cavalry Corps, the Division then held a position on the KLEIN ZILLEBEKE RIDGE (parallel to the BASSEVILLE RIVER) until nightfall, when it was relieved by the 4th Brigade.

From October 31st to November 4th, the Division has acted as Corps Reserve to the 1st Army Corps, and has been called upon seven times to re-inforce the infantry line which had been reported broken. The whole Division was so employed on the 31st October, and on the 1st November, one Brigade on the 2nd November, and two squadrons on the 3rd November. On each occasion the troops have counter-attacked successfully on foot, and the infantry line has been restored.

I regret to report the loss of 2 squadrons on 30th October. The Officers and men remained in the trenches at ZANVOORDE until the

2.

enemy's infantry, exterminated them in practically hand to hand fighting.

Lord Hugh Grosvenor, 1st Life Guards, and Captain Vandeleur, 2nd Life Guards, the two squadron leaders, and their men, as far as we can gather, met their deaths with the finest gallantry.

Since that date our loss has been less severe, casualties occurring mostly amongst horses, from shell fire.

The Division is now located in close support to the infantry line from GHELUVELT to KLEIN ZILLEBEKE.

Major General
Commanding 3rd Cavalry Division

The G.O.C.
Cavalry Corps.

"A" Form. Army Form
MESSAGES AND SIGNALS.

Prefix **An** Code **LA** m. Words **81** Charge — This message is on a/c of: Recd. at ___ m.
Office of Origin and Service Instructions

R.C.A.

Sent at W.D. 4/11 1-0 pm
47

TO: 1st 2nd & 3rd Divisions
3rd Cav Division

Sender's Number: G.A. 126.
Day of Month: 4
AAA

It has been brought to notice that a person calling himself a staff officer came to certain units last night, and gave alarming reports and orders to withdraw. aaa — It is quite in keeping with German methods to employ people to personate our officers and consequently if there is any doubt as to the identity of anyone giving orders, he should be detained until enquiries are made.

H. Gough BG
1st Corps

11. A.M

"A" Form.

MESSAGES AND SIGNALS. No of Message _____

Prefix _____ Code _____ m. Words | Charge
Office of Origin and Service Instructions

Sent
At _____ W _____ m.
To
By

This message is on a/c of:

D 5/4 Service.
(Signature of "Franking Officer.")

Recd. at 7.30 p.m.
Date 4th
From
By

TO— 1st Div.
2nd "
7th Div.
3rd Cav Div
Lord Cavan

Sender's Number: G.691
Day of Month: 4th
In reply to Number:
AAA

The fighting throughout the whole area of operations has been satisfactory today AAA. Some German guns were captured N. of DIXMUDE The French attack on the WYTSCHAETE — MESSINES line continued satisfactorily AAA. Some attacks were made against various parts of 1st Corps line which were all repulsed AAA

Reinforcements will arrive for the 1st Corps tomorrow AAA

Our present positions will be maintained & strengthened.
One Bde. R.F.A + 1 Batty 4.5 Howitzers from the 1st & 2nd Divs. also 1 R.F.A Bde from 7th Div.

From
Place
Time

The above may be forwarded as now corrected. (Z)

Censor. Signature of Addressor or person authorised to telegraph in his name
*This line should be erased if not required.

	Sent		Date
At	m.	Service.	From
To			
By		(Signature of "Franking Officer.")	By

TO	2
Sender's Number	Day of Month	In reply to Number	**A A A**

will be concentrated tomorrow about ~~Dick~~ DICKEBUSH and billet and bivouac in an area immediately N.W. of that place AAA. Details regarding this area are being forwarded direct to Divs. AAA The Senior Bde. Comdr. will command in the area and f. instructions will be issued to him later. AAA Arty. from 1st Div. will pass the road junction just E of YPRES at 3 a.m. AAA That from 2nd Div at 4 a.m. and that from 7th Div. at 5 a.m. AAA Report to CHATEAU DE TROIS TOURS Acknowledge

From: 1st Corps
Place:
Time: 6.30 p.m.

W.D.
3rd Cav. Div. Operation/Routine Order No. 20   Copy No. 1. 56

Reference 1/40,000.   YPRES.
Nov. 4th 1914

Information 1. The fighting throughout the whole area of operations has been satisfactory today. Some German guns were captured N. of DIXMUDE.
The French attack on the WYTSCHAETE-MESSINES line continued satisfactory.

Intention 2. Our present positions will be maintained & strengthened tomorrow.

Distribution 3. Brigades will rendezvous tomorrow at the same places as today at 6.30 a.m.

Reports 4. Div. Hd. Qrs. will be at the same place as today from 6.30 a.m., and a Staff Officer from each Brigade will meet the G.O.C there.
Up till 6.30 a.m. Hd. Qrs. will be 200 yds S.W of the YPRES-MENIN, YPRES-ZONNEBEKE Rd. junction.

J W Gage Lt Col.
for 3 C.D.

Issued at 8.40 p.m.

"A" Form.　　　　　　　　　　　　　　　　Army Form C. 2121.
MESSAGES AND SIGNALS.　　　No. of Message

Prefix	Code	Words	Charge	This message is on a/c of:	Recd. at	m.
Office of Origin and Service Instructions.		174 Sent		W.D. 1/5	Date	
		At　　m.			From 5-X-14 10	
1st A&Q		To		(Signature of "Franking Officer.")	By	
		By				

TO — 3rd Cav Division.　　　　Brig Gen McCracken

Sender's Number	Day of Month	In reply to Number	AAA
G.A. 127	5th		

The following moves will take place to-night in accordance with arrangements which have been made. aaa.

The 3rd Cav Divn with one brigade will relieve the troops of the 1st division south of the YPRES – MENIN road. aaa. The 1st Divn will arrange for a reserve to remain behind the cavalry line.

Brigadier General McCracken with the 7th and 15th Inf Brigades will relieve the 7th division. aaa. The following units troops of the 7th Division will remain and come temporarily under General McCracken. The divisional cyclists — one Coy Divl R.E. Divisional Artillery (less 35th R.F.A Brigade)

MESSAGES AND SIGNALS.

Prefix	Code	m.	Words	Charge	This message is on a/c of :	Recd. at	m.
Office of Origin and Service Instructions.			Sent			Date	
			At m.		Service.	From	
			To				
			By		(Signature of "Franking Officer.")	By	

TO { 2. }

| * | Sender's Number | Day of Month | In reply to Number | AAA |

The 22nd Infantry brigade will, when relieved, march to billets & bivouacs just South of YPRES and West of the Canal and will form part of the Corps reserve (The exact billeting area will be notified later).
The remainder of the 7th Division will proceed to LOCRE and come into Army Reserve and will report direct to G.H.Q aaa The 35th R.F.A. Brigade have been ordered to rejoin the 7th division at LOCRE.

From 1st Corps
Place
Time 1. P.M.

"A" Form. Army Form C. 2121.
MESSAGES AND SIGNALS. No. of Message _____

Prefix ___ Code ___ m.	Words	Charge	This message is on a/c of:	Recd. at **8.10 p.** m.
Office of Origin and Service Instructions.	Sent		W D ½ Service.	Date **5**th
	At ___ m.			From
	To			By
	By		(Signature of "Franking Officer.")	

TO ~~1st Corps~~ ~~2nd Divn~~ ~~7th Divn~~   3rd Cavy Divn Cavy Corps

| Sender's Number | Day of Month | In reply to Number | A A A |
| G 718 | 5th | | |

The General situation ~~is to~~ remains satisfactory but detailed information as to the progress made by the allied troops on our right and left is not yet to hand aaa The 1st Corps will continue to hold and strengthen the line now occupied particular attention being given to the strengthening of the POINT D'APPUI along old line aaa It is to be clearly understood that the troops forming the Corps Reserve are not to be called upon by subordinate commanders except in a case of extreme emergency aaa Further reliefs of troops of the 1st Corps will be carried out tomorrow, details

From			
Place			
Time			

The above may be forwarded as now corrected. (Z)

Censor. Signature of Addressor or person authorised to telegraph in his name
*This line should be erased if not required

	Sent		Service	Date	
	At m.			From	
	To				
	By		(Signature of "Franking Officer.")	By	

TO		2			
	Sender's Number	Day of Month	In reply to Number	**A A A**	

of which will be notified later aaa
Report Centre remains at CHATEAU
de TROIS TOURSE aaa
Acknowledge

From 1st Corps
Place
Time 6 30 pm

The above may be forwarded as now corrected.   (sd) H.C. Gough BG

"A" Form. Army Form C. 2121.

MESSAGES AND SIGNALS.   No. of Message _____

Prefix	Code	m.	Words	Charge	This message is on a/c of:	Recd. at	m.
Office of Origin and Service Instructions.			Sent			Date	
			At	m.	____Service.	From	
			To			By	
			By		(Signature of "Franking Officer.")		

TO
C. o C. 7ᵗʰ Cav Bᵈᵉ   c/o 3ʳᵈ Field Squadron
C.R.A.   3 Signal Squadron
O/C A.C.   A.A. 9149 - Hdqrs.

Sender's Number	Day of Month	In reply to Number	AAA
G. 106	5 Nov		

The general situation remains
satisfactory AAA The 1ˢᵗ Corps will continue
to hold and strengthen the line now
reached and the 7ᵗʰ Cav Bᵈᵉ will be
in Corps Reserve tomorrow at the
same place as today § 6 signal office
Report centre will be at _____ from
5 to ? YPRES - MENIN - YPRES -
ZONNEBEKE road junction until ? am
and then at WHITE HOUSE _____
3 Mi YPRES - MENIN road _____

From 3 Cav Bde
Place
Time 6.15 _____

The above may be forwarded as now corrected. (Z)

115

G.S.O. I   3rd Cav. Div 11th Quarles
Nov 2nd. 1914.
10. am

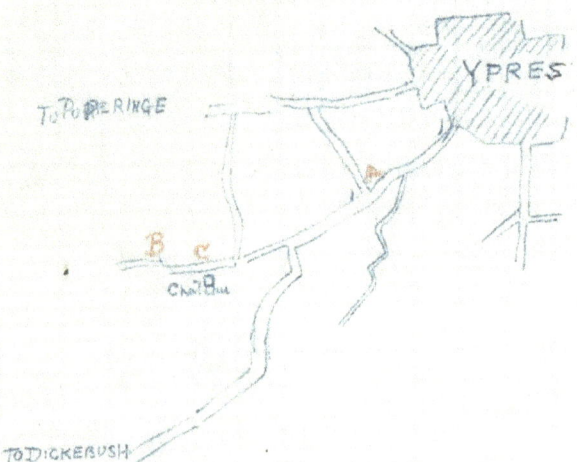

The motors are parked at corner of road 3/4 of a
kilometre S.S.W of YPRES on the road YPRES -
DICKEBUSH marked. A   under Sergt. Kirby
All the rest of the Transport is in a field marked B
O.C.A.S.C is at a cottage marked. C
Laurie is also there

"A" Form.   Army Form C. 2121.

MESSAGES AND SIGNALS

No. of Message 77

Prefix — Code — Words 89 — Charge —
Office of Origin and Service Instructions.
Sent At — To — By —
This message is on a/c of:
Service.
Recd. at 12.60 p.m.
Date 6/11
From

TO ~~1st Divn~~ ~~2nd Divn~~ 3rd Cavy Divn. Lord Cavan

Sender's Number G 739 | Day of Month 6th | In reply to Number | AAA

Four battalions 2nd Corps will relieve part of the First Corps to-night One battalion strength 500 will relieve left battalion of Lord Cavan's line AAA The remaining three battalions will take over that part of the line at present held by the cavalry AAA 3rd Cavalry Division and Lord Cavan will send officers to 1st Division head quarters at midday to arrange details of exchange with officers of 2nd Corps. AAA Lord Cavan's battalion will be relieved by K.O.S.B's.

From 1st Corps
Place
Time 11.25 a

"A" Form.   Army Form C. 2121.

MESSAGES AND SIGNALS.

Prefix	Code	m.	Words	Charge	This message is on a/c of:	Recd. at	m.
Office of Origin and Service Instructions			Sent		W.D-6	Date	
			At	m.	Service.	From	
			To				
			By		(Signature of "Franking Officer.")	By	

TO 7th Cavalry Brigade

Sender's Number	Day of Month	In reply to Number	AAA
G/81	6/11/14		

The following reliefs will probably be carried out to-day aaa Lord Cavan's Command by troops of 2nd Corps aaa C. Cavalry Brigade by 2nd Corps aaa These troops will go into Corps Reserve aaa 1st Infantry Brigade by 7th Cavalry Brigade aaa Officers from relieving troops will meet at Woods at an hour to be notified later where they will be met and all details arranged for taking over the trenches aaa If this order is confirmed it would probably be convenient for Col. & Staff of 7th Cav Bde to meet Col. & Officers at Woods

From
Place
Time

The above may be forwarded as now corrected. (Z)

Censor. Signature of Addressor or person authorised to telegraph in his name
This line should be erased if not required.

"A" Form. Army Form C. 2121.

MESSAGES AND SIGNALS. No. of Message ____

Prefix	Code	m.	Words	Charge			
Office of Origin and Service Instructions.					This message is on a/c of:	Recd. at	m.
			Sent			Date	
			At	m.	Service.	From	
			To			By	
			By		(Signature of "Franking Officer.")		

TO {

Sender's Number	Day of Month	In reply to Number	**A A A**

at 3 pm to-day and for regimental
Commanders and Squadron leaders to
meet Company Commanders of 1st Infantry
Brigade at the same place at
3.45 p.m. aaa The actual relief
of the trenches will probably take
place between 8.30 pm and 9.30 pm.
aaa The 1st Brigade would be required
to remain in the trenches (N of the YPRES-
MENNIN road) for 24 hours and since
it would not be possible for wagons to
bring supplies (?) S of the YPRES-
MENNIN road and it will be necessary
for troops of your brigade to carry their
food for to-morrow into the trenches will
you please state at what hour and
place it would be most convenient

From
Place
Time

The above may be forwarded as now corrected.   (Z)

Censor.   Signature of Addressor or person authorised to telegraph in his name
* This line should be erased if not required.
8350 S. B. Ltd Wt. W4842/542—50,000. 9/14. Forms C2121/10.

Censor.   Signature of Addressor or person authorised to telegraph in his name
* This line should be erased if not required.
8350 S. B. Ltd Wt. W4842/542—50,000. 9/14. Forms C2121/10.

MESSAGES AND SIGNALS.

Prefix	Code	m.	Words	Charge	This message is on a/c of:	Recd. at	m.
Office of Origin and Service Instructions			Sent			Date	
			At	m.	Service.	From	
			To			By	
			By		(Signature of "Franking Officer.")		

No. of Message _____

TO

Sender's Number	Day of Month	In reply to Number	A A A

for four Supply column to be sent to-day aaa Can you also please state what number of rifles of J.C.B. will be available for the trenches to-night there are now estimated at 600 aaa Have your 2 squadrons been relieved yet from [pre Cavaly] trenches [?] aaa the G.O.C. has gone to see C in C at ST OMER and is not expected back until 5 p.m. aaa.

From
Place YPRES MENIN RD 3 Kilo
Time 11.30 a.m.

The above may be forwarded as now corrected. (Z)

Censor. Signature of Addressor or person authorised to telegraph in his name
* This line should be erased if not required.

"A" Form. Army Form C. 2121.
MESSAGES AND SIGNALS. No of Message 837

Prefix	Code	Words	Charge	This message is on a/c of:	Recd. at	m.
Office of Origin and Service Instructions		119 Sent		W.J.6	Date	
1st A&C	At m. To By			Service.	From 5-XII 1·40	

TO ~~3rd~~ ~~~~
3rd Cav Div

Sender's Number	Day of Month	In reply to Number	AAA
GD 20	5th		

Following	reliefs	will	probably be
carried	out	tomorrow AAA	Lord
Cavans	command	by	troops of
2nd	Corps AAA	Cav.	at
present	in	trenches	S. of MENIN
road	by	Second	Corps and
will	ja	side	Corps relief
AAA	1st	Inf.	Bde by
troops	of	Cav.	Div. AAA
Troops	at	present	under Lord
Cavan	will	rejoin	their division
AAA	The	1st Bde	will probably
be	withdrawn S.W	of	YPRES
AAA	officers	from	relieving troops
will	arrive	(at HOOGE)	at an
hour	to be notified later	as now	they will be
met	and	shown	over ground

From Addressed all Divs 4th Bde MGn
Place ~~~~ only thought to possible ~~~~
Time a.a.a. 1st Corps 10·10 p.m.

The above may be forwarded as now corrected. (Z)   ... Capt
                                          Censor.   Signature of Addresser or person authorised to telegraph in his name
*This line should be erased if not required.
3662 M.& Co. Ltd. Wt. W929/549—100,000. 6/14. Forms C2121/10.

Time 1 pm
The above may be forwarded as now corrected. (Z) Nuill Capt BM
                                          Censor. Signature of Addresser or person authorised to telegraph in his name
*This line should be erased if not required.
3662 M.& Co. Ltd. Wt. W929/549—100,000. 6/14. Forms C2121/10.

                                          Censor. Signature of Addresser or person authorised to telegra
*This line should be erased if not required.
3662 M.& Co. Ltd. Wt. W929/549—100,000. 6/14. Forms C2121/10.

this quarter & the retirement of the French

3rd Cav Dn.
5th Dn
1st Dn

"A" Form.
MESSAGES AND SIGNALS.
Army Form C. 2121.

Prefix	Code	m.	Words	Charge	This message is on a/c of:	Recd. at 1/V m.
Office of Origin and Service Instructions.			Sent		W.D. ²/Service	Date 6/XI/14
			At	m.		From W
			To			
			By		(Signature of "Franking Officer.")	By N/L

TO THIRD CAV DIV

Sender's Number	Day of Month	In reply to Number	AAA
BM 3	Sixth	Ga 106	

Number of available rifles six hundred AAA Squadrons have been relieved from Lord Cavan's trenches AAA Refill at same place as three o'clock yesterday

From SEVENTH CAV BDE
Place ZILLEBEKE
Time 1 pm

The above may be forwarded as now corrected.

Censor. Signature of Addressor or person authorised to telegraph in his name

this quarter & the retirement of the French

A. Form.   Army Form C. 2121.

MESSAGES AND SIGNALS.   No. of Message____

Prefix____ Code____ m.	Words	Charge	This message is on a/c of:	Recd. at 5.40 m.
Office of Origin and Service Instructions	Sent		WO 3/6 Service.	Date____
	At____ m.			From 6
	To		(Signature of "Franking Officer.")	By
	By			

TO { 3rd Cavalry Division
~~22nd Infantry Brigade~~

| Sender's Number | Day of Month | In reply to Number | AAA |
| GC 8 | 6th | | |

Lord Cavan reports French on
his right falling back to
the line astride brown road
and railway just East of
last N of YERBRANDEN MOLEN
AAA ~~you must give him~~
~~all support necessary~~ 2nd Divn
also reports enemy inf action
in the direction of REUTEL

From 1st Corps
Place
Time   4.25pm

The above may be forwarded as now corrected.   (Z) Malcolm Lt
                                                      Censor. Signature of Addressor or person authorised to telegra

*This line should be erased if not required.
3662 M. & Co. Ltd   Wt. W929/549—100,000. 6/14. Forms C2121/10.

this quarter & the retirement of the French

To G.O.C.
   I Corps.
     Chateau de Trois Tours
Ga. 117. Nov. 8.

The following is a brief account of the operations in which the 7th Cav. Bde. was engaged on Nov. 6th.

About 3·15 p.m. the retirement of the French, who were on Lord Cavan's right, was reported and Gen. Kavanagh was sent with the 7th Cav. Bde. to protect this flank.

At the time of the alarm, Gen. Kavanagh's Bde. was in the woods about 1 mile E. of ZILLEBEKE. He galloped back towards ZILLEBEKE, dismounted his Bde. on the outskirts of that village and advanced down the KLEIN-ZILLEBEKE Rd. with the 1st & 2nd Life Gds. in front & the Blues in Reserve.

This advance encouraged the French to re-assume the offensive and all went well until the Bde. arrived in the vicinity of the road running N.E. through the woods from ZWARTELEEN. Gen. Kavanagh then halted the Bde. to allow the French to re-occupy their trenches.

Suddenly, without any warning, the French began to retire rapidly followed by Germans.

Gen. Kavanagh sent 2 Sqds. at the double across the road to protect his right, a certain number of men being lost in so doing. Considerable confusion ensued in this quarter & the retirement of the French

carried our men back about 100 yds. to some
reserve trenches in which the Brigade was able
to re-establish itself.
 The 7th Cav. Bde. held this line until it was
relieved by the 22nd Inf. Bde., the 1st Life Gds.
not being withdrawn until about 4-0 a.m.
on Nov. 7th.
 During the above operation the Bde. lost 17
Officers killed & wounded and some 60 men.
 The Bde. was brilliantly led by its General and
all ranks displayed the utmost gallantry.
I wish to bring Gen. Kavanagh's name particularly to the notice of the Commander-
in-Chief, and also the gallant behaviour
of the following officers, Gen. Kavanagh's
account of which I append.
 Col. Wilson – Royal Horse Guards – killed.
Maj. The Hon. Hugh Dawnay – 2nd Life Gds. – killed.
Maj. The Hon. A. Stanley – 1st Life Gds.
Lieut. S. Menzies – 2nd Life Gds.

J. Byng Maj Gen
3rd Cav Div

YPRES.
Nov. 8th 1914.

"A" Form.
Army Form C. 2121.

MESSAGES AND SIGNALS.

No. of Message 84

TO: 3rd Cavalry Division

Sender's Number: 2757
Day of Month: 06

AAA

Sir Douglas Haig wishes to thank General Kavanagh's Brigade for the splendid support given to the infantry today at a very critical moment

From: 1st Corps
Time: 8.35 am

Time: 11-30 am

"A" Form. Army Form C. 2121.
MESSAGES AND SIGNALS.

TO 3rd Cavalry Div

Sender's Number: A.782
Day of Month: 6th

AAA

The following has been received from the C in C.

Please thank Bryng & Kavanagh on my behalf for the help they have given to the French Cav. I am making very strong representations to Foch on the subject.

Sir John has received your reports on the operations and deeply regrets the heavy loss incurred.

From: 1st Cav Corps
Time: 11-30 pm

"A" Form.   Army Form C. 2121.

MESSAGES AND SIGNALS.   No. of Message _____

Prefix	Code	m.	Words	Charge			
Office of Origin and Service Instructions.					This message is on a/c of:	Recd. at	m.
			Sent			Date	
			At	m.	W.D.	From	
			To		Service.		
			By		(Signature of "Franking Officer.")	By	

TO { 7 Cavalry Brigade

Sender's Number	Day of Month	In reply to Number	
G/92	7/XI/14		A A A

The following messages are (forwarded)
with the G.O.C'S congratulations AAA
1) From Sir Douglas Haig to G.O.C 3 Cav Div
7/XI/14 9.25pm. begins AAA Sir Douglas
Haig wishes to thank 7 Cavalry
Brigade for the splendid support given
to the infantry today at a very critical
period AAA ends AAA (2) From C in C
to G.O.C 1 army Cab Office 7/XI/14 begins
AAA Please thank Gough and
Kavanagh on my behalf for the help they
have given to the 4th Div AAA I am
making very strong representation to French
on the subject AAA ends AAA
Sir Douglas adds that he deeply
regrets the heavy loss incurred AAA

From 3 Cav Division
Place ST ELOI YPRES MESSINES
Time 11 AM

The above may be forwarded as now corrected.   (Z)

"A" Form.
Army Form C. 2121.

MESSAGES AND SIGNALS.

Prefix	Code	m.	Words	Charge	This message is on a/c of:	Recd. at 11/- m.
Office of Origin and Service Instructions.		Sent			W.D. Service.	Date 6/xi/14
At		m.				From
To				(Signature of "Franking Officer.")	By
By					

TO ~~1st Div~~ 3rd Cav Div
~~2nd Div~~ 4th Bde

| Sender's Number | Day of Month | In reply to Number | |
| G 748 | 6th | | AAA |

The attack made against the French ~~~~~~~~~~~~~~ left and our right has been checked AAA The line has now been re-established & every as [unclear] pressure is being brought to bear on the French to make a counter attack tomorrow morning in order to entirely re-establish their line AAA The relief of the Cavalry Division and left battalion of Lord Cavan's force will be carried out as arranged tonight AAA The 7th Cavalry Brigade when relieved will

From
Place
Time

The above may be forwarded as now corrected. (Z)

Censor. Signature of Addressor or person authorised to telegraph in his p.

From First Div
Place
Time 10.36. P.m.

H S Jeudwine
Col. G.S.

The above may be forwarded as now corrected. (Z)

Censor. Signature of addressor or person authorised to telegraph in his name.

Copy.

From 3 Cav Div
Place 3 Kms YPRES-MENIN
Time 16.18

M'Gage Lt Col

The above may be forwarded as now corrected. (Z)

Censor. Signature of Addressor or person authorised to telegr.

			Service	Date
At	m.			From
To				
By		(Signature of "Franking Officer.")	By	

TO

(2)

Sender's Number	Day of Month	In reply to Number	A A A
143			

join the rest of the Cavalry Division which will be as before in Corps Reserve about HOOGE. AAA The 2nd Worcesters will be sent at once by the 7th Brigade to just north of HOOGE where they will come under orders of 2nd Division to whom they will report for instructions AAA The 22nd Brigade will remain temporarily under the orders of Lord Cavan AAA The 1st Div. will maintain as large a Divl Reserve as possible & will report strength & location of this reserve. AH Report as before

From 1st Corps
Place
Time 8.pm

The above may be forwarded as now corrected.   (Z)

Censor.   Signature of Addressor or person authorised to telegraph in his name

*This line should be erased if not required

Co. Ltd. Wt. W929/549-100,000. 6/14. Forms C2121/10.

From First Div
Place
Time 10.36. P.m.

The above may be forwarded as now corrected.   (Z)

H.S. Jeudwine
Col. G.S.

Censor.   Signature of addressor or person authorised to telegraph in his name.

*This line should be erased if not required.

Copy.

From 3 Cav Div.
Place 3 K.de YPRES MENIN
Time 10.10 pm

The above may be forwarded as now corrected.   (Z)

Censor.   Signature of Addressor or person authorised to telegr

*This line should be erased if not required.

8350 S.B. Ltd. Wt. W4842/541 50,000. 9/14. Forms C2121/10.

Duplicate

"A" Form.
MESSAGES AND SIGNALS.

Army Form C. 2121.
No of Message 35

Prefix **M** Code **am** m. Words **110** Charge
Office of origin and Service Instructions.
Sent
At ____ m.
To
By
1st A&Q

This message is on a/c of: Recd. at R ___ m.
W.D ___ Service. Date
From 7-
(Signature of "Franking Officer.") By

TO) First Corps.

Sender's Number	Day of Month	In reply to Number	AAA
G.439	6th	G.948	

Have warned 6th Cav. Bde that relief will now take place & am endeavouring to regain touch with 9th Bde which was placed at disposal of 2nd Divn. in accordance with your G.130 as reported in my G.429 aaa. 3rd Bde still acting under orders of Lord Cavan & L.N. Laws relieving Berkshires in 1st Bde Sections aaa. Divnl reserves will therefore consist of S.W.B. strength 4 Officers 250 other ranks who will be at HOOGE together with Divnl Mounted Troops strength about 200. & Northrs. when relieved strength 10 Officers 470 other ranks aaa. Addressed First Corps repeated Third Cav. Div.

From First Div
Place
Time 10.36. P.m.

H S Jeudwine
Col. G.S.

The above may be forwarded as now corrected. (Z)
Censor. Signature of addressor or person authorised to telegraph in his name.
* This line should be erased if not required.

Copy.

From 3 Cav Div
Place 3 Kds YPRES MENIN
Time 16.10

The above may be forwarded as now corrected. (Z)
M'Gage
Censor. Signature of Addressor or person authorised to telegr
* This line should be erased if not required.

Received 2.15am 16

W.D. 2/7

General Staff   7.XI.14
3rd Cav. Div.

1. The relief of the trenches has now been concluded, and the last squadron will be back in camp in half an hour's time.

2. Will you please send orders re off saddling today?

B. D. Fisher
B.M. 6 C.B.
6.35pm.

From 3rd Cav Div
Place 3 Kms YPRES — MENIN
Time 16.10

G/46 MESSAGES AND SIGNALS №2

Prefix: GOC I AC   W.D 2/7

The 6th Cav Bde were relieved from the trenches at 5 a.m. today. They are now in Corps Reserve near my Head Quarters.

J Byng. M.Gen.
3rd Cav Divn

1 mile W. of HOOGE.

8-25
7.XI.14.

From: 3 Cav Div
Place: ...
Time: ...

	Sent		Service.	Date	
	At ___ m.		W.D.	From	
	To		(Signature of "Franking Officer.")	By	
	By				

TO: 7th Cavalry Brigade

Sender's Number	Day of Month	In reply to Number	
G/93	7/XI/14		AAA

Your Brigade will be relieved by the 6th Cavalry B^{de} at 12 noon. The situation permits me to [?] them like you to move to or to the vicinity of the area now occupied by 6th Cavalry B^{de} a.a.a.

From: 3 Cav Div
Place: 3 Kd. Yrge...
Time: 10.10 a.m.

The above may be forwarded as now corrected. (Z)

A Form.   Army Form C. 2121.

MESSAGES AND SIGNALS.

Prefix	Code	m.	Words	Charge	This message is on a/c of:	Recd. at	m.
Office of Origin and Service Instructions.			Sent		W.D. Service	Date	
			At	m.		From	
			To			By	
			By		(Signature of "Franking Officer.")		

TO
- G.O.C. 6th Cav. Bde.
- " 7th "
- C.R.A. 3rd Cav. Div.
- H.Q. A.S.C. 3rd Cav. Div.
- 3rd F.U. Sqd. R.E.
- 3rd Sig. Sqd.
- A. Bde. & M.G. 3rd Cav. Div.

Sender's Number: GA 114   Day of Month: 7th Nov.   In reply to Number: AAA

1. The 3rd Cav. Div. will be in Corps Reserve tomorrow and Brigades will rendezvous in their present billetting areas.

2. Report Centre :- Chateau 1 mile W. of KRUISSTRAAT till 7-0 a.m., and after that to White house, 3rd Kil.tre YPRES - MENIN Rd.

3. An officer from each Brigade will report at 3rd Cav. Div. H.Q. at 8-0 a.m. tomorrow as liason Officer.

4. It is particularly requested that any German arms or ammunition captured may be forwarded at once to Div. H.Q. Ars.

From: 3rd Cav. Div.
Place: Chateau 1 m. W. of KRUISSTRAAT.
Time: 8.40 pm

The above may be forwarded as now corrected.

From: 1st Corps
Place:
Time: 12.45 pm

The above may be forwarded as now corrected.

From:
Place:
Time:

The above may be forwarded as now corrected.

Prefix	Code	m.		This message		Date
Office of Origin and Service Instructions						From
	Sent At	m.		Service		
	To					
	By		(Signature of "Franking Officer.")			By

TO

Sender's Number	Day of Month	In reply to Number	AAA
G 806	7th		

Owing to the splendid behaviour of General Kavanagh's Brigade last night and also that of the 22nd Infantry Bde to-day we have practically regained the ground lost owing to the French troops on our right giving way aaa. The French have had severe fighting on our right and are about MESSINES and have gained about a mile aaa. General FOCH has given orders that further French reinforcements are to come up on our right so as to ~~make~~ re-establish the original line aaa The Corps Reserve tomorrow will consist of 3rd Cav: Division and one Battalion of Zouaves about HOOGE aaa Reports as before acknowledge.

From: 1st Corps
Place:
Time: 6.30 p.m

From: 1st Corps
Place:
Time: 12.45 pm.

"A" Form.　　Army Form C. 2121.

MESSAGES AND SIGNALS.

No. of Message 123

Words: 68

Service Instructions: MK

Sent At: AHQ
To:
By: WJ

This message is on a/c of

(Signature of "Franking Officer.")

Recd. at
Date
From

TO — 3rd Cavalry Divn.

Sender's Number: G.832
Day of Month: Eighth
In reply to Number:
AAA

General VIDAL with eight battalions is now entrenching a line from HOOGE through ZILLEBEKE to Canal due south of YPRES to VORMEZEELE to form a base for an advance AAA He has also been ordered to send two battalions to co-operate with Genl MOUSSY in an attack which is to be made on KLEIN ZILLEBEKE at 1 p.m.

From: 1st Corps
Place:
Time: 12-45 pm.

The above may be forwarded as now corrected. (Z)

"A" Form. Army Form C. 2121.

MESSAGES AND SIGNALS.   No. of Message _____

Recd. at 3.30 p.m.
Date 8

TO { Third Cav Div.

Sender's Number	Day of Month	In reply to Number	AAA	
Cmn	forwarding	ninth	state	of
2nd	Life	Guards	as	requested.
AAA.	There	are	three	trained
Officers	left	in	the	Regiment.
AAA.	Two	of	these	are
Indian	Army	Officers	who	only
joined	10	days	ago	and
are	therefore	know	none	of
the	men	AAA.	In	my
opinion	their	Regiment	must	have
some	time	to	be	reinforced
and	reorganized	AAA.		

From
Place
Time

The above may be forwarded as now corrected. (Z)

3.30

are of the 2nd Life Guards.

Commanding Officer   1.
Adjutant   1.
2Lt   2.
Other Ranks   300. of these
15 are signallers, 8 are machine gunners,
15 are farriers & shoeing smiths.

There are no clerks in the Regt.

The Regt has lost 29 good NCO's.

There is no M.G. officer or NCO

A Kearsey
Capt
acting BM 7th Cav Bde.

8.xi.'14

"A" Form.
Army Form C. 2121.

MESSAGES AND SIGNALS.

No. of Message 162

Prefix AM Code BBS Words 118 Charge

Office of Origin and Service Instructions

AHQ

Sent
At
To
By

This message is on a/c of:

3.20 p.m.

(Signature of "Franking Officer.")

Recd.

[stamp: ARMY TELEGRAPHS 9-XI-14]

TO 1st Division
~~2nd Division~~ Lord Cavan
3rd Cav Divn

Sender's Number Day of Month In reply to Number
G.42   9th   AAA

Relief will be continued tonight on the lines laid down in G.85 of last night AAA The Cav Divn will arrange to relieve its 500 rifles now in the trenches those relieved returning to Corps Reserve AAA 1st Division will relieve from their Divnl Reserve as much as possible of line still held by Lord Cavan AAA Troops relieved will go into Corps Reserve near HOOGE and Divnl Reserve will be filled up from those troops now in Corps Reserve AAA 1st Division to report what numbers can be relieved tonight details of relief being arranged direct Addressed 1st Div 3rd Cav Divn Lord Cavan, repeated 2nd Div.

From 1st Corps
Place
Time 1.40 pm

The above may be forwarded as now corrected   (Z)

Place 1st A YPRES MENIN RD
Time 3.45 pm

The above may be forwarded as now corrected.   (Z)

Time
The above may be forwarded as now corrected.   (Z)

Time 6.0 pm
The above may be forwarded as now corrected.   (Z)

"A" Form. Army Form C. 2121.

MESSAGES AND SIGNALS.   No. of Message

Prefix	Code	m.	Words	Charge			
Office of Origin and Service Instructions.			Sent		This message is on a/c of:	Recd. at	m.
			At	m.		Date	
			To		/g Service.	From	
			By	W.D	(Signature of "Franking Officer.")	By	

TO { 6" Cav Bde Cav Bde 9
7" Cav Bde
C.R.A

Sender's Number	Day of Month	In reply to Number	
G102	Nov 9"		AAA

The 7" Cav Bde will furnish 520 rifles
to relieve the troops of the 6" Cav Bde.
now in the trenches in the ZILLEBEKE
area AAA The relieving troops to be in
the vicinity of ZILLEBEKE by 7-0 pm
today AAA The GOC 7" Cav Bde will detail
an officer to communicate with 6" Cav Bde
as to the taking over of the trenches AAA
The 6" Cav Bde will detail a liaison officer
to report to Lord Cavan by 8-0 pm & to
remain at his HQ during the night
AAA The 7" Cav Bde will arrange for
close inter-communication between the
troops detailed for the trenches and Lord
Cavan's HQ until relieved tomorrow
Orders for tomorrow the same as for
today unless otherwise notified

From 3rd Cav Bde
Place 2 KM YPRES-MENIN RD
Time 3-45 p.m.

The above may be forwarded as now corrected.   (Z)

Censor.   Signature of Addressee or person authorised to telegraph in his name

*This line should be erased if not required.

Time

The above may be forwarded as now corrected.   (Z)

Censor.   Signature of Addressee or person authorised to telegraph in his name

*This line should be erased if not required.

Time 6.0 pm

The above may be forwarded as now corrected.   (Z)

Censor.   Signature of Addressee or person authorised to telegraph in his name

*This line should be erased if not required.

Censor.   Signature of Addressee or person authorised to telegraph in his name

*This line should be erased if not required.

"A" Form.   Army Form C. 2121.

MESSAGES AND SIGNALS.

No. of Message _____

Prefix _____ Code _____ m. | Words | Charge | This message is on a/c of: | Recd. at _14/_ m.
Office of Origin and Service Instructions | Sent | | W.D / 10 Service. | Date 9/21/14
 | At _____ m. | | | From _____
 | To _____ | | (Signature of "Franking Officer.") | By _____
 | By _____ | | |

TO: 1st Division, 2nd Division, 3rd Division, 3 Cav. Division, G. Corps Troops

Sender's Number: 9.876   Day of Month: 9   In reply to Number: AAA

There is no change in the situation in our immediate front.
The following information is published for the information of the troops

1) On the 7th November the 22nd Inf. Brigade captured 6 German machine guns and brought them away

2) The Northumberland Fusiliers repulsed an attack yesterday and inflicted considerable loss on the enemy who left about 40 dead in front of the trenches

3) An attack was made yesterday north of the MENIN road by a force of Germans estimated at 2000

From _____
Place _____
Time _____

Time 6.0 pm.

"A" Form.   Army Form C. 2121.

MESSAGES AND SIGNALS.

No of Message _____

| Prefix ___ Code ___ m. | Words | Charge | This message is on a/c of : | Recd. at ___ m. |
| Office of Origin and Service Instructions | Sent At ___ m. To By | | Service. (Signature of "Franking Officer.") | Date ___ From ___ By ___ |

TO

| Sender's Number | Day of Month | In reply to Number | **AAA** |

This attack was also beaten off, the enemy's dead numbering fully 150

4) To-day the 15th Brigade reports that a few men of the Bedfords under a Sergeant recovered machine guns which they had lost a few days ago

5) The shelling of the GHELUVELT road to-day is reported by our observers to have been very effective

6) The German port of KIAO-CHAU has been captured AAA Acknowledge

From 1st Corps

Place

Time 6.0 pm

The above may be forwarded as now corrected.   (Z)

Censor.   Signature of Addressor or person authorised to telegraph in his name

MESSAGES AND SIGNALS.

TO	G.O.C. 6: Cav. Bde. C.R.A. 3° Cav. Div. 3° Fd. Sqd. R.E	
	" 7: Cav. Bde. A.D.M.S. " 3° Sig. Sqd.	
	A.A. & Q.M.G. H.Q.A.S.C.	

AAA

Ga 122   Nov. 10th

The 6: Cav. Bde. will ~~relieve the~~ take over the trenches from the 7th Cav. Bde. at 7·0 p.m. today and will occupy them for 48 hours under Bde. arrangements.

Report centres will remain as at present and no further orders will be issued today unless fresh instructions are received from Army Hd. Qrs.

Both Bdes. will arrange liaison with Genl. Lord Cavan's force by day & night until further orders.

From   3rd Cav. Div.
Place 2½ Kil. YPRES-MENIN Rd.
Time   12·30 p.m.

"C" Form (Duplicate). Army Form C. 2123
MESSAGES AND SIGNALS. No. of Message

| Charges to Pay | Office Stamp |
| £ s. d. | |

Service Instructions.

Handed in at the ___AHQ___ Office, at _9.35_ a.m. Received here at _9.42_ a.m.

TO: 3rd Cav Div

Sender's Number.	Day of Month.	In reply to Number.	AAA
G993	13th		
French	on	Cavans	right
being	shelled	aaa	In
view	of	information	from
two	sources	that	Germans
intend	to	press	in
today	at	this	point
please	keep	in	close
touch	with	Lord	Cavan
and	have	your	division
ready	to	support	him
at	once		

FROM: 1st Corps.
PLACE:
TIME: 9.30 am / Received 9.40 am

Time _9.50 am_
The above may be forwarded as now corrected. (Z) _McGaye Lt Col_
Censor. Signature of Addressor or person authorised to telegraph in his name

Time _frontier_
The above may be forwarded as now corrected. (Z)
Censor. Signature of Addressor or person authorised to telegraph in his name

Time _10-40 AM_
The above may be forwarded as now corrected. (Z) _McGaye Lt Col_
Censor. Signature of Addressor or person authorised to telegraph in his name

TIME:

MESSAGES AND SIGNALS.

TO: 1st Cav Bde

Sender's Number	Day of Month	In reply to Number	AAA
G 123	13		

Trench on Cavan's right being shelled aaa in view of this information from two sources that Germans intend to-day to press in at this front please keep ready to move at a moment's notice aaa

From: G Cav Bde
Time: 9.50 am

Time: 10-40 am

"A" Form.   Army Form C. 2121.

MESSAGES AND SIGNALS.

Prefix	Code	m.	Words	Charge	This message is on a/c of:	Recd. at	m.
Office of Origin and Service Instructions.			Sent		W.O. / 13 Service.	Date	
			At m.			From	
			To			By	
			By		(Signature of "Franking Officer.")		

TO { 6th Cav. Bde.   A.A. & Q.M.G. 3rd Cav. Div.
     7th Cav. Bde.
     C.R.A. 3rd Cav. Div.

Sender's Number	Day of Month	In reply to Number	AAA
Ga 130	13th Nov.		

1. Generally speaking the position last night remained unchanged. The French on our right have been reinforced. An attack on Lord Cavan's right was repulsed by Inf. & Cav. Early yesterday the French lost some ground E. of ZONNEBEKE but it was all recovered later owing largely to the support of the 6th Inf. Bde. & 2nd Div.n Art.y, and the enemy is known to have suffered very heavily. Farther north the situation was practically unchanged but on the whole the general position of the Allies had improved. The number of Germans killed on the 11th inst. is known to be large & efforts are being made to get an accurate estimate. According to official returns the German losses to the end of September were 507,000. It is probable that at least 250,000 more have been killed & wounded since that date.

From   In the East the Russian advance continues
Place   & Russian troops are now well within the German
Time   frontier.

The above may be forwarded as now corrected.   (Z)

Censor.   Signature of Addressor or person authorised to telegraph in his name

Time 10-40 A.M.

The above may be forwarded as now corrected.   (Z)   McGax Lt. Col.

"A" Form. Army Form C. 2121.

MESSAGES AND SIGNALS.   No. of Message

Prefix	Code	m.	Words	Charge	This message is on a/c of:	Recd. at	m.
Office of Origin and Service Instructions.			Sent			Date	
			At	m.	Service.	From	
			To				
			By		(Signature of "Franking Officer.")	By	

TO ②

* Sender's Number | Day of Month | In reply to Number | AAA

2. The 7th Cav. Bde. will relieve those troops of the 6th Cav. Bde. now in the trenches, tonight, under Brigade arrangements. Tour of duty 48 hours. Should a supporting reg" be required for tonight, it will be found by the 7th Cav. Bde.

From 3rd Cav. Div.
Place YPRES.
Time 10-40 A.M.

The above may be forwarded as now corrected.   (Z) [signature]
Censor.   Signature of Addressor or person authorized to tele
* This line should be erased if not required.

"C" Form (Duplicate)
MESSAGES AND SIGNALS

2B BEW 38

Service Instructions. Priority

Handed in at the ___ Office, at 2.28 pm Received here at 2.35 pm

TO 3rd Cav Div

Sender's Number.	Day of Month.	In reply to Number.	AAA
G1008	13		
7th	Bde	report	1.40
pm	Considerable	bodies	of
enemy	advancing	to	attack
aaa	Keep	in	close
touch	with	situation	aaa
1st	Divn	and	Lord
Cavan	have	been	informed

FROM 1st Corps
PLACE
TIME 2.25 pm

"A" Form.
Army Form C. 2121.

MESSAGES AND SIGNALS.

No. of Message

Prefix	Code	m.	Words	Charge	This message is on a/c of:	Recd. at 3.45 m.
Office of Origin and Service Instructions.			Sent		W.O³/13 Service	Date 13 XI 14
			At m.			From
			To			
			By		(Signature of "Franking Officer.")	By

TO 3rd Cavalry Division

Sender's Number	Day of Month	In reply to Number	AAA
S.100g	13th		

Cavan reports 2-10 pm enemy
attacking through K 24 C & A AAA
One regiment 7th Cavalry Bde. has
gone up in support of infantry AAA
Move your other brigade towards
Cavan so as to be ready if required

From 1st Corps
Place
Time 3-10 pm

The above may be forwarded as now corrected. (Z)

Censor. Signature of Addressor or person authorised to telegraph in his name

Place
Time 2-50 pm

The above may be forwarded as now corrected. (Z)

Censor. Signature of Addressor or person authorised to telegraph in his name

the Brigade should put

FROM
PLACE
TIME

Recd 3.40 pm

13-11

Place
Time 6 pm

The above may be forwarded as now corrected. (Z)

Censor. Signature of Addressor or person authorised to telegraph in his name

TO 3rd Cav: Bde HQrs

Sender's Number: BM/914 Day of Month: 13th

Please send 7th Cav: Bde to wood immediately north of these Head Qrs to position occupied by 2nd Life Guards last night as I have already had to call on this Regt to reinforce London Scottish

From Lord Cavan
Time 2-50 pm

the GOC Brigade should put

Recd 3.40 pm
13.11

Time 6 p.m.

"C" Form (Duplicate).   Army Form C. 2123
MESSAGES AND SIGNALS.   No. of Message

1B Bde 1417

W.D 5/13

Service Instructions. Priority

Handed in at the 1st A.H.Q. Office, at 2pm. Received here at 3pm.

TO 3rd Cav Div

Sender's Number: G 1007   Day of Month: 13th   AAA

The following reliefs will take place tonight the 3rd Div will extend its right so as take over the left of Lord Cavans command about 400 men will be available for this duty aaa. The 3rd Div will also extend its left so as to relieve R Queens regt which will return to 1st Div aaa 2 the 1st Cav div will send one brigade to take over part of Lord Cavan line the Brigade should put

Received 3.40pm

13·11

Time 6 p.m.

Charges to collect	£ s. d.	From	At	m.
Service Instructions.		By	To	
			By	

Handed in at the _____ Office, at _____ .m. Received here at _____ .m.

TO ②

*Sender's Number. | Day of Month. | In reply to Number. | AAA

in about 550 to 600 rifles
aaa This is in addition to
the 500 rifles from 3rd
Cav Div already in the
trenches aaa 9. 3rd
Div 1st Cav bde
have been instructed to send
officers to lord Cavans
hq to arrange details
aaa acknowledge aaa
Addressed 1st Div repeated 2nd
& 3rd Divns 1st and 3rd
Cav Divs and Lord Cavan

FROM
PLACE 1st Corps
TIME 2.30 pm

Time 6/n.

"A" Form.   Army Form C. 2121.

MESSAGES AND SIGNALS.   No. of Message ____

Prefix	Code	m.	Words	Charge	This message is on a/c of:	Recd. at	m.
Office of Origin and Service Instructions.			Sent		W D	Date	
			At m.		Service.	From	
			To				
			By		(Signature of "Franking Officer.")	By	

TO   1st Army Corps

Sender's Number	Day of Month	In reply to Number	AAA
G.128	13		

Cavan reports situation normal aaa
6th Cav Bde have been allowed to return
to bivouac aaa Vaughan 2/? now
in trenches and goes in support aa
Cavan left aaa remainder of 2 Divs
aaa Somerset Yeomanry have arrived

From 3rd Cav Div.
Place
Time 6/12.

"A" Form.   Army Form C. 2121.
MESSAGES AND SIGNALS.   No. of Message

Prefix	Code	m.	Words	Charge		Recd. at	11 p	m.
Office of Origin and Service Instructions.					This message is on a/c of:	Date	11.11.14	
			Sent			From		
		At		m.	W D / ⅓ Service			
		To						
		By			(Signature of "Franking Officer.")	By		

TO { 1st 2nd 3rd Divisions } Lord Cavan
     { 3rd Cavalry Division. }

| Sender's Number | Day of Month | In reply to Number | |
| G.A. 138 | 11 | | AAA |

~~The situation~~ Portions of the German Guard division took part in the attack against us to-day aaa Other units of this Guards division located against French on our left AAA. Some of the trenches between POLYGONE wood and VELDHOEK have not been ~~yet~~ retaken yet & an attack to capture them has been arranged for 1. a.m. aaa The enemy lost heavily especially in front of 7th and 15th Brigades. AAA Two British Cavalry brigades will be arriving to reinforce during the night and will proceed to about BELLEWAARDE Farm.

Reports as before

From 1st Corps
Place
Time 9.45.p.m.

The above may be forwarded as now corrected. (Z)   H Gough BG
     Censor.   Signature of Addressee or person authorised to telegraph in his name

FROM	7th Cav Bde on HOOGE
PLACE	Road E of CHATEAU
TIME	wood 5.30 am

Recd 7.00 A.M.

"A" Form.   Army Form C. 2121.

MESSAGES AND SIGNALS.   No. of Message 46

Code	Words	Charge	This message is on a/c of	Recd. at 7a m.
of Origin and Service Instructions	Sent			Date From By
AHQ	At m. To By		(Signature of "Franking Officer")	

TO ~~1st~~ ~~2nd~~ ~~3rd Divisions~~
3rd Cav. Div.   Lord Cavan

Sender's Number	Day of Month	In reply to Number	AAA
G.A.140	12th		

Situation as follows ~~enemy~~ First Brigade unable regain trenches new line being formed from POLYGONNE wood along S.E edge of NONNE BOSCHEN wood to join left of 3rd division near MENIN road AAA. All available infantry have been detailed to occupy and support this line with General KAVANAGH brigade in reserve and one brigade DELISLES cavalry division has been ordered N.W corner of NONNE BOSCHEN wood as further reserve the remaining brigade this cavalry division being in reserve at BELLEWAARDE farm AAA. Particular attention should be paid by 3rd division to keeping their left strong ~~along~~ near the MENIN road.

From 1st Corps
Place
Time 6.15 am

The above may be forwarded as now corrected. (Z)

Gough BG

Censor. Signature of Addressor or person authorised to telegraph in his name

*This line should be erased if not required

2662 M. & Co. Ltd. Wt. W929/549—100,000. 6/14. Forms C2121/10.

FROM PLACE TIME	7th Cav Bde on HOOGE Road E of CHATEAU wood 5.30 am

Recd 7.00 A.M.

(5840) W₀. W 451-1591. 5-11. 10,000 Pads. WY. & S., Ltd. Sch. 78.   Army Form C 2123.

G Form. (Duplicate.)   **MESSAGES & SIGNALS.**   No. of Message ....

Inquiries respecting this Message, or application for repetition of the same, may be made at the Delivering Office; but any complaint as to its delay, &c., should be made in writing and addressed to the officer in charge. In either case this form must accompany such inquiries or complaint.

Service Instructions: Buckley   WD 72   Charges to pay

Handed in at the .... Office at 7.14 a.M.   Received here at 7.27 .M.

TO Third Cav Div

Sender's Number	Day of Month	In reply to Number	A. A. A.
BM 3	12th		

In accordance with orders received from Gen. Landon the 1st Life Guards paraded dismounted at 1.45a and marched to 1st Div HQ aaa At 4.30am this Regt was sent forward to support the Gloster Regt N. W of VELDTHOEK aaa The Remainder of bde is now in position E. of CHATEAU wood

FROM PLACE TIME	7th Cav Bde on HOOGE Road E of CHATEAU wood 5.30 am

Rcd 7.20. A.M.

"A" Form.
Army Form C. 2121.

MESSAGES AND SIGNALS.

No. of Message ____

Prefix	Code	Words	Charge	This message is on a/c of:
		56	4	

Office of Origin and Service Instructions.

Sent At W ____ 9-30 ____
To ____
By ____ (Signature of "Franking Officer")

1st AHQ

[Stamp: ARMY TELEGRAPHS 12.XI.14 HQ]

TO
1st ~~2nd 3rd Army~~
3rd Cav Divn. ~~South Cavan~~

Sender's Number	Day of Month	In reply to Number	AAA
GA 144	12th		

Prisoners state that the German Guard regiments were brought up to relieve their XXVII corps and were told to make supreme effort yesterday to break through as their other corps had failed AAA French reinforcements are at hand and everything depends on our holding our positions today

Copies to 6" 17" Cav Bdes.
Nr GA 127.
11.30 A.M.
Nov. 12.

From 1st Corps
Place ____
Time 7.35 A M

The above may be forwarded as now corrected. (Z) (Sd) JE Gough BG

Censor. Signature of Addressor or person authorised to telegraph in his name

*This line should be erased if not required
3662 M. & Co. Ltd. Wt. W929/549—100,000. 6/14. Forms C2121/10.

"A" Form. Army Form C. 2121.

MESSAGES AND SIGNALS.   No of Message____

Prefix	Code	m.	Words	Charge	This message is on a/c of:	Recd. at	m.
Office of Origin and Service Instructions			15			Date	
			Sent		7-40 a	From	
At	WD	12 m.			12 z Service.		
To					(Signature of "Franking Officer.")	By	
By							

TO { Col Cunliffe Owen   3rd Cav Divn
     7th Cav Bde

Sender's Number	Day of Month	In reply to Number	AAA
664			

3rd Divn coming 9 am between left
of 6th Bde and right of French heavily
attacked and have been obliged to
withdraw some troops from POLYGONE
wood to support 6th Bde. Tubs Col
Cunliffe Owen will make the most
thorough reconnaissance possible
in his front and will take every
opportunity of offensive action.
Addressed Col Cunliffe Owen 7th
Cavalry Bde 3rd Div.

Byng ? sent

From
Place
Time 9.20   H S Landon ?

The above may be forwarded as now corrected.   (Z)
                                    Censor.   Signature of Addressor or person authorised to telegraph in his name

"C" Form (Duplicate).
MESSAGES AND SIGNALS.

Army Form C. 2123.

TO: 3rd Cav Div

Sender's Number.	Day of Month.	In reply to Number.	AAA
GM 867	12		

Understand 3rd Dragoon Guards are going into trenches tonight aaa Hope you will be able to give me another regt to replace them aaa 3rd Dragoon Gds are now in wood just behind these hdqrs aaa The new regt should take up same similar position aaa understand that Germans are massing for

		Charges to Pay.	Office Stamp.
Service Instructions.		£ s. d.	

Handed in at the _____ Office, at 3.5 m. Received here at ___ m.

TO _____

Sender's Number.	Day of Month.	In reply to Number.	AAA
an	night	attack	

FROM: Lord Cavan
PLACE:
TIME: 3·10 pm

"A" Form.　　　　　　　　　　　　　　　　　　　　　Army Form C. 2121.

MESSAGES AND SIGNALS.　　No. of Message

Prefix	Code	m.	Words	Charge	This message is on a/c of:	Recd. at	m.
Office of Origin and Service Instructions.			Sent			Date	
			At	m.	W O	From	
			To		Service	By	
			By		(Signature of "Franking Officer.")		

TO　Lord Cavan

Sender's Number	Day of Month	In reply to Number	AAA
G 117	12.XI.14	B M 867	

a regiment from 7th Cavalry Brigade is relieving the 3rd Dragoon Guards who are in the trenches. The relieving regiment will be in support at the same place as 3rd [Dragoons] [was]. The balance of the 6th Cavalry Brigade and the 7th Cavalry Brigade (the regiment at your H.Q.) will form a reserve at your call during the night. [illegible] changes for 7th Cav. Brigade will be handed to 6th Cavalry Brigade under the [illegible]. Do you require to hear further from each before tonight. Telephone [illegible] to telephone?

From 2 Cav. Div.

Place

Time

The above may be forwarded as now corrected.　(Z)

Censor.　Signature of Addressor or person authorised to telegraph in his name

* This line should be erased if not required.

"C" Form (Duplicate). Army Form C. 2123
MESSAGES AND SIGNALS. No. of Message _____

Charges to Pay. Office Stamp.
£   s.   d.

Service Instructions.

Handed in at the _____ Office, at 6.15 __.m. Received here at 8.30 __.m.

TO 3rd Cav Div

Sender's Number. Day of Month. In reply to Number.
  457   12   AAA

have been round my trenches and seen Lord CAVAN who had seen General Haig this afternoon Lord Cavan expects the 6th Cavalry Brigade to be in support close behind his headquarters by 6 am tomorrow AAA I shall be in position with the remainder of my brigade 500 yds east of ZANDVOORDE by 5 am

FROM   AAA C Battery RHA
PLACE   will be in position about
TIME   the centre of K 11 by

TIME

artillery and the enemy is known to have suffered very heavily farther north the situation is practically unchanged

From
Place
Time

The above may be forwarded as now corrected   Z

Censor. Signature of Addressor or person authorised to telegraph in his name
*This line should be erased if not required.

"C" Form (Duplicate). Army Form C. 2123
MESSAGES AND SIGNALS. No. of Message _____

| Service Instructions. | Charges to Pay. £ s. d. | Office Stamp. |

Handed in at the _____ Office, at 5.16 p.m. Received here at 5.30 p.m.

TO. (2)

| Sender's Number. | Day of Month. | In reply to Number. | AAA |

5.45 am aaa my reason for these precautions is that Lord Cavan expects a general attack at dawn tomorrow aaa

FROM   GOC 6th Cav
PLACE   Bde
TIME

Artillery and the enemy is known to have suffered very heavily. Farther north the situation is practically unchanged

From
Place
Time

The above may be forwarded as now corrected. Z

Censor. | Signature of Addressor or person authorised to telegraph in his name

*This line should be erased if not required.

MESSAGES AND SIGNALS.
"A" Form.   Army Form C. 2121.

TO — 1st Divn, 2nd Divn, 3rd Divn, 1st Cav. Divn, 3rd Cav. Divn, Lord Cavan

Sender's Number: G.982   Day of Month: 13th

Generally speaking the position on our front remains unchanged. The French on our right flank held the position taken up yesterday and have been reinforced. During the day an attack on Lord Cavan's Brigade was repulsed by infantry and cavalry. The 7th and 9th Infy. Bdes were subjected to bombardment about 2.30 pm but slack but the one attack was easily beaten off. Early in the day the French lost some ground east of ZONNEBEKE but it was all recovered later largely owing to the support by the 6th Infy. Bde 4th Divn. artillery and the enemy is known to have suffered very heavily. Further north the situation is practically unchanged

	At m.	Service.	Date
	To		From
	By	(Signature of "Franking Officer.")	By

TO		2	

Sender's Number   Day of Month   In reply to Number   **A A A**

but on the whole the general position of the
Allies has improved. The number of
Germans killed in yesterdays fight is
known to be large and efforts are being
made to get an accurate estimate.
According to official returns the German
losses to the end of September were
507,000. It is probable that at least
250,000 more have been killed and wounded
since that date. In the east the Russian
advance continues and Russian troops
are now well within the German frontier.
2. Reinforcements. The Composite Regt
of Household Cavalry join 4th Cav.
Bde last night. The R. Hertfordshire
Territorial Batt. has joined the 2nd
Division. Two Yeomanry regts arrive

From
Place
Time

The above may be forwarded as now corrected   (Z)

Censor.   Signature of Addressor or person authorised to telegraph in his name

*This line should be erased if not required.

	At	m.	Service.	From
	To			By
	By		(Signature of "Franking Officer.")	

TO

	3		
Sender's Number	Day of Month	In reply to Number	**A A A**

tonight and two regular infantry battalions come up tomorrow. Further reinforcements are expected

3. Troops will hold the ground they are now on. The Grenadier Guards which have been acting under 1st Div. will return to Corp. Reserve near HOOGE at first opportunity. The 1st and 3rd Cavalry Divns. will also be in Corp. Reserve as follows:—

1st Cav. Divn: 1 Bde N. of HOOGE ready to support infantry. The other brigade near BELLEWAARDE FM.

3rd Cav. Divn.— One regt. or more in close support of Lord Cavan. Remainder about HOOGE. Report as before. Acknowledge.

From
Place Co. H.
Time 2/pm

H Gough B.G.

W.D. 8/12

TO:- 1st Div., 2nd Div., 3rd Div., 1st Cav. Div., 3rd Cav. Div., Lord CAVAN.

G.983. 12th November, 1914. The Commander-in-Chief has asked me to convey to the troops under my command his congratulations and thanks for their splendid resistance to the German attack yesterday. This attack was delivered by some 15 fresh Bns. of the German Guard Corps which had been specially brought up to carry out the task in which so many other Corps had failed, viz to crush the British and force a way through to YPRES.

Since its arrival in this neighbourhood the 1st Corps, assisted by the 3rd Cav. Div., 7th Div., and troops from the 2nd Corps, has met and defeated the 23rd, 26th and 27th German Reserve Corps, the 13th Active Corps, and finally a strong force from the Guard Corps. It is doubtful whether the annals of the British Army contain any finer record than this.

(Signed) DOUGLAS HAIG, Lieutenant-General,
Commanding 1st Army Corps.

"A" Form. Army Form C. 2121.

MESSAGES AND SIGNALS.

No. of Message _____

Prefix _____ Code _____ Words _____ Charge _____

Office of Origin and Service Instructions.

Sent At _____ m.
To _____
By _____

This message is on a/c of:
W.D.
(Signature of "Franking Officer.")

Recd. at 7.50 m.
Date _____
From _____
By _____

TO 3rd Cav Divn.

Sender's Number: BM 1974
Day of Month: 14th
In reply to Number:
AAA

Reliefs successfully carried out last night. AAA All quiet so far this morning.

From Lord Cavan
Place
Time 8 AM

The above may be forwarded as now corrected

Censor. Signature of Addressor or person authorised to telegraph in his name

W Cuthversan

"A" Form. Army Form C. 2121.
MESSAGES AND SIGNALS.

TO: 1st Division   1st Cav: Divn.
2nd Division   3rd Cav: Divn.
3rd Division   Lord Cavan

Sender's Number: 228   Day of Month: 13th   AAA

The whole front was heavily shelled today from about 10am till dark. Infantry attacks were made all along the front from left of Lord Cavan's section to the ME NN road inclusive, but were repulsed with loss to the enemy aaa Owing to the fact that the French troops on our left lost some ground near BROODSEINDE the 6th Infantry Brigade withdrew its advanced points to the main defensive line after inflicting heavy loss upon the enemy who was attacking in this quarter. At one point a German company succeeded in establishing itself in a wood behind the French line, 40 were killed and the rest then surrendered. Two German deserters who came to our lines today

	Sent		Date
	At ___ m.	Service ___	From ___
	To ___		
	By ___	(Signature of "Franking Officer.")	By ___

TO {

Sender's Number | Day of Month | In reply to Number | **A A A**

reported that considerable number of their comrades have left their units and have escaped into Holland aaa. To the south the French have gained a little ground near ST ELOI. aaa.

2. Troops will hold their ground tomorrow – Corps Reserve will be as follows :–
(a) The London Scottish and Lincoln's Fusiliers south of the HOOGE road near 1st Divn; H.Q.
(b) 1st Cavalry Divn: less one brigade N. of the HOOGE road.
(c) 3rd Cavalry Divn: less 500 rifles (in the trenches) near BELLEWAARDE FARM.
1st Cavalry Divn. will establish its H.Q. tomorrow near * H.Q. 2nd Divn.
Reports as before.

* near

From: 1st CORPS
Place:
Time: 8 P.M.

The above may be forwarded as now corrected   Z   [signature]

Censor.   Signature of Addressor or person authorised to telegraph in his name

*This line should be erased if not required.

G.130

W.D. 3/14.

1. Until further orders the 3rd Cavalry Division will form a Corps Reserve as follows:—
   (a). <u>Mobile Reserve</u> One Brigade billeted in an area W. of YPRES.
   (b). <u>Reserve</u> One Brigade (dismounted) in the area near the railway crossing at HALTE on the YPRES- MENIN road, with its horses in an area W. of YPRES.

The "Mobile Reserve" will have one regiment saddled up, both by day and night.

The "Reserve Brigade" will furnish
   (c) 500 rifles for the trenches.
   (d) 300 rifles in immediate support to Lord Cavan's line.
   (e) 400 rifles as a reserve ~~to Lord Cavan~~ Corps

"Dug-outs" are now being constructed in the railway cutting immediately S.W. of HALTE to accommodate the H.Q. and units of the Reserve Brigade, and should be completed by to morrow afternoon.

Brigadiers are held responsible that proper sanitary precautions are observed, and that the "dug-outs" are handed over to the relieving Brigade in reasonably clean condition.

2. (a) Under normal conditions the Mobile Reserve Brigade will relieve the

Telephone with Lord Cavan will be maintained as at present (i.e. at the farm evacuated by H.Q. 6th Cav. B.), and in addition, the H.Q 3rd Signal

14.11.14
3/h.h.

G.S. 3 Cav...

Reserve Brigade crossed hours, at 6.30 p.m.

Horses, Assembly Place.
(b). The horses of the Reserve Brigade will be brought to the open space of the railway station in YPRES, and the troops of this brigade will be marched there, by the railway line when relieved.

Similarly, the troops of the Mobile Reserve Brigade will be dismounted at the same place, and conducted to the trenches by the same route, the horses being promptly taken back to their billeting area, so as to clear the roads and assembly place for the led horses of the brigade to be relieved.

Communications
3.(a) The O/C 3rd Signal Squadron will take immediate steps to connect the H.Q. of the "Mobile Reserve Brigade" by telephone and cyclist to those of the 3rd Cav. Division. He will also connect the H.Q. of the "Reserve Brigade" at the railway cutting near HALTE to-morrow, with Lord Cavan's H.Q, and with Divl. H.Q.

(b). To-night, the communication by telephone with Lord Cavan will be maintained as at present (i.e. at the farm evacuated by H.Q. 6th Cav. Bde), and in addition, the O/C 3rd Signal

G.S. Brewer

14.11.14
3 p.m.

Squadron will have a suitable post for transmitting messages to Divl. H.Q. in the event of a break occurring in the line.

(c). The G.O.C. 7th Cavalry Brigade will, by 6 p.m. to night, detail an officer and the necessary orderlies to stay at this communication post to transmit messages from Lord Cavan, and will also maintain liaison between the latter's H.Q. and the Post.

(d) All messages received, dealing with the situation in Lord Cavan's line will be transmitted by the communication Post to Divl. H.Q. for the G.O.C's information.

(4). The 7th Cavalry Brigade will move to a billeting area W. of YPRES, on relief by 6th Cavalry Bde to-morrow. The location of this area will be notified later.

Mullcage Lieut. Col
G.S. 3rd Car Div.

YPRES
14.11.14
3 p.m.

"C" Form (Duplicate).
MESSAGES AND SIGNALS.   Army Form C. 2123.

Service Instructions: Priority

Handed in at the 1st Div Office, at 1.38 pm.   Received here at 1.49 p.m.

TO   3rd Cav Div

Sender's Number.	Day of Month.	In reply to Number.	AAA
G 33	14th		

Enemy are making an attack front of 13th and 9th Bdes aaa Corps Commander orders you to be ready

Received 2 pm

FROM   1st Div
PLACE
TIME   1·20 pm

PLACE
TIME   2·35 pm

"C" Form (Duplicate).
MESSAGES AND SIGNALS.
Army Form C. 2123.

No. of Message

Service Instructions: Priority

Handed in at the 1st Army 9.45p Office, at ......m. Received here at ...... m.

TO: 3rd Cav Divn

Serial Number.	Day of Month.	In reply to Number.	AAA
534	14th		

Positions east of YPRES at present held by British troops under Command of Sir Douglas Haig are to be taken over by the French aaa The relief will begin tomorrow night at the latest

Received 3p

FROM: 1st Corps
PLACE:
TIME: 2.35pm

"A" Form.   Army Form C. 2121.

MESSAGES AND SIGNALS.

Prefix	Code	m.	Words	Charge			
Office of Origin and Service Instructions					This message is on a/c of:	Recd. at 11.30/p m.	
			Sent		W.D. /s Service	Date 14.XI	
			At	m.		From 1st AC	
			To			By	
			By (sgd)		(Signature of "Franking Officer.")		

TO { acknowledge / une / message /

Sender's Number	Day of Month	In reply to Number	AAA
G.51	14th		

1. Prisoners of the Guard Division now in our front state that the 2nd Grenadier Guards Regt. has only 5% of its original serving soldiers and regular reservists left. Casualties have been replaced by Ersatz and Landwehr troops. A draft of Ersatz troops originally sent to Russia for garrison duty has been recalled to this part of the theatre of operations to reinforce the 15th Corps. A boy of 15½ years old serving in the ranks has been taken prisoner. All the Germans that crossed the left bank of the YSER yesterday were driven back by a night attack.

From

Place

Time

The above may be forwarded as now corrected.   (Z)

Censor. | Signature of Addressor or person authorised to telegraph in his name

*This line should be erased if not required

2662 M. & Co. Ltd. Wt. W929/549—100,000. 6/14. Forms C2121/10.

Time

The above may be forwarded as now corrected.   (Z)

Censor. | Signature of Addressor or person authorised to telegraph in his name

*This line should be erased if not required

2662 M. & Co. Ltd. Wt. W929/549—100,000. 6/14. Forms C2121/10.

The above may be forwarded as now corrected.   (Z)

Censor. | Signature of Addressor or person authorised to telegraph in his name

*This line should be erased if not required

2662 M. & Co. Ltd. Wt. W929/549—100,000. 6/14. Forms C2121/10.

Censor. | Signature of Addressor or person authorised to telegraph in his name

*This line should be erased if not required

2662 M. & Co. Ltd. Wt. W929/549—100,000. 6/14. Forms C2121/10.

"A" Form.   Army Form C. 2121.

MESSAGES AND SIGNALS.   No. of Message____

Prefix____Code____m.	Words	Charge	This message is on a/c of:	Recd. at____m.
Office of Origin and Service Instructions				
	Sent			Date____
	At____m.		____Service.	From____
	To			
	By		(Signature of "Franking Officer.")	By____

TO {

| Sender's Number | Day of Month | In reply to Number | A A A |

There has been heavy fighting to the N. and S. of our position. On the north the French have gained a little ground on the S the situation is practically unchanged. Our own position was heavily shelled and the front of the 3rd Division was attacked. Some ground was lost but has now been recovered. The 6th Bde was also attacked during the afternoon but has held its own without difficulty. Yesterday a series of attacks were made on the front of Lord Cavan's line and many of the enemy were killed within 5 yards of

From
Place
Time

The above may be forwarded as now corrected. (Z)

Censor. | Signature of Addressor or person authorised to telegraph in his name
*This line should be erased if not required
3662 M. & Co. Ltd. Wt. W929/549—100,000. 6/14. Forms C2121/10.

The above may be forwarded as now corrected. (Z)

Censor. | Signature of Addressor or person authorised to telegraph in his name
*This line should be erased if not required
3662 M. & Co. Ltd. Wt. W929/549—100,000. 6/14. Forms C2121/10.

Censor. | Signature of Addressor or person authorised to telegraph in his name
*This line should be erased if not required
3662 M. & Co. Ltd. Wt. W929/549—100,000. 6/14. Forms C2121/10.

"A" Form.　　　　　　　　　　　　　　　Army Form C. 2121.

MESSAGES AND SIGNALS.　　　No. of Message_____

of the trenches.

2. The C in C has informed the G.O.C. 1st Corps that the position now held east of YPRES are to be taken over by the French and that the relief will begin tomorrow night.

3. Tomorrow the troops will hold the position they are now in but tonight the 2nd Grenadier Guards and the Irish Gds. will replace the S.W. Borderers and the Munster Fusiliers under Lord Cavan's command. The S.W.B and Munsters will go into Corps Reserve. Details of relief and bivouacs will be arranged by the 1st Division.

4. It is understood that the ZOUAVE

MESSAGES AND SIGNALS.

Prefix	Code	m.	Words	Charge		This message is on a/c of :	Recd. at	m.
Office of Origin and Service Instructions			Sent				Date	
			At	m.		Service.	From	
			To				By	
			By			(Signature of "Franking Officer.")		

TO {

* Sender's Number	Day of Month	In reply to Number	A A A

Battalion on the MENIN road is being withdrawn tonight under orders from General D'Urbal.
5. Reports as before. Acknowledge
6. It is noted for information that the cavalry is distributed as follows:-
1st Division. One Bde in the trenches under Lord Cavan. One Bde and two guns near HOOGE of which one regt. only is mounted.
2nd Division:- 500 in the trenches under Lord Cavan, one regt in support of Lord Cavan. 400 rifles in reserve near HALTE. Remaining Bde. W. of YPRES.

From 1st Corps
Place
Time 10.0 pm
The above may be forwarded as now corrected.   (Z)   B.G.
Censor.   Signature of Addressee or person authorised to telegraph in his name
*This line should be erased if not required

"A" Form. Army Form C. 2121.

MESSAGES AND SIGNALS.   No. of Message 192

Prefix	Code	m.	Words	Charge	This message is on a/c of:	Rec'd.	m.
Office of Origin and Service Instructions			Sent		W.D 2/15	Date	
Priority 1st Corps			At ... m. To By		Service. (Signature of "Franking Officer")	From 14.XI.14 HQ ARMY TELEGRAPHS	

TO { 1st Cavalry ~~Div~~
3rd Cavalry Div } Rec 12.45 am 15/XI

Sender's Number | Day of Month | In reply to Number | AAA

3rd Division report indications
enemy may renew attack in the morning
along the 3rd Division front aaa The
Cavalry Brigade of 1st Cavalry Division
should be prepared to support
closely, and should keep close
communication with 3rd Division
Head Quarters so as to be able
to counter attack at once if
required aaa The 1st Cavalry Division
will send one regiment from its reserve
west of YPRES to about BELLEWAARDE PARK
at 6.30 am. The remainder of the brigade should
be in readiness to move at short notice. aaa
Acknowledge

From 1st Corps
Place
Time 11.40 pm

The above may be forwarded as now corrected. (Z)

Censor. Signature of Addressor or person authorised to telegraph in his name
*This line should be erased if not required
2663 M. & Co. Ltd. Wt. W929/549—100,000. 6/14. Forms C2121/10.

Time
The above may be forwarded as now corrected. (Z)
Censor. Signature of Addressor or person authorised to telegraph in his name
* This line should be erased if not required.
8350 S. B. Ltd. Wt. W4842/541—50,000. 9/14. Forms C2121/10.

PLACE	
TIME	

W. 5375—423. 75,000 Pads—12/12—B. & F.—Forms/C.2123/1.

TIME	

W. 5375—423. 75,000 Pads—12/12—B. & F.—Forms/C.2123/1.

"A" Form.   Army Form C. 2121.
MESSAGES AND SIGNALS.

Prefix	Code	m.	Words	Charge	This message is on a/c of:	Rec'd. at	m.
Office of Origin and Service Instructions.			Sent		W.D. /15	Date	
At		m.			Service.	From	
To							
By				(Signature of "Franking Officer.")	By	

TO { 6th Cavalry Brigade

Sender's Number	Day of Month	In reply to Number	AAA
G/44	15.XI.14		

Germans expect attack in
morning a a a the 6th Cavalry
Brigade will send one regiment
to defend BELLEWARDE FARM
at 6:30 a.m. to-day, and the
remainder of the Brigade will
be in readiness to move at
short notice a a a the O/C
regiment should report at once
by telephone or messenger
from your H.Q. of yesterday
if called into action will
acknowledge

From 2 Cav Div
Place
Time 1 a.m.

"C" Form (Duplicate).   Army Form C. 2123.
MESSAGES AND SIGNALS.   No. of Message

SD MKK 19

Service Instructions. Priority

Received 1.30 p

Handed in at the AHQ Office, at 12.15 m. Received here at 4.1 p.m.

TO 3 Cav Divn   WD 15

Sender's Number.	Day of Month.	In reply to Number.	
G6	15		AAA

The following reliefs will take place tonight aaa The french 9th corps will relieve the left of 2nd Divn up to N edge of POLYGONE wood the 2nd division relieves the troops of the 1st Division in their trenches the 1st cavalry Divn will relieve the left of the 3rd Division with as many

FROM

PLACE

TIME

W. 5375—423. 75,000 Pads—12/12—B. & F.—Forms/C.2123/1.

TIME

W. 5375—423. 75,000 Pads—12/12—B. & F.—Forms/C.2123/1.

"C" Form (Duplicate). Army Form C. 2123.
MESSAGES AND SIGNALS.   No. of Message

| | Charges to Pay. | Office Stamp. |
| | £ s. d. | |

Service Instructions.

Handed in at the _____ Office, at _____ m. Received here at _____ m.

TO

Sender's Number.	Day of Month.	In reply to Number.	AAA
troops	as	possible	and
the	exact number	to	
be	notified	to	the
3rd	Division the		3rd
Cavalry	Division will	relieve	
the	troops	of	the
1st	Cavalry	division	which
are	now	in	the
trenches	in	Lord	Cavans
section	aaa	2	the
1st	Division	(less	artillery
and	one	infantry	brigade
and	the	battalion	with

FROM

PLACE

TIME

Service Instructions.

Handed in at the _____ Office, at _____ .m. Received here at _____ .m.

TO

Sender's Number. | Day of Month. | In reply to Number. | AAA

ford (Cavan) will march to Billets which will be notified later aaa One brigade of the first division will billet west of YPRES and will be in corps reserve 3 The 2nd division will keep its divisional reserve near HOOGE 4 The 1st Cavalry Division will arrange that its troops in Lord Cavan trenches will

FROM

PLACE

TIME

Service Instructions.

Handed in at the _____ Office, at _____ m. Received here at _____ m.

TO

Sender's Number.	Day of Month.	In reply to Number.	AAA
On	relief move	~~on~~	~~on~~
in	to corps	reserve	in
billets	west	of YPRES 5	
The details of these reliefs will			
be arranged between the units			
concerned			

FROM 1st Corps
PLACE
TIME 12.30 pm

"C" Form (Duplicate).   Army Form C. 2123 A.

MESSAGES AND SIGNALS. No. of Message...........

Sig AC 19 WD B

Charges to Pay — Received 1.8pm

Office Stamp — 15 / 14 / 14

Service Instructions.

Handed in at the 4th Bde Office, at 15.5 p.m. Received here at 1.21 p.m.

TO: 3rd Cav Divn

Sender's Number	Day of Month	In reply to Number	AAA
BM974	15th		
500	Rifles	will	be
required to	relieve	2nd	
Cavalry	Bde		

FROM / PLACE / TIME: Lord Cavan 12.5 pm

---

by this Divn. is being taken over by 1st Cav. Bde.
(C) The 1st Cav. Bde. will form an independent section astride the MENIN road.
(d) The 2nd Inf. Divn is holding from

From / Place / Time

(Sd) JK Gough BM

G.152

W D 5/15

G.O.C. I a.c.

The following will be the distribution of my Division tonight

6" Cav Bde

500 Rifles in trenches now occupied by 7" Cav Bde

500 Rifles in trenches now occupied by 2nd Cav Bde

200 Rifles Support to L. Cavan at his Head Qrs.

7" Cav Bde

400 Rifles at Railway Bridge J 10 D in Corps Reserve

Remainder in present forms in Corps Reserve

HALTE
3-15
15 XI-14

J Byng. M Gen
Comdg 3rd Cav Divn

were pounded with an lyddite today — no attacks on my line so far. Cavan. M.S. 4.45 pm

by this Divn. is being taken over by 1st Cav. Bde.

(c) The 1st Cav Bde. will form an independent section astride the MENIN road.

(d) The 2nd Inf. Divn. is holding from

(Sd) Hh Gough BH

3rd Cav. Divn. W.N. 6/75 Received 5 pm 15.xi.

Your instructions to 7th Cav Bde passed on to [Cap? Dawnie?] & [?] C Battery to 6th [?] Bde. Our Artillery has had a successful day & effectually prevented enemy from so positively shifting 1st Life Guards. Also an officer of 4th D.G. have reconn[oitred] & patient personal reconnaissance & found German trench in my immediate front with exactly 50 dead in it - 136th & 55th Regts. Brown Road trenches of enemy have also been very well pounded with our lyddite today - No attacks on my line so far. Cavan. M/S. 2.45 pm

by this Divn. is being taken over by 1st Cav. Bde.

(c) The 1st Cav. Bde. will form an independent section astride the MENIN road.

(d) The 2nd Inf. Divn. is holding from

From
Place
Time

The above may be forwarded as now corrected. (Z)

Censor. Signature of Addressor or person authorised to telegraph in his name

This line should be erased if not required.

3662 M. & Co. Ltd. Wt. W929/549—100,000. 6/14. Forms C2121/10.

(Sd) JK Gough BM

Censor. Signature of Addressor or person authorised to telegraph in his name

This line should be erased if not required.

3662 M. & Co. Ltd. Wt. W929/549—100,000. 6/14. Forms C2121/10.

"A" Form. Army Form C. 2121.

MESSAGES AND SIGNALS

Prefix	Code	m.	Words	Charge	This message is on a/c of:	Recd. at **9·0 p** m.
Office of Origin and Service Instructions			Sent		W.D/16	Date **15**
			At Operation m.		Orders Service	From
			To 1st Army Corps		(Signature of "Franking Officer.")	By

TO:
- 1st Divn.
- 2nd Divn.
- 3rd Divn.
- 1st Cav. Divn.
- 3rd Cav. Divn.
- Lord Cavan

Sender's Number	Day of Month	In reply to Number	AAA
G.79	15.11.14		

1. The general situation continues to be satisfactory. The Allied Armies are being strongly reinforced.

2. The relief of our troops by the French commences this evening and other reliefs are also being carried out between ours in accordance with arrangements which have been made.

3. Tomorrow the line will be held as follows:—
   (a) Lord Cavan's Command as before.
   (b) 3rd Inf. Divn. The left of the line held by this Divn. is being taken over by 1st Cav. Bde.
   (c) The 1st Cav. Bde. will form an independent section astride the MENIN road.
   (d) The 2nd Inf. Divn. is holding from

From
Place
Time

The above may be forwarded as now corrected. (Z)

(Sd) JE Gough BM

MESSAGES AND SIGNALS

the left of the 1st Cav. Bde. to the N. corner of the POLYGONE wood where it is in touch with the right of the 9th French Corps.

(c) The Corps Reserve consists of :-
The 3rd Inf. Bde. at N.W. outskirts of YPRES.
The 1st Cav. Divn. (less one Bde) about BRIELEN.
The 3rd Cav. Divn. (less 6th Bde) about 1½ miles E. of YPRES.

4. The 1st Inf. Divn. (less 3rd Bde.) & certain artillery units of the 2nd Divn will leave tonight for the new concentration area in accordance with arrangements which have already been made.

5. Reports as before. Acknowledge.

From: 1st Corps
Place:
Time: 7.30 pm

(Sd) J E Gough BG

"A" Form.   Army Form C. 2121.

MESSAGES AND SIGNALS.   No. of Message _____

Prefix ___ Code ___ m.	Words	Charge	This message is on a/c of:	Recd. at ___ m.
Office of Origin and Service Instructions.	Sent		W.D.	Date ___
	At ___ m.		Service.	From ___
	To ___		(Signature of "Franking Officer.")	By ___
	By ___			

TO { 6° Cavalry B^de

Sender's Number	Day of Month	In reply to Number	AAA
G.159	16		

Unless otherwise ordered the 6th
Cavalry Brigade will hold its
present line of trenches to-night

From 3 C.D.
Place
Time 1.5 pm

The above may be forwarded as now corrected.   (Z) McGage Lt Col
                                      Censor. Signature of Addressor or person authorised to telegraph in his name

Time 1.47 pm
The above may be forwarded as now corrected.   (Z) McGage Lt Col
                                      Censor. Signature of Addressor or person authorised to telegraph in his name

TIME

Time 5.80 pm
The above may be forwarded as now corrected.   (Z)
                                      Censor. Signature of Addressor or person authorised to telegraph in his name

"A" Form.
Army Form C. 2121.

MESSAGES AND SIGNALS.

No. of Message _____

Prefix _____ Code _____ m. | Words | Charge | This message is on a/c of: | Recd. at _____ m.
Office of Origin and Service Instructions. | Sent | | | Date _____
| At _____ m. | | W.D. | From _____
| To _____ | | (Signature of "Franking Officer.") | By _____
| By _____ | | |

TO { 7ᵗʰ Cavalry Brigade

| Sender's Number | Day of Month | In reply to Number | **A A A** |
| G.160 | 16 | | |

Unless further orders are received the 6ᵗʰ Cavalry Brigade will hold its present line to-night and the 7ᵗʰ Cavalry Brigade will furnish a reserve of 400 rifles to be posted in the vicinity of HALTE on the YPRES - MENIN road aaa There will be some 20 'dug-outs' available for shelter for this force near the railway bridge at HALTE aaa G.O.C. will inform G.O.C. 3ʳᵈ Cav. Div. what portion (if any) of this reserve is posted on the railway line, and of the disposition of the remainder for the night. aaa O/C 3ʳᵈ Signal Squadron will establish a communication post at HALTE aaa

From 3ʳᵈ Cav. Div.
Place _____
Time 1.45 pm.

The above may be forwarded as now corrected. (Z) W H Gage Lt Col.

Censor. Signature of Addressor or person authorised to telegraph in his name

*This line should be erased if not required.

3662 M. & Co. Ltd. Wt. W929/549—100,000. 6/14. Forms C2121/10.

TIME

W. 5375—423. 75,000 Pads—12/12—B. & F.—Forms/C.2123/1.

Ph.
Time 0.80 pm

The above may be forwarded as now corrected. (Z)

Censor. Signature of Addressor or person authorised to telegraph in his name

*This line should be erased if not required.

3662 M. & Co. Ltd. Wt. W929/549—100,000. 6/14. Forms C2121/10.

"C" Form (Duplicate).   Army Form C. 2123.
MESSAGES AND SIGNALS.   No. of Message

Service Instructions.

Handed in at the 1st A.H.Q. Office, at 2.29 p.m. Received here at 2.45 p.m.

TO 3rd Cav Div

Sender's Number: G 101   Day of Month: 16th   In reply to Number: 538   AAA

No change in your line of trenches tonight but you are free to make any reliefs you please with your own troops in cooperation with Lord Cavan

FROM: 1st Corps
PLACE:
TIME: 2.30 pm

"A" Form. Army Form C. 2121.

MESSAGES AND SIGNALS.   No. of Message_____

TO: Corps ~~1st Corps~~ 3rd Low Run

Sender's Number: Rm 905   Day of Month: In reply to Number: AAA

All quiet along my line at 3-30 pm

From: Lord Cavan
Place:
Time: 3-30 pm

"A" Form. Army Form C. 2121.
MESSAGES AND SIGNALS. No. of Message_____

Prefix ___ Code ___ m.	Words	Charge	This message is on a/c of:	Recd. at 8.30 p m.
Office of Origin and Service Instructions	Sent		W.D. 16	Date 16.XI.14
	At ___ m.		Service.	From
	To			
	By		(Signature of "Franking Officer.")	By

TO { 1st ~~A~~ / 2nd ~~A~~ / 3rd ~~A~~   Ld Corps / 1st Corps / 3rd Cav D

| Sender's Number | Day of Month | In reply to Number | AAA |
| G 106 | 16th | | |

1/ German prisoners report that our H E shell did great execution yesterday, blowing in several trenches. 130 dead were counted today in front of the line held by this command AAA German deserters continue to arrive in our lines AAA The Russians are making very satisfactory progress.

French troops took over some of the line held by 1st Corps last night — the relief of our troops will be continued tonight as far as the MENIN Road inclusive.

2/ The following troops will be in Corps Reserve tomorrow —
(a) 1st Cav Div (less 1 Bde) near BRIELEN
(b) 3rd Cav Div (less 1 Bde) in a position W of YPRES to be fixed by G O C 1st Cav Div

"A" Form.   Army Form C. 2121.

MESSAGES AND SIGNALS.   No. of Message_____

Prefix____Code_____m.	Words	Charge	This message is on a/c of:	Recd. at____m.
Office of Origin and Service Instructions	Sent			Date_____
_____	At____m.		_____Service.	From_____
	To			By
	By		(Signature of "Franking Officer.")	

TO {   ②

*	Sender's Number	Day of Month	In reply to Number	A A A

but about 200 rifles will be stationed near HALTE on MENIN Road.
(C) 5ᵗʰ Inf. Bde. with Hdqrs near the MENIN Road between HALTE & HOOGE.

3/ The 1ˢᵗ Div. will march under its own arrangements to billets in the following area :- (reference map 1/100000)
Southern Boundary. HAZEBROUCK exclusive along ARMENTIERES railway to OULTERSTEENE
Northern Boundary. a line East & West through MOOLENAEKER
Western Boundary HAZEBROUCK - CAESTRE railway
Eastern Boundary OULTERSTEENE - BAILLEUL road

From
Place
Time

The above may be forwarded as now corrected. (Z)

Censor. Signature of Addressor or person authorised to telegraph in his name

*This line should be erased if not required
3662 M. & Co. Ltd. Wt. W929/549—100,000. 6/14. Forms C2121/10.

Censor. Signature of Addressor or person authorised to telegraph in his name
*This line should be erased if not required
3662 M. & Co. Ltd. Wt. W929/549—100,000. 6/14. Forms C2121/10.

TIME

W. 5375—423. 75,000 Pads—12/12—B. & F.—Forms/C.2123/1.

MESSAGES AND SIGNALS.

Prefix	Code	m.	Words	Charge	This message is on a/c of:	Recd. at	m.
Office of Origin and Service Instructions		Sent				Date	
		At	m.		Service.	From	
		To					
		By			(Signature of "Franking Officer.")	By	

TO { (3)

Sender's Number | Day of Month | In reply to Number | **AAA**

The 2nd Div. will not move tomorrow.

4/ Reports as before

Acknowledge

From 1st Corps
Place
Time 7.20 p.m.

Signature: J. Gough BG

"C" Form (Duplicate). Army Form
MESSAGES AND SIGNALS. No. of Message

Service Instructions. W D / Charges to Pay. £ s d 4.45 p

Handed in at the XX Office, at ___ m. Received here at ___ m.

TO   3rd Cav Div

Sender's Number. Day of Month. In reply to Number.
ga 605   AAA

Lord Cavan reports 1.35 pm enemy in some strength collecting about K 24 D and attacking aaa all well so far except all my communications destroyed aaa 3rd D Gds were blown out of their front trench aaa have ordered 2nd Coldstreams to be ready to support them at once if required and told 3rd D Gds to call on them direct aaa First attack on Irish and Grenadier

FROM
PLACE
TIME

Service Instructions.

Handed in at the _____ Office, at _____ m. Received here at _____ m.

TO

Sender's Number. | Day of Month. | In reply to Number. | AAA

Charge in K23B repulsed with heavy loss but enemy are again advancing and my hq with 10th Hussars reserve N.W. of wood in K17a

FROM 3rd Div
PLACE
TIME 2.20 pm

"C" Form (Duplicate). Army Form C. 2123.
MESSAGES AND SIGNALS. No. of Message

Service Instructions.

Charges to Pay. Office Stamp.
£ s. d.
2-0
p.m.

Handed in at the 1st Corps Office, at 1.20 m. Received here at 1.50 m.

TO 2nd Cav Divn

| Sender's Number. | Day of Month. | In reply to Number. | AAA |
| G133 | 17th | | |

Lord Cavans hq now moving to farm just NW of wood in K 14 A aaa 500 rifles Hertfordshire Battn T.F. will relieve Royals and 10th Hussars tonight aaa Please inform Col Westmacott & arrange for officer to settle details with Lord Cavan

FROM 1st Corps
PLACE
TIME 1.25 pm

MESSAGES AND SIGNALS.

Prefix	Code	m.	Words	Charge			
Office of Origin and Service Instructions.					This message is on a/c of	Recd. at	m.
			Sent			Date	
			At	m.	W.D. Service.	From	
			To				
			By		(Signature of "Franking Officer.")	By	

TO { 7 Cavalry Bde

Sender's Number	Day of Month	In reply to Number	AAA
G 160	17		

Lord Cavan's HQ are now moving to farm just NW of wood in K.17.A. aaa 500 rifles Staffordshire Batt T.F. will relieve the Royals and 10th Hussars to-night aaa the 7th Brigade will therefore furnish 500 rifles on the right of Lord Cavan's line as before and 300 men as local reserve near Lord Cavan's HQ aaa 400 men will remain as a reserve on the railway line to be detailed from 7th Cavalry Brigade instead of from the 6th C.B. aaa ~~Please arrange~~ ~~for a Staff officer to accompany~~

From 3 Cav. Div.
Place
Time 2.10 p.m.

The above may be forwarded as now corrected. (Z)

Censor. Signature of Addressee or person authorised to telegraph in his name

Time 7.30 pm

The above may be forwarded as now corrected. (Z)

Hough bgl

"A" Form. Army Form C. 2121.

MESSAGES AND SIGNALS.

No of Message _____

Prefix ____ Code ____ m. | Words | Charge | This message is on a/c of: | Recd. at ____ m.
Office of Origin and Service Instructions. | | | W. D. 3/17 | Date ____
 | Sent | | Service. | From ____
At ____ m. | | | |
To ____ | | (Signature of "Franking Officer.") | By ____
By ____ | | | |

TO —

Sender's Number: G 148 | Day of Month: 17th | In reply to Number: | AAA

1. After a heavy artillery bombardment two infantry attacks were made on our whole front and were repulsed with heavy loss to the enemy. On the right the enemy approached to within a few yards of the Grenadier Guards who were shelled and fell back leaving many dead. One of our officers buried in the ruins of the cottages. The 3rd L. G. reinforced by one coy of 2nd Coldstream also repulsed a determined attack in which 50 of the enemy were left dead in front of the trenches. We captured the 15 German prisoners and 3 heavy howitzers have been put out of action by the Allied artillery. Our own casualties up to 11 AM are also heavy, two of our men have been buried alive—

From ____
Place ____
Time ____

The above may be forwarded as now corrected. (Z)

Censor. Signature of Addressor or person authorised to telegraph in his name

*This line should be erased if not required.

Time 7.30 pm

The above may be forwarded as now corrected. (Z)

Clough Bey

Censor. Signature of Addressor or person authorised to telegraph in his name

MESSAGES AND SIGNALS.

No. of Message _____

Prefix	Code	m.	Words	Charge	This message is on a/c of:	Recd. at	m.
Office of Origin and Service Instructions.			Sent			Date	
			At	m.	Service	From	
			To				
			By		(Signature of "Franking Officer.")	By	

TO {

Sender's Number	Day of Month	In reply to Number	AAA

found on a dead German which states that only 2 officers and 150 men were left in his battalion. Russian troops have penetrated more than 80 miles into German territory and are now only 46 miles from CRACOW.

2. The HQ 1st Div. left this afternoon for POPERINGHE the 6th Inf Bde marches tomorrow to WESTOUTRE and LOCRE, the Cavalry Bde at Cav Divn HQ 2nd Cav Bde near ST JEAN CAPELLE under Gen ALLENBY, the 2nd Cav Bde under the command of the 3rd Cav Divn.

3. My Cav Advance tomorrow will be to follow to ST JEAN ?? to be brought

From		
Place		
Time		

The above may be forwarded as now corrected. (Z)

_____
Censor.   Signature of Addressee or person authorised to telegraph in his name

This line should be erased if not required.

2662 M. & Co. Ltd. Wt. W929/549—100,000. 6/14. Forms C2121/10.

Time 7.30 pm

The above may be forwarded as now corrected. (Z)

_____
Censor.   Signature of Addressee or person authorised to telegraph in his name

This line should be erased if not required.

2662 M. & Co. Ltd. Wt. W929/549—100,000. 6/14. Forms C2121/10.

The above may be forwarded as now corrected. (Z)

_____
Censor.   Signature of Addressee or person authorised to telegraph in his name

This line should be erased if not required.

2662 M. & Co. Ltd. Wt. W929/549—100,000. 6/14. Forms C2121/10.

"A" Form.   Army Form C. 2121.

MESSAGES AND SIGNALS.   No of Message ___

Prefix ___ Code ___ m.	Words	Charge	This message is on a/c of:	Recd. at ___ m.
Office of Origin and Service Instructions.	Sent			Date ___
	At ___ m.		___ Service.	From ___
	To			By
	By		(Signature of "Franking Officer.")	

TO {

Sender's Number   Day of Month   In reply to Number   **A A A**

1/Q near level crossing in K.20
b) The 3rd Can R.W. has about 500
rifles under Revd Cavan. [struck through]
with 4 m.c. rifles now HALTE an
the remainder in billets south of
VLAMERTINGHE
Report us before
Acknowledge

From _____
Place _____
Time _____

The above may be forwarded as now corrected.   (Z)

Censor.   Signature of Addresser or person authorised to telegraph in his name

*This line should be erased if not required.
3662 M. & Co. Ltd. Wt. W929/549—100,000. 6/14. Forms C2121/10.

The above may be forwarded as now corrected   (Z)

Censor.   Signature of Addresser or person authorised to telegraph in his name

*This line should be erased if not required.
3662 M. & Co. Ltd. Wt W929/549—100,000. 6/14. Forms C2121/10.

"A" Form.   Army Form C. 2121.

MESSAGES AND SIGNALS.   No. of Message_____

Prefix _____ Code _____ m.	Words	Charge	This message is on a/c of :	Recd. at _____ m.
Office of Origin and Service Instructions.				Date_____
_____	Sent		_____ Service.	From_____
_____	At _____ m.			
_____	To_____			
_____	By_____		(Signature of "Franking Officer.")	By_____

TO {
_____
_____
_____
}

Sender's Number	Day of Month	In reply to Number	
			A A A

The G.O.C. 7th Infy. Brigade
has reported that in the course
of the fighting today the Wiltshire
Regt. counter-attacked with the
bayonet and drove the enemy
before them for 500 yards killing
many.
This was a fine soldier-like
performance and has been so reported
to Sir John French.

Sd. H. Gough B.G.

From			
Place			
Time			

The above may be forwarded as now corrected   (Z)

Censor. | Signature of Addressor or person authorised to telegraph in his name

*This line should be erased if not required.
3662 M. & Co. Ltd. Wt W929/549—100,000. 6/14. Forms C2121/10.

AND SIGNALS. Army Form C.2121.

TO: ~~3rd Division~~ ~~Lord Cavan~~ 3rd Cavalry Division

Sender's Number: GA 157
Day of Month: 17
AAA

The enclosed copy of telegram to GHQ is forwarded for your information

HGough BG
SGSO 1st Corps

7.45 pm

GES AND SIGNALS.   No of Message _____

Code ___ m.	Words	Charge	This message is on a/c of :	Recd. at ___ m.
				Date ___
Office of Origin and Service Instructions.	Sent			
Priority	At ___ m.		___ Service.	From ___
	To ___			
	By ___		(Signature of "Franking Officer.")	By ___

TO   G H Q   Copy

| Sender's Number | Day of Month | In reply to Number | AAA |
| GA 156 | 17 | | |

Our front heavily shelled all day increasing in afternoon aaa. Determined infantry attacks were made during afternoon against Lord Cavans and 3rd division line AAA. All attacks beaten off with heavy loss to enemy AAA 3rd division report that Wilts regiment made fine counter attack with bayonet gallantly led by Major ROCHE the enemy were followed up for 500 yards AAA The Wilts have done fine work while under my command and I regret to report Major ROCHE killed he is a great loss. AAA Lord Cavan reports enemy arrived within five yards of trenches held by Grenadiers who inflicted heavy loss on enemy as also did our artillery AAA. 3rd dragoon guards reinforced by one

From ___
Place ___
Time ___

The above may be forwarded as now corrected.   (Z)

Censor. Signature of Addressor or person authorised to telegraph in his name

This line should be erased if not required.
2652 M. & Co. Ltd. Wt. W929/549—100,000. 6/14. Forms C2121/10.

Time 1.15 p.m.

The above may be forwarded as now corrected.   (Z)

Censor. Signature of Addressor or person authorised to tele

This line should be erased if not required.
2652 M. & Co. Ltd. Wt. W929/549—100,000. 6/14. Forms C2121/10.

MESSAGES AND SIGNALS.

TO — 2

Company 2nd Coldstreams also beat off an attack in which enemy left 50 dead in front of trench. AAA Without doubt a very satisfactory days work. AAA 1st Cavalry brigade march to ST JEAN on being relieved in trenches to-night AAA 6th infantry brigade also marching at 4 am en route for concentration area.

From 1st Corps.
Time 7.15 pm

Signature: H Gough BG

G'd I a C.   W.D. G/182/18

I have just received rather fuller particulars of yesterday's fight

The line held by the 6' Cav Bde was twice heavily attacked and I am glad to report never broken.

At 1 pm the attack was fairly easily repulsed but at 4 pm it was more critical.

I have tried to get a fairly accurate report of the German losses and I am inclined to believe the following is fair

In front of the Royals & 10' Hussars — 200 dead
"   "   of the N. Somerset I Y   120 "
"   "   of the 3rd Dn Gds   50 "

These have been counted by Officers and I think there must be many more

early in this morning another series of determined attacks were made when the French 164th ??? on our right. These have been repulsed and the enemy have ceased to ??? ???

11.30 am

I regret to say my losses are severe

3rd Dn Gds   1 off killed 2 severely wd
              60 NCOs & men killed & wounded.

Royals   1 off wded   5 NCOs & men
                            killed & wded.

10 Hussars   2 offs killed
              12 NCOs & men K & wded

N Somerset   2 offs killed
              45 NCOs & men K & W

The Brigade was relieved last night
and is now back in billets —

                    J Byng, M. Gen
18/XI/14   Comdg 3 Cav Bde

"A" Form.
Army Form C. 2121.

MESSAGES AND SIGNALS.

No. of Message

Prefix	Code	m.	Words	Charge			
Office of Origin and Service Instructions.			Sent		This message is on a/c of:		Recd. at 8.20 p.m.
			At	m.	W D 78		Date 18
			To			Service.	From
			By		(Signature of "Franking Officer.")		By

TO { 1st Division, 2nd Division, 3rd Division — 3rd Cavalry Division, Cav. Bde. }

Sender's Number	Day of Month	In reply to Number	
G 171	18		AAA

It is estimated that in yesterday's attack the enemy had certainly 600 killed and probably more. Compared with this figure our own casualties were slight. From the way in which the enemy came on it seems clear that the attacking force consisted of new troops and that the 2nd German Corps may now be added to those who have failed to take YPRES. Prisoners state that their orders were to hold their own but the British lines at all costs. Yesterday's attack was of a most determined nature and the fact that it failed at every point is most satisfactory. In the early hours of this morning another series of determined attacks were made when the French 16th Corps on our right... Three hours were repeated and the enemy was ordered persistently.

... The 28th Indian Brigade ...

From				
Place				
Time				

The above may be forwarded as now corrected (Z)

Censor. Signature of Addressor or person authorised to telegraph in his name
*This line should be erased if not required.

FROM		
PLACE		
TIME		11.30 am

Place
Time

The above may be forwarded as now corrected. (Z)

MESSAGES AND SIGNALS. No. of Message

Prefix	Code	m.	Words	Charge			
Office of Origin and Service Instructions			Sent		This message is on a/c of :	Recd. at	m.
			At	m.		Date	
			To		Service.	From	
			By		(Signature of "Franking Officer.")	By	

TO

| Sender's Number | Day of Month | In reply to Number | AAA |

1. Battery, 57th Battery less one section and the 111th Heavy Battery will proceed to the new column area — usual arrangements.
2. The Cure d'Larve companies will be the same as before.
4. Reports as before. Acknowledge.

From: ......
Place: ......
Time: 1 pm

The above may be forwarded as now corrected (Z)

FROM
PLACE
TIME .... 11·30 am

Place
Time
The above may be forwarded as now corrected (Z)

"C" Form (Duplicate). Army Form C. 2123.

MESSAGES AND SIGNALS.   No. of Message

Service Instructions.	xH On	Charges to Pay. £ s. d. Rec. 12 Nov	Office Stamp

Handed in at the 1st A&G Office, at 11.29 a.m. Received here at 11.40 a.m.

TO Genl Byng
    3rd Cav Divn

Sender's Number.	Day of Month	In reply to Number.	
G 165	17		AAA

Thanks for your telegram giving account of yesterdays fighting please congratulate the 6th Cavalry Bde for me upon the excellent fight they put up aaa I regret to hear your losses were so heavy but its very satisfactory to know that the enemys casualties are so much heavier

FROM   Gen Haig
PLACE
TIME   11.30 am

Place
Time
The above may be forwarded as now corrected.   (Z)
                                    Censor. Signature of Addressor or person authorised to telegraph in his name
*This line should be erased if not required.

"A" Form.
Army Form C. 2121.

MESSAGES AND SIGNALS.

Prefix	Code	m.	Words	Charge	This message is on a/c of:	Recd. at	m.
Office of Origin and Service Instructions.			Sent		W.D. 4/8 Service.	Date	
			At ____ m.			From	
			To				
			By		(Signature of "Franking Officer.")	By	

TO { 6ᵗʰ Cavalry Brigade

Sender's Number	Day of Month	In reply to Number	A A A
G.163	18		

Following from Sir Douglas Haig AAA begins Please congratulate the 6ᵗʰ Cavalry Brigade for me for the excellent it was work your not it has lot to been losses it so heavy to very satisfactory know little to that musn known enemy's casualties are so heavier AAA

From 3ʳᵈ Cav Div
Place
Time

The above may be forwarded as now corrected. (Z)

Censor. Signature of Addressor or person authorised to telegraph in his name

*This line should be erased if not required.

GOC I AC W.D. 5/78

I attach the reports of the Brigadier and the two Commanders of Sections of trenches on the attack ~~on~~ on the 6th Cav Bde on Nov 17.

My reason for doing so is to draw attention to the conduct of the North Somerset Yeomanry. This Regt has only been in the area of operations three days and it was its first experience in the trenches.

I consider that the return of their casualties viz: 21 killed and 27 wounded is a clear proof of ~~the~~ staunch behaviour in action.

I would also draw attention to the plucky and valuable reconnaissance of Lt. Kennard Frenfell. No 5241 Sergt MacMillan and No 231 Corporal Kelman — all of the R.L Dragoons on the 16th & 17th November.

I would also mention the gallant conduct of Capt Wright and L. Chapman (both killed) 3rd Dn Guards in the recapture of some farm buildings in the possession of the Germans.

J. Byng M Gen
3rd Cav Divn

20. XI. 14.

H.q. 6th Cav. Bde.
18th
(17) X/14
W.D./18

General Staff
3rd Cav. Div.

1. The Brigade returned to bivouac between 1 A.M. and 3 A.M. this morning.

2. The line of trenches, held yesterday by my Brigade, was heavily attacked yesterday but was not broken. Two distinct attacks, one about 1 pm and the other about 4 pm, were made against the trenches on the ZILLEBEKE - KLEINZILLEBEKE Road.

3. Our Casualties were approximately as under.

Royals — Lt BROWN severely wounded and 5 N.C.O's and men killed & wounded.

3rd D.G's — Capt WRIGHT killed, Capt STEWART and Lieut CHAPMAN dangerously wounded, R.S.M. STEWART killed and about 60 N.C.O's & men killed & wounded.

10th Hussars — Capt PETO and Lt DRAKE killed and 12 N.C.O's and men killed and wounded.

N. Somersetshire Y. — Capt LIEBERT and another Officer killed, and 45 N.C.O's and men killed & wounded.

I will forward detailed figures later.

...the relief of the last of the 2nd Div. troops S. of the MENIN road by the 1st Div. ...

45

4. The German Casualties were very heavy. 200 dead being counted in front of the 10th Hussars and Royals, 120 in front of the N. Somersetshire Yeomanry, and 50 in front of the 3rd D.G's. These numbers were all counted by officers. There were undoubtedly heavier casualties, as the dead in front of one Squadron 3rd D.G's could not be counted owing to the darkness.

5. I will forward a fuller report as soon as I have been able to collect details.

6. As the Brigade has had an exceptionally hard time during the last 48 hours, I hope if possible they may not be called upon today.

David M Campbell
Lt Col.

9.20 A.M.

the relief of the last of the 2nd Div. troops S. of the MENIN road by the 1st Div. ???

From			
Place			
Time			

"A" Form. Army Form C. 2121.

MESSAGES AND SIGNALS.

Prefix	Code	m.	Words	Charge	This message is on a/c of:	Recd. at 12.5 a m.
Office of Origin and Service Instructions.			Sent		W.D. 11	Date 11/XI/14
			At	m.	Service.	From
			To			
			By		(Signature of "Franking Officer.")	By

TO 1/D 3 Cav Divn
    2/D
    3/D

Sender's Number	Day of Month	In reply to Number	AAA
G.902	10th		

The news from Russia continues
good AAA. The Russian Cavalry are over
the frontier & within 40 miles of
POSEN AAA. There are many indications
that the Germans are transferring
troops from here to the Eastern theatre
AAA. The Germans after heavy shelling
during the night made a violent
attack on the French about BIXSCHOOTE
& recovered some of the ground they lost
yesterday although this does not amount to
much AAA. The situation however is
quite satisfactory AAA.
Reliefs will be carried out tonight
as arranged AAA. They will consist in
the relief of the last of the 2nd Div. Korps
S. of the MENIN road by the 1st Div. AAA

From
Place
Time

The above may be forwarded as now corrected. (Z)

Censor. Signature of Addressor or person authorised to telegraph in his name
*This line should be erased if not required.
2652 M. & Co. Ltd. Wt. W929/549—100,000. 6/14. Forms C2121/10.

	At	m.	Service.	From
	To			
	By	(Signature of "Franking Officer.")	By

TO

| Sender's Number | Day of Month | In reply to Number | A A A |

From 1st Corps
Place
Time 6.15 p.m.

The above may be forwarded as now corrected. (Z)

Censor. | Signature of Addressee or person authorised to telegraph in his name

*This line should be erased if not required.

"A" Form.
Army Form C. 2121.

MESSAGES AND SIGNALS.

Prefix	Code	m	Words	Charge	This message is on a/c of:	Recd. at m.
Office of Origin and Service Instructions.			Sent		W D	Date 11/XI/14
			At m		Service.	From
			To		(Signature of "Franking Officer.")	By
			By			

TO — THIRD CAV. DIV

Sender's Number	Day of Month	In reply to Number	AAA
G (C) 1	11th		

Enemy attacking in Great force along MENIN road AAA Corps Reserve Infantry have been moved up.

From FIRST DIV
Place
Time 9.37 am
The above may be forwarded as now corrected. (Z) [signature] Lt Col.

Place
Time 10 am.
The above may be forwarded as now corrected. (Z) [signature]

PLACE — L
TIME — 3.22 pm

"A" Form. — Army Form C. 2121.
MESSAGES AND SIGNALS. No. of Message _____

Prefix ___ Code ___ m	Words	Charge	This message is on a/c of:	Recd. at 10·7 _ m
Office of Origin and Service Instructions.	Sent		W.D. / Service	Date 11ᵗʰ
	At ___ in			From
	To		(Signature of "Franking Officer.")	By
	By			

TO   THIRD CAV DIV

| Sender's Number | Day of Month | In reply to Number | |
| G.(c) 3 | ELEVENTH | | A A A |

Enemy reported to have broken
thro' FIRST BDE line between
S.W. corner of POLYGON wood
and MENIN road A.A.A. Corps
Reserve moving to wood E
of HOOGE CHATEAU

From   FIRST DIV
Place
Time   10 a.m.

The above may be forwarded as now corrected. (Z)

PLACE   ʌ   3·22 pm
TIME

THIRD CAV DIV

"C" Form (Original).
MESSAGES AND SIGNALS.
Army Form C. 2123

TO 3rd Cav Div

Sender's Number: Bm 815 Day of Month: 11th   AAA

Am asking 6th Brigade to send me a regt for the night as situation in front of London Scottish very difficult AAA regt can have its cookers at my hqrs at dark

FROM Lord Cavan
PLACE
TIME 3.22 pm

"C" Form (Duplicate).   Army Form C. 2123.
MESSAGES AND SIGNALS.   No. of Message

Im FW 69
Im DF 31

Charges to Pay.   Office Stamp.

WD 5/11   6.35 pm 11.XI.14

Service Instructions.

Handed in at the 3D Office, at ......m. Received here at......m.

TO: 3rd Cav Div and 6th Cav

Sender's Number.	Day of Month.	In reply to Number.	AAA
	11th		
Situation	improved	aaa	London
Scottish	much	harassed	all
day	by	enfilade	fire
from	50	yards	so
charged	trenches	and	now
occupy	it	aaa	I
have	sent	third	D
G	home	and	hope
not	to	call	on
them	aaa	Fear	6th
bde	got	very	heavily
shelled	all	day	in
trenches	aaa	I believe	our line

FROM
PLACE
TIME

Service Instructions.			

Handed in at the _____ Office, at _____ m. Received here at _____ m.

TO

Sender's Number.	Day of Month.	In reply to Number.	AAA
is	now	same	as
last	night		

FROM PLACE TIME: Lord Cavan 5.45 pm

"A" Form.   Army Form C. 2121.
MESSAGES AND SIGNALS.   No. of Message_____

TO 3rd Cav. Divn.

Sender's Number	Day of Month	In reply to Number	AAA
G.618	11th		

2nd Divn reports 3.50 pm begins 5th Bde. reports 3.35 pm begins. Oxfords now occupy trenches vacated this morning by Black Watch aaa Am watching movement of enemy and have H.L.I. machine guns at S.W. corner POLYGONE wood aaa Two Coys. H.L.I. still in hand and am in touch with Genl. FitzClarence and Oxfords — Ends

From First Divn.
Place
Time 4·15 pm
The above may be forwarded as now corrected.   (Z)   Capt. G.S.

Time
The above may be forwarded as now corrected.   (Z)

Time 6.15 P.M.
The above may be forwarded as now corrected.   (Z)   (Sd) J.E. GOUGH B.G.

Time 7.30
The above may be forwarded as now corrected.   (Z)

"A" Form. Army Form C. 2121.

MESSAGES AND SIGNALS. No. of Message 1

Prefix SB Code EC m. Words 72 Charge

Office of Origin and Service Instructions. [illegible] AHQ

Sent At m. To By

This message is on a/c of: W.D. Service. (Signature of "Franking Officer.")

Recd. at m. Date From By

TELEGRAPHS 5 X 14 HQ

TO [illegible]

Sender's Number	Day of Month	In reply to Number	AAA
2			

Relief will be carried out tomorrow night by French [illegible] aaa Officers to make previous reconnaissance [illegible] be at 3rd [illegible] H.Q. at 7 A.M. tomorrow [illegible] arrange to meet them aaa [illegible] arranged for today [illegible] for tomorrow aaa You can inform [illegible] that [illegible] is arranged aaa [illegible] to Capt WESTMACOTT [illegible] Major VAUGHAN

ACKNOWLEDGE

From [illegible]
Place
Time 5.50 pm

The above may be forwarded as now corrected. (Z) [illegible]

Censor. Signature of Addressor or person authorised to telegraph in his name

*This line should be erased if not required.

2652 M. & Co. Ltd. Wt. W929/549—100,000. 6/14. Forms C2121/10.

Time 6.15 P.M.

The above may be forwarded as now corrected. (Z) (Sd) J.E. GOUGH. B.G.

Censor. Signature of Addressor or person authorised to telegraph in his name

*This line should be erased if not required.

2652 M. & Co. Ltd. Wt. W929/549—100,000. 6/14. Forms C2121/10.

Time 7.30 pm

The above may be forwarded as now corrected. (Z) [illegible]

Censor. Signature of Addressor or person authorised to telegraph in his name

*This line should be erased if not required.

2652 M. & Co. Ltd. Wt. W929/549—100,000. 6/14. Forms C2121/10.

"A" Form.
Army Form C. 2121.

MESSAGES AND SIGNALS.

No of Message _____

Prefix _____ Code _____ m.
Office of Origin and Service Instructions.

Words | Charge
Sent
At _____ m.
To
By

This message is on a/c of:

W D/19 Service.
(Signature of "Franking Officer.")

Recd. at 7.35p m.
Date
From 19
By

TO {
1st Divn.
2nd Divn.
3rd Divn.
}
~~Lord Cavan~~
3rd Cav. Divn.
~~3rd Cav Bde~~

Sender's Number | Day of Month | In reply to Number
G. 206 | 19th | AAA

1. The enemy were reported about 8 A.M. to be massing in front of the 7th Bde., but the attack if one was intended must have been stopped by our artillery fire as no advance was made. ~~by the French~~

2. The relief of the rest of our ~~line~~ originally timed to take place tonight will take place tomorrow night.

3. Corps Reserve as before (less one bn.)

4. Reports as before. Acknowledge.

From 1st Corps
Place
Time 6.15 P.M.

The above may be forwarded as now corrected.
(Z) (Sd) J.E. GOUGH B.G.
Censor. Signature of Addressor or person authorised to telegraph in his name

Time 7.32 ___

The above may be forwarded as now corrected.
(Z) [signature]
Censor. Signature of Addressor or person authorised to telegraph in his name

"A" Form.   Army Form C. 2121.
MESSAGES AND SIGNALS.

TO: 7th Cavalry Brigade

Sender's Number: G 169
Day of Month: 19

AAA

The French are taking over our trenches tomorrow night aaa An officer from each Cavalry Regiment in the trenches to be at Lord Cavan's H Q at 7 a.m. tomorrow to explain position to their units and if necessary conduct French officers round the trenches aaa

From 3 Cav Div
Time 7.32 p.m.

GOC. I AC ~~H. to~~ F.

I forward these reports on the
gallant conduct displayed
yesterday by No 1125
Corporal of Horse WARREN R.H.G⁵

I consider his action deserving
of recognition. the more so, as his
Squadron Leader in the Composite
Regiment informs me that this
is not the only occasion on which
he has displayed coolness and
courage under the heaviest fire

J Byng. M.G.
3rd Cav Div

HALTE
20. XI. 14

W.D. 2/19

Ga.144.   19th.   ***.

1. The following units will march to-morrow to the concentration area:-

(a) "C" By. R.H.A. independently at 7-0 a.m.

(b) 6th Cav. Bde. independently at 3-30 p.m. Should the 6th Cav. Bde. transport precede the troops, it must be clear of the Rd. junction 1 mile South of VLAMERTINGHE by 8-0 a.m. The 6th Cav. Bde. will continue to be a Mobile Reserve until the hour of march.

(c) Hd.Qrs. and Divnl. Troops at 8-0 a.m., in order of march:-

Head Quarters,
3rd Sig. Sqd.,
Nos. 6 and 7 Fd. Amb. (less Secs. detached),
H.Q. 3rd Cav. Div. A.S.C.

The above will be under the command of Col. SWABEY, A.S.C. Starting Pt. X roads at WEMGROENEM (I.15.C.).

(d) 3rd Fd. Sqd. independently in rear of Div. Troops.

2. Route:-   OUDERDOM, RENINGHELST, WESTOUTRE, LA MANCHE, METEREN, and thence by STRAZEELE.

3. The 7th Cav. Bde. and "K" By. R.H.A. & Amm. Col. on relief to-morrow evening by French troops will move into their present billets and march under Bde. arrangements into the concentration area on the 21st instant.

4. On reaching the concentration area, the Royal Horse Guards and the X Hussars will move into the 8th Cav. Bde. area. "C" and "K" Bys. R.H.A. and Sections Cav. Fd. Amb. at present attached to Brigades will rejoin Head Quarters.

5. The R.H.G. and X Hussars will send on billeting parties to-morrow to report to Capt. RITSON, Staff Capt. 8th Cav. Bde. at the Ry. Transport Office, HAZEBROUCK Station by 12-0 Noon.

6. The Communicating Post will be maintained at the Railway Cutting until the relief of the 7th Cav. Bde. A Report Centre will be opened at the CHATEAU DE LA MOTTE at 2-0 p.m. Reports to Comm. Post up to 2-0 p.m. and then to Report Centre.

(Signed)   M.F. GAGE, Lt. Colonel,

General Staff, 3rd Cavalry Division.

8.30 p.m.

W.D. 1/10.III COPY NO: 4

SECRET.

OPERATION ORDER No: 17.

by

Lieut-General Sir EDMUND ALLENBY, K.C.B.

Commanding Cavalry Corps.

9th March, 1915.

1.(a). The First Army will take the offensive as soon after 9th March as the condition of the ground permits. Its mission is to break through the enemy's line on its front.

(b). The Second Army will take such action as will prevent the enemy from withdrawing troops from its front.

(c). The Cavalry Corps, Indian Cavalry Corps and North Midland Division will form the General Reserve.

2. From 6 a.m. 10th March Cavalry Divisions will be ready to move to positions of readiness as follows at one hours notice :-

    1st Cavalry Division.. .. MONT DES CATS

    2nd Cavalry Division.. .. An area just N.W. of ESTAIRES.

    3rd Cavalry Division.. .. BOIS D'AVAL.

3. Cavalry Corps report centre will remain at LA MOTTE until further notice.

Noel Buck

Brig.General,
General Staff.

Issued at 3.40 p.m.

Recd. 4.0 p.m.
9.III.15.

SECRET.

OPERATION ORDER No. 18
by LIEUT.GENERAL SIR EDMUND ALLENBY, K.C.B.
COMMANDING   CAVALRY   CORPS.

10th March, 1915

1. (a) First Cavalry Division will continue to maintain the same degree of readiness as today.

(b) Second Cavalry Division will be assembled in a position of readiness just N.W. of ESTAIRES by seven a.m.

(c) Third Cavalry Division will be assembled in a position of readiness in the BOIS D'AVAL by seven a.m.

2. General Officer Commanding First Army has been authorised to make a direct call upon Second Cavalry Division for the services of one Cavalry Brigade only, should he consider that circumstances necessitate it.

3. Cavalry Corps report centre will remain at LA MOTTE till further notice.

Issued at 6.15 p.m.

Brig.General,
General Staff.

"A" Form.   Army Form C. 2121.

MESSAGES AND SIGNALS.

TO: 6th, 7th, 8th Cav Bdes. S.O. R.H.A. 3rd Cav Div.
3rd Fld. Sqn. R.E., 3rd Sig. Sqn., A.A. & Q.M.G.
D.S.C. A.D.M.S.

Sender's Number: G 435
Day of Month: 10th
AAA

The Division has been ordered to concentrate at the Div'l rendezvous BOIS D'AVAL in accordance with my G 425 by 7-0 a.m. tomorrow AAA Reference para 3 of G 425 "B" Echelon transport of Divisional troops (less R.H.A. & Am. Col.) will assemble at the same hour in its present billets.

From: 3rd Cav Div.
Time: 7-10 p.m.

W.D. 2/11.III

No. G. 425.

1. Should the 3rd Cavalry Division be ordered to move to the Divisional rendezvous in the BOIS D'AVAL, Brigades, etc., will concentrate at the rendezvous' shown in the attached table. They will be accompanied by 'A' Echelon transport.

2. At the rendezvous' they will be met by a Staff Officer and conducted to the Divisional rendezvous.

Brigades will not take their 'A' Echelon transport beyond the Brigade rendezvous shown in attached table.

3. 'B' Echelon transport (also 3rd Cavalry Divisional Ammunition Column) will be assembled in Brigade Billetting areas. at places to be fixed by Brigadiers and notified to Div. H.Q.

Major
General Staff,
10th March, 1915. 3rd Cavalry Division.

Unit.	Rendezvous.	Route.
6th Cavalry Brigade.	Road junction 200 yds N.W. of the I in FORET DE NIEPPE, where the RUE DES MORTS joins the LA MOTTE - MERVILLE Rd.	STEENBECQUE - LE PARC - RUE DES MORTS.
7th Cavalry Brigade.	X roads ½ mile S.W. of S in SWARTENBROUCK on LA MOTTE - VIEUX BERQUIN road.	LA KREULE - L'HOFFAND - K in HAZEBROUCK - O of AU SOUVERAIN.
8th Cavalry Brigade.	Entrance to BOIS CLEBERT, on main HAZEBROUCK - LA MOTTE road. ¾ m. S. of first A in LE TIR ANGLAIS.	SERCUS - S. portion of HAZEBROUCK - HAZEBROUCK - LA MOTTE main road.
R.H.A. Brigade.	Road junction (not marked on map 5A) where road running along N.E. edge of BOIS CLEBERT joins main HAZEBROUCK - LA MOTTE road.	MORBECQUE - N.E. edge of BOIS CLEBERT.
3rd Field Squadron, R.E.	Field on S. of HAZEBROUCK - LA MOTTE road ¾ m. S. of T in LE TIR ANGLAIS.	Main road - to precede 8th Cavalry Brigade.
3rd Signal Squadron.	Field in grounds of LA MOTTE AUX BOIS CHATEAU.	Main road - to precede 3rd Field Squadron.

Headquarters,
    Cavalry Corps.

    Herewith the report called for in your Gb 118 of May 5th.

    Rough sketches have not been attached, as they would not help to elucidate the movements of the Division during the dates specified.

Headquarters, 3rd Cavalry Division.
    7 May, 1915.

                                    [signature]
                                            General Staff,
                                        3rd Cavalry Division.

②

Report on the part taken by the 3rd Cavalry Division, commanded by Brigadier-General D.Campbell vice Major-General Sir J.Byng, officiating in command of the Cavalry Corps, in the operations of April 22nd to May 4th.

- - - - - -

April 23rd.   On April 23rd the Division received orders to rendezvous South of POPERINGHE; it accordingly concentrated in the neighbourhood of LE BREARDE and marched via CAESTRE and GODEWAERSVELDE to ABEELE, eventually bivoucking between the latter place and EECKE.

April 24th.   On the 24th the Division marched at 8-30 a.m. to a position of readiness South of VLAMERTINGHE remaining there until the evening, when it moved into billets in the neighbourhood of BOESCHEPE and RENINGHELST.

April 25th.   By 6-30 a.m. on April 25th, the Division was saddled up ready to move, and about noon, marched to the vicinity of HAMHOEK with the idea of billetting in that area. Counter-orders were, however, received, and the Division moved into billets in the area HOUTKERQUE - WATOU - WINNEZEELE.

April 26th.   On the following morning, Brigades rendezvoused by 6-30 a.m. ready to move off at ½ hours notice and at 10-0 a.m. were ordered to proceed to a position of readiness West of the St.JANS-TER-BIEZEN - ABEELE ridge, where they remained until 7-30 p.m. when the Division, leaving the horses West of POPERINGHE, marched to VLAMERTINGHE and went into billets.

April 27th.   The 27th passed uneventfully until 5-30 p.m. when the enemy commenced an intermittent shelling of the village and neighbouring rest camps. This necessitated the move of the 6th Cavalry Brigade out of VLAMERTINGHE into farms and fields in the vicinity.

At 8-20 p.m. preliminary orders were received for the Division to move at once to the support of General JOPPE'S Turcos, who were reported to be falling back in disorder over the pontoon East of BRIELEN. However, before a move could

could be made, this order was cancelled and a quiet night ensued.

April 28th.   At 8-30 a.m. the next morning, a further bombardment ensued and it was considered advisable to move troops out into the fields. However, shortly afterwards, the Division was ordered to move back to its horses. Some 20 casualties had been suffered during the two bombardments.

The men had a hot and dusty march back to their horses, reaching them about 3-0 p.m. and later moved into billets South of ST. JANS-TER-BIEZEN.

April 29th
to
May 2nd.
Nothing of interest occurred during the next few days. Brigades rendezvoused each day West of the ST. JANS-TER-BIEZEN - ABEELE ridge returning in the evenings to their billets, the area of the latter being slightly modified on May 2nd.

May 3rd.   During the afternoon, just as the Division was preparing to move into a new billetting area, orders were received for an immediate move to VLAMERTINGHE so as to be able to support the 11th Infantry Brigade if necessary, part of the latter having been severely handled near FORTUIN.

Brigades were concentrated South of VLAMERTINGHE by 7-45 pm, and, leaving their horses there, marched to a position of readiness 1200 yards West of YPRES STN.

May 4th.   By 4-0 a.m. the next day the situation permitted of their withdrawal, they accordingly marched back to their horses and moved into a billetting area extending from near ST. JANS-TER-BIEZEN through HOUTKERQUE to HERZEELE.

Major-General Sir J.Byng then re-assumed command of the Division, Sir E.Allenby having returned from sick leave.

Summary of Operations of 3rd Cavalry Division during period
23rd April to 6th June, 1915.

On 23rd April the French line North of YPRES having been broken, the 3rd Cavalry Division was ordered to move up towards YPRES to a position of readiness. It remained in a position of readiness a few miles West of YPRES until 4th May when it returned to billets near HOUTKERQUE.

On the night of 5th May the Division assisted in digging trenches East of YPRES under the Vth Corps returning next day to billets.

On the 9th May the Division moved up to VLAMERTINGHE and came under the orders of the Vth Corps, and on 12th May took over a line of trenches East of YPRES.

On 13th May the Division was heavily shelled and suffered severe losses. A gallant counter-attack in which the 8th Cavalry Brigade took part recovered the trenches which had been evacuated, but owing to the heavy hostile shell-fire it was found impossible to hold them, and a new line was dug in rear.

On the night of 14th/15th the Division was relieved in the trenches by the 2nd Cavalry Division and went into Corps Reserve.

On 21st May the Division returned to billets.

On the night of 29th/30th the Division relieved the 2nd Cavalry Division in the trenches and remained there until the night of 5th/6th June. During this period there was some considerable fighting in and around the village of HOOGE.

The R.H.A. 3rd Cavalry Division were during the period under mention in action near KEMMEL attached to the 2nd Army.

The

The 3rd Field Squadron R.E. did good work during the period under mention in assisting and supervising the digging of entrenchments.

Casualties.

From April 23rd to June 8th.

About 103 Officers and 1817 other ranks, the majority of these were on the 13th May.

Approximate Casualties incurred by the 3rd Cavalry Division, during period 22nd April to 4th May, both dates inclusive.

	Killed.	Wounded.	Missing.
Officers.	Nil	Nil	Nil.
Other ranks.	5	18	Nil.

Summary of Operations of 3rd Cavalry Division during period
23rd April to 6th June, 1915.

On 23rd April the French line North of YPRES having been broken, the 3rd Cavalry Division was ordered to move up towards YPRES to a position of readiness. It remained in a position of readiness a few miles West of YPRES until 4th May when it returned to billets near HOUTKERQUE.

On the night of 8th May the Division assisted in digging trenches East of YPRES under the Vth Corps returning next day to billets.

On the 9th May the Division moved up to VLAMERTINGHE and came under the orders of the Vth Corps, and on 12th May took over a line of trenches East of YPRES.

On 13th May the Division was heavily shelled and suffered severe losses. A gallant counter-attack in which the 8th Cavalry Brigade took part recovered the trenches which had been evacuated, but owing to the heavy hostile shell-fire it was found impossible to hold them, and a new line was dug in rear.

On the night of 14th/15th the Division was relieved in the trenches by the 2nd Cavalry Division and went into Corps Reserve.

On 21st May the Division returned to billets.

On the night of 29th/30th the Division relieved the 2nd Cavalry Division in the trenches and remained there until the night of 5th/6th June. During this period there was some considerable fighting in and around the village of HOOGE.

The R.H.A. 3rd Cavalry Division were during the period under mention in action near YPRES attached to the 2nd Army.

The

The 3rd Field Squadron R.E. did good work during the period under mention in assisting and supervising the digging of entrenchments.

Casualties.

From April 23rd to June 6th.

About 108 Officers and 1317 other ranks, the majority of these were on the 13th May.

Summary of Operations of 3rd Cavalry Division during period
23rd April to 6th June, 1915.

On 23rd April the French line North of YPRES having been broken, the 3rd Cavalry Division was ordered to move up towards YPRES to a position of readiness. It remained in a position of readiness a few miles West of YPRES until 4th May when it returned to billets near HOUTKERQUE.

On the night of 5th May the Division assisted in digging trenches East of YPRES under the Vth Corps returning next day to billets.

On the 9th May the Division moved up to VLAMERTINGHE and came under the orders of the Vth Corps, and on 12th May took over a line of trenches East of YPRES.

On 13th May the Division was heavily shelled and suffered severe losses. A gallant counter-attack in which the 8th Cavalry Brigade took part recovered the trenches which had been evacuated, but owing to the heavy hostile shell-fire it was found impossible to hold them, and a new line was dug in rear.

On the night of 14th/15th the Division was relieved in the trenches by the 2nd Cavalry Division and went into Corps Reserve.

On 21st May the Division returned to billets.

On the night of 29th/30th the Division relieved the 2nd Cavalry Division in the trenches and remained there until the night of 5th/6th June. During this period there was some considerable fighting in and around the village of HOOGE.

The R.H.A. 3rd Cavalry Division were during the period under mention in action near YPRES, attached to the 2nd Army.

The 3rd Field Squadron R.E. did good work during the period under mention in assisting and supervising the digging of entrenchments.

Casualties.

From April 23rd to June 6th.

About 103 Officers and 1317 other ranks, the majority of these were on the 13th May.

General Headquarters.

I forward herewith a report on certain operations in which the Cavalry were concerned during May 11th - 14th. A copy of this report was sent to General Officer Commanding 5th Corps.

In submitting it to General Headquarters I venture to suggest that the following lessons of a tactical nature may be deduced :-

(1). the undesirability of siting trenches upon the forward slopes of the ground or in localities where the enemy are able to obtain direct observation from more commanding points. The line taken up by the Cavalry on the morning of 13th May was, for instance, in full view of the enemy occupying the high ground West and South-west of FREZENBERG.

(2). the importance of adhering to our usual custom of reconnaissance by Officers of relieving troops prior to actual relief.

(3). the undesirability of attempting to reoccupy trenches from which troops have been driven by shell-fire and shell-fire only - If the enemy's artillery is sufficiently powerful and well enough directed to be able to render a line untenable at 4 a.m., only lack of ammunition (a factor upon which we cannot rely) is likely to prevent him from rendering them untenable again at 3 p.m. It would seem preferable so to arrange our batteries, our supporting points, and the lines of fire of our rifles and machine guns that the loss of a portion of the front line, if that portion happens to be naturally weak (e.g. exposed), may not be of vital

importance

importance; and that the enemy may himself suffer when he attempts to make good with infantry the position captured by his gun fire.

O.26

3rd Cavalry Division.
G. 735.

G 657A

Headquarters,
    Cavalry Corps.

    Herewith a Report on the Operations between the 11th and 14th instant in which the 3rd Cavalry Division took part.

Headquarters, 3rd Cavalry Division.   *M F Gage*   Lieutenant-Colonel,
18th May, 1915.   General Staff,
                                                            3rd Cavalry Division.
                                                            for G.O.C.

G. 735.

3rd CAVALRY DIVISION.

General Report on Operations, May 11th - 14th, 1915.

Reference - Sheet 28 (Belgium), 1/40,000.

11th May.
3rd Cav.Dvn comes
under orders of
27th Division.

1. At 10 a.m. on the 11th May, 1915, the 3rd Cavalry Division came under the orders of the 27th Division. At an interview with the G.O.C. 27th Division, at 2 p.m. on the same date, the G.O.C. 3rd Cavalry Division was ordered to relieve the 80th Infantry Brigade in trenches East of YPRES on the following night, with troops of the 3rd Cavalry Division, and in the meanwhile it was arranged that the latter should :-

(a) Relieve two squadrons of the 1st Cavalry Division then in support to 80th Infantry Brigade at I.11.b. on the night 11th/12th May, and also

(b) Send reconnoitring officers into 80th Infantry Brigade trenches the same night who should remain in the following day.

(c) Relieve the 80th Infantry Brigade on the night 12th/13th May on the following line -

100 yards N. of the main road in I.18.b. to and including the railway line in I.6.c.

The arrangements under (a) and (b) were duly carried out, and the Officer Commanding, 3rd Field Squadron, R.E. reconnoitred the area held by the 80th Infantry Brigade, and arranged for certain necessary improvements and additions in the defence line to be carried out by the troops of the 3rd Cavalry Division.

12th May.
3rd Cav.Dvn.deprived
of 3rd Fd, Sdqn.

2. On representation being made by the Officer Commanding 3rd Field Squadron, R.E. that he was being detailed to carry out work unconnected with the Division on the night of the 12th May, and since his assistance would be urgently required with the 3rd Cavalry Division, the 27th Division was asked to arrange that the Squadron

might

might be held available for work in the trench line that night. The request was subsequently refused by the 5th Corps and the 3rd Cavalry Division was thus deprived of the services of it's Field Squadron at a time when they were most urgently required.

May 12th. Counter-Order.

At 10 a.m. preparatory orders were received which to a great extent cancelled those of the 11th, under which the 3rd Cavalry Division was to take over the 80th Infantry Brigade line. The 3rd Cavalry Division was now to relieve only a portion of the latter's line, namely, from the BELLEWAARDE Lake to the ROULERS Railway line, and in addition, that of the 85th Brigade from the above railway line to about VERLORENHOEK. The Division was, by the same order, to come under the command of Major-General De Lisle, and to take over the newly allotted line on the night of 12th/13th May. This order was subsequently confirmed.

In an interview with Major-General De Lisle, the G.O.C. 3rd Cavalry Division pointed out that his Division would now, under the new order, have to take over a line of trenches which had not been previously reconnoitred, that owing to the impracticability of entering the trenches by daylight it was not possible to carry out any such reconnaissance, and that the troops would therefore have to move into the trenches in the dark and would be at a serious disadvantage if any attack should be made by the enemy the next morning. The G.O.C. 3rd Cavalry Division therefore protested against the new arrangement and asked that the 3rd Cavalry Division might be allowed to relieve the 80th Infantry Brigade as already arranged, especially so since officers of the 3rd Cavalry Division were already in these trenches and were making themselves acquainted with the local conditions.

A

Situation at 4.15 a.m.
13th May 1915

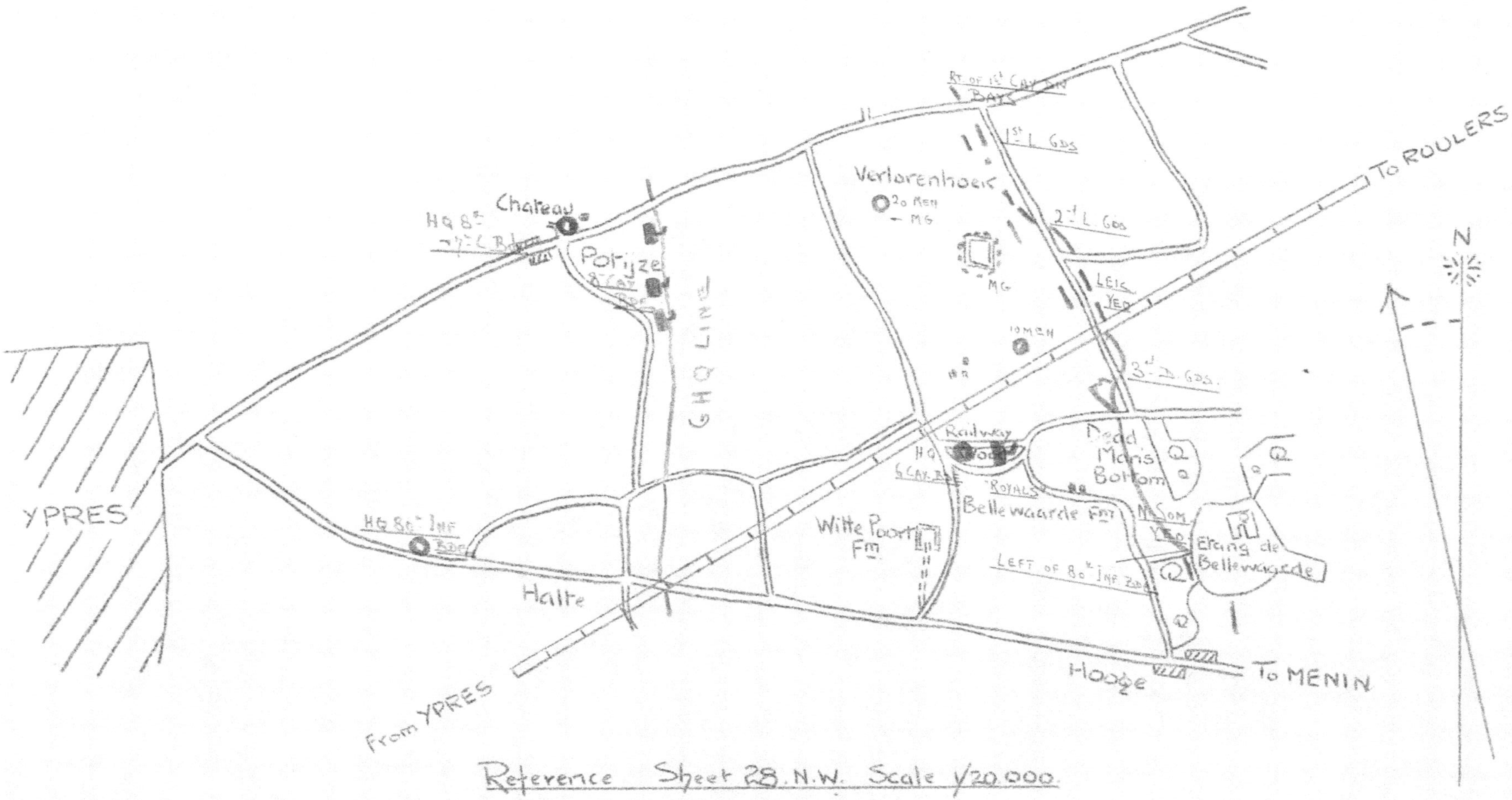

Reference Sheet 28 N.W. Scale 1/20,000

The confirmatory order to relieve the 85th Infantry Brigade however, was received at 3-50 p.m. and the relief took place the same night.

The 3rd Field Squadron, R.E. having been taken away from the Division it was essential that some R.E. should take their place, and Cavalry Force Order No. GA. 740 notified that an R.E. officer and a section would be available to supervise defences and communications, and that the officer was to report at the 85th Infantry Brigade Headquarters that evening. This officer, however, did not report at the time notified, and the 7th Cavalry Brigade had to take up its line without any R.E. assistance.

In the Appendix are copies of various reports which show how seriously handicapped the 7th Cavalry Brigade was owing to :-

    (a) Lack of opportunity for previous reconnaissance of trench line, and

    (b) Absence of any R.E. assistance.

13th May.

3. The relief of the 85th Infantry Brigade by the 3rd Cavalry Division was completed by 2 a.m. 13th May. The disposition of the Division is shown on the accompanying sketch, marked 'A'.

4-15 a.m.

Soon after dawn, the G.O.C. started from his Headquarters, (H.11.d), to visit Brigadiers, and on arriving at the Eastern exits of YPRES, a heavy bombardment of the sector WIELTJE - YPRES - HOOGE was found to be in progress. Proceeding along the MENIN road

4-35 a.m.

with a view to visiting the G.O.C. 6th Cavalry Brigade at I.11.b., the shell fire became so severe that the G.O.C. was unable to proceed further than Headquarters, 80th Infantry Brigade (I.9.d). Here it was found that telephone communication with the front line was already

cut,

4.

7-15 a.m.   cut, but shortly afterwards the Brigade-Major, 6th Cavalry Brigade, arrived with a verbal message to the effect that the front of this Brigade, and the area in rear of it to the outskirts of YPRES, was being very heavily shelled, and that the 3rd Dragoon Guards had been buried in their trenches. He further stated that reports, when he left, indicated that the Germans had succeeded in piercing the line, and the G.O.C. 6th Cavalry Brigade, was therefore sending forward the Royal Dragoons to re-establish it.

It transpired later that the report as to the breaking of the 6th Cavalry Brigade line was incorrect, but this was not discovered until reconnaissance in front of the Royal's counter-attack had reached the front line. The advance of the Royal's was carried out most gallantly, under a heavy shell fire, and very heavy casualties were incurred.

7-30 a.m.   The G.O.C. Division now proceeded to the Headquarters of the 7th and 8th Cavalry Brigades which were in dug-outs near POTIJZE Chateau. In the meanwhile reports had reached the Advanced Report Centre, which was still W. of YPRES, that the 7th Cavalry Brigade front was also being heavily bombarded, and that the troops were suffering severely. The trenches near VERLORENHOEK were said to have been blown in, the hostile infantry to be attacking the left front, and 7th Cavalry Brigade support to have been sent forward.

7-45 a.m.   The G.O.C. reached POTIJZE about 7-45 a.m. and an Advanced Report Centre was established there.

8-25 a.m.   In re-iteration of the Vth Corps order of the previous day, a further order was now received from the 1st Cavalry Division to the effect that if the line were broken it was to be re-established at whatever cost, and soon afterwards Major-General Briggs was

delegated

delegated to command the Reserves of the 1st and 3rd Cavalry Divisions, in the event of the situation demanding a counter-attack in either of the sections occupied by those Divisions.

It was, under this order, most desirable that a counter-attack to regain the lost trenches should be organized at the earliest possible moment, but before any orders for such an attack could be issued, it was equally essential that more definite information on the situation should be obtained, in order that the attack might be given a correct direction. At present, the width of the gap in the 3rd Cavalry Division line was a matter of speculation only; the G.O.C. knew that at 7 a.m. the situation was critical with the 6th Cavalry Brigade according to the Brigade-Major's report, and now that on the left of the line appeared equally critical. Until therefore, things had assumed a more definite shape, it would be obviously undesirable to formulate a plan for a counter-attack. The permanent success of an attack launched under existing conditions, however, was doubtful for even though the trenches, if lost, might be recaptured it seemed doubtful if the troops would be able to remain in them owing to the accurate registration and observation of the hostile artillery, which had already caused such damage.

9-30 a.m.

The situation was now very obscure, communication with the front being most difficult. It appeared, however, that practically the whole of the trenches occupied by the 7th Cavalry Brigade had been destroyed, and that the remnants of the Brigade, some 50 of the 1st Life Guards under their Commanding Officer, had fallen back on the Bays (near 3rd kilo. stone North of the VERLORENHOEK road), about 100 2nd Life Guards with 6

officers,

Situation at 12.45 pm
13th May 1915

Reference Sheet 28.N.W. Scale 1/20,000.

6.

officers, behind the G.H.Q. line, whilst of the Leicester Yeomanry all that could be ascertained was that the remains of 1 squadron were N. of the railway line in H.11.b.

10-25 a.m.   At 10-25 a.m. another order was received from Cavalry Force to counter-attack, together with certain suggestions for carrying out this operation. Preparatory steps had already been taken towards this end, but it was necessary that the situation should become clearer before any such attack took place.

The preparatory steps referred to consisted in :-

(a) Warning the Cavalry Force that if the Reserves under General Briggs were thus employed, the G.H.Q. line would be left unoccupied.

(b) Despatching the 10th Hussars of the 8th Cavalry Brigade to connect the G.H.Q. line with the right of the Bays (1st Cavalry Brigade) which had become exposed owing to the retirement of the 7th Cavalry Brigade. It would then be in a position to make a counter-attack to recover the lost trenches South of VERLORENHOEK, in co-operation with a similiar attack which it was intended to launch from the left of the 6th Cavalry Brigade to recover the trenches on the left of that Brigade.

(c) Ordering the 8th Cavalry Brigade to send one Regiment (Royal Horse Guards) to similiarly protect the left of the 6th Cavalry Brigade, and to reconnoitre the ground preparatory to counter-attack.

At 12-45 p.m. the situation having become clearer, the orders for the counter-attack, which was to commence at 2-30 p.m. were issued. The G.O.C. 8th Cavalry Brigade was to command this attack, which was to be carried out by his Brigade, supported by all the Artillery which was then supporting the Cavalry line, and by armoured motor-cars. One regiment of the 9th Cavalry Brigade was also detailed to be ready to support the attack, or if it failed to close the gap.

The counter-attack was carried out with the utmost gallantry and vigour, under very heavy fire from shrapnel and H.E. shell. The enemy did not wait to meet it, but fled in disorganized bodies, and are believed to have suffered heavy loss from our artillery, which acted all through in close co-operation.

[margin note: Requires confirmation; very doubtful if more than a few hostile scouts were actually seen.]

B

Situation at 4:45 pm
13th May 1915.

N
To ZULLER
To MENIN
To YPRES
YPRES

Bays Small Party 1st Gds
Remnants 10th Hussars
3rd D. Gds
N Som Yeo
Small Parties 8th Cav Bde
19th Hussars
Small Parties 2nd C. Bde
HQ 6th Cav Bde
Blues
Royals
Wilts 3rd Regt
1 Bn DLI
GHQ LINE
HQ 3rd Cav Div 7 + 8 Corps
HQ 8g Inf Bde
Hooge road
Halte

Reference Sheet 28 N.W. South 1/20000

7.

The lost trenches were regained, but they had been destroyed by the morning's bombardment and afforded no cover against the terrific artillery fire which was now opened on the troops of the 8th Cavalry Brigade, small bodies of which managed to remain in the trenches until dark, but it was found impossible to consolidate the position or to organize any regular defence in face of such a bombardment.

The armoured motors did valuable work in the counter-attack, both offensively on the left flank of the advance, and subsequently in ascertaining the dispositions of the front line as far as they could be seen from the VERLORENHOEK road.

4-45 p.m.

At 4-45 p.m. the situation was as shown in the accompanying sketch 'B'.

Endeavours were now made to protect the left of the 6th Cavalry Brigade by pushing forward the remnants of the 7th Cavalry Brigade, and the Blues (8th Cavalry Brigade) to a position along the road running N.N.W. from Railway Wood (I.11.b)., and a report on the situation was sent to Cavalry Force.

The G.O.C. 6th Cavalry Brigade reports that he received the greatest assistance from the Officer Commanding, Royal Irish Fusiliers in reinforcing his firing line towards evening when all his reserves had been used up, and in providing a company to connect his exposed left flank with the 7th Cavalry Brigade. The Officer Commanding, 60th Rifles, was also of great assistance in helping the North Somerset Yeomanry when the extreme right trenches of the 6th Cavalry Brigade had been blown in.

7-30 p.m.

At 7-30 p.m. fresh orders were received from the G.O.C. Cavalry Force. As it did not appear possible from these orders that the G.O.C. was aware of the actual

situation

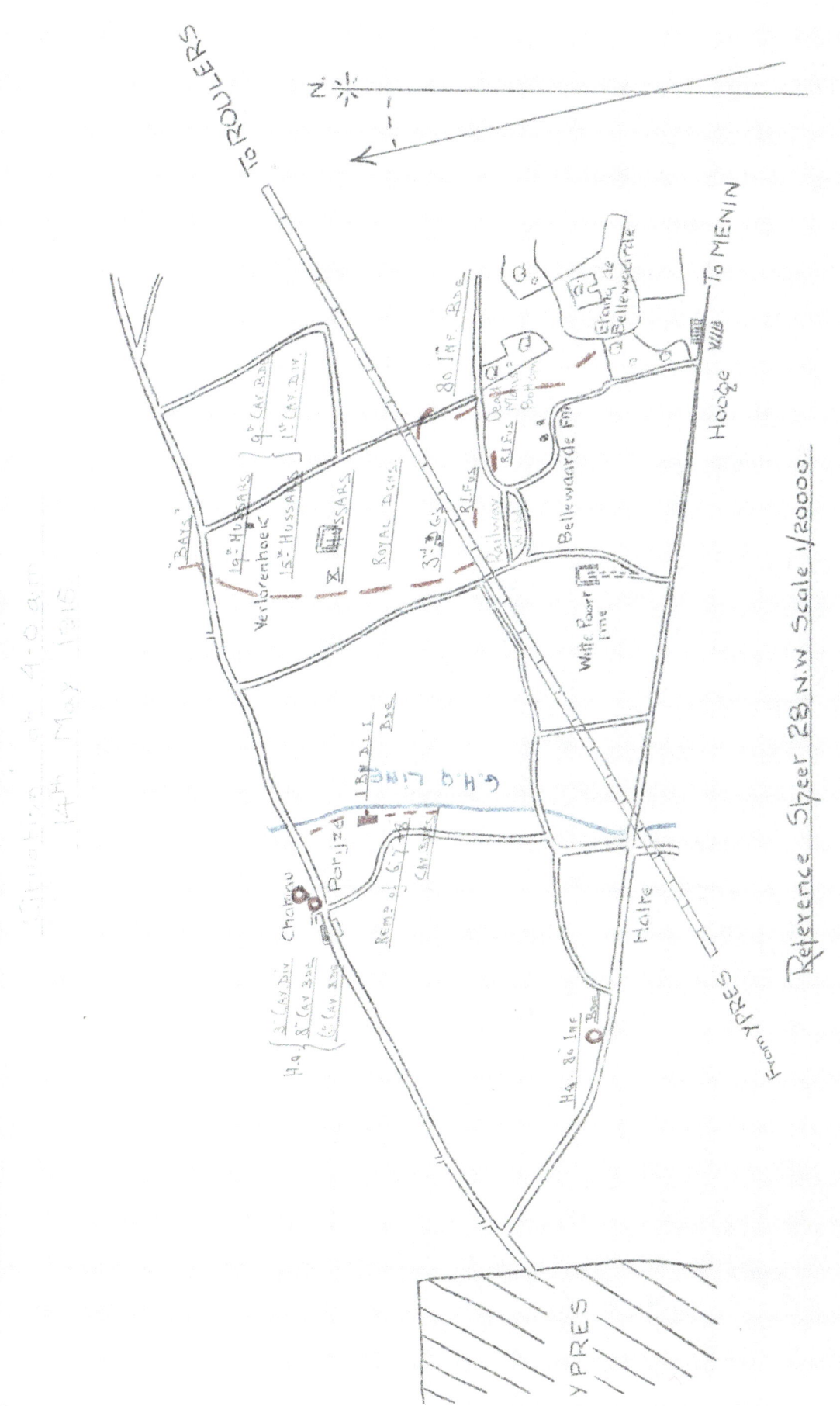

8.

situation, a Staff Officer was sent to explain same to him, with the result that further orders were subsequently
10-10 p.m. received. The result of these was that the 27th Division took over the right up to the Railway inclusive. The 6th Cavalry Brigade (less North Somerset Yeomanry and inclusive of the 10th Hussars) took up a new line parallel to and in front of the road running from near WITTE POORT Fme to 2½ kilo. POTIJZE - VERLORENHOEK road to within 600 yards of the latter, whilst the remaining troops were collected as a Reserve in the G.H.Q. line under General Bulkeley-Johnson.

May 14th.
12.40 a.m. 4. A digging party of 600 men from the Durham Light Infantry Brigade had been sent out to assist in digging the new line under the supervision of the R.E., it was found necessary to ask the Officer Commanding this party to leave out 300 men to maintain the line until the arrival of the 6th Cavalry Brigade.

2-30 a.m. The relief of the 6th Cavalry Brigade by the 80th Infantry Brigade was completed by 2-30 a.m. when the new line was occupied as follows :- on the right, 3rd Dragoon Guards., in the centre, Royal Dragoons., on the left, 10th
4 a.m. Hussars.

Fortunately the night was a quiet one and the troops were enabled to consolidate their positions somewhat. The heavy rain which had fallen at intervals during the previous 24 hours had tended to make the condition of things for the troops most uncomfortable. Many (especially in the 7th and 8th Cavalry Brigades) had lost their coats and were wet to the skin and caked in mud. In addition the 7th Cavalry Brigade had lost their rations during the early morning bombardment, and many of the rifles had become so caked in mud as to be temporarily unserviceable.

1-30 p.m. The morning passed quietly, and about midday orders were received that the Division would be relieved by the 2nd

Cavalry

Cavalry Division in the evening, and would return to huts in the neighbourhood of VLAMERTINGHE. The necessary orders
4 p.m. were issued as soon as Staff Officers from the relieving troops had arranged details.

3-20 p.m. A verbal message from the 3rd Dragoon Guards, confirmed later by the 80th Infantry Brigade, reported considerable numbers of Germans massing in Dead Man's Bottom (I.6.b) near the West edge of the wood. The guns were turned on to the wood referred to, a certain amount of firing on both sides
5 p.m. took place, but eventually died down. Patrols were sent out to see if it would be possible to occupy a new line somewhat in advance of the one hurriedly taken up last night.

7-30 p.m. A Staff Officer from the Cavalry Force Commander arrived with a message regarding the line which the 27th Division and he had decided should be taken up - at the same time a corresponding message arrived from the 27th Division. As the G.O.C. 2nd Cavalry Division, had in the meantime issued his own orders, and the occupation of the line referred to above would necessitate a covering force for the working party, a certain amount of difficulty ensued. The 2nd Cavalry Division had had officers out reconnoitring their line in the evening under the supervision of the Officer Commanding, 2nd Field Squadron, R.E., and as this line approximated to the one previously referred to, it was
9-15 p.m. finally adopted. Patrols subsequently reported that only hostile snipers appeared to be in the immediate front, and that the new line which extended from the railway in I.11.b. west of the farm in I.5.d. to the main road in I.5.a.8.8. was feasible.

The relief of the Division was carried out without incident by midnight, and the troops marched to the huts (7th and 8th Cavalry Brigades) South of VLAMERTINGHE, and to billets (6th Cavalry Brigade) in the village. Headquarters returned to the farm previously occupied 1200 yards West of YPRES Station.

3rd Cavalry Division.

APPENDIX TO G. 735.

Notes by the General Officer Commanding, 7th Cavalry
        Brigade, on Trench Line.

The <u>1st Life Guards</u> relieved the East Surrey's on the left. Here the support trenches had only just been started and were not two feet deep. The whole of the front was not protected by trenches. A farm intervened and there was a gap there of about 70 yards.

There were no communicating trenches at all. There was no wire in front.

It was quite impossible to communicate with the squadron on the right.

From the hour of taking over until 3 a.m. everyone worked hard digging to improve the trenches and communications.

At a depth of three feet water appeared in the trenches. This was previously reported to me when taking over from the 85th Brigade, the troops of that Brigade having only taken over the line 24 hours previously.

There was some barbed wire attached to posts lying behind the trenches, but at night it was not possible to see how much.

Getting in or out of the trenches was a very hazardous proceeding even at night owing to the lack of cover on the terrain and the absence of communicating trenches. The enemy kept up a constant fire over the area to be crossed. Colonel Stanley was not at all satisfied with the trenches and did his utmost to improve them. Nobody in the Brigade had seen them previous to arrival in the dark.

I enclose reports from the other two C.O's.

They were told previous to leaving POTIJZE that R.E. stores were being sent up to that place and that they would have to send parties back to carry up what they required

for

for the trenches.

I cannot give you much more information at present, but am endeavouring to glean further details from officers who were in the trenches. The 2nd Life Guards were in the centre and relieved the Buffs, whilst the Leicestershire Yeomanry relieved the Royal Fusiliers on the right.

15.v.15

* * *

Report by the Officer Commanding, Leicestershire
      Yeomanry, on the Trench Line.

We have occupied trenches as held by the Royal Fusiliers from the Railway Crossing on right flank to point near Farm which is destroyed. I have two squadrons in front trench and both machine guns. The support trench, held by remaining squadron, is too much on left flank and too far in rear, but any new trench within reasonable distance of front line will be very much exposed to shell fire. The front trench is much exposed to enfilade fire since the enemy occupied high ground to S.E., and in consequence I require all the sandbags I can get to improve cover.

I have located the "Point d'Appuis" which I will occupy as soon as I can get the water out. It is close to the support trenches.

Reference communication with flanks, left flank is not in communication with trench on our left. I have ordered the squadron on that flank to get touch and cut communication trench. I got touch with troops on my right over the Railway, they had not been relieved by the Cavalry, but the North Somerset Yeomanry have passed here some time ago to take these trenches over.

Communication trenches to the support from the firing line will be a large work to undertake owing to distance but am starting the work. Since leaving the trenches my telephone has ceased to work, so report by orderly.

I am still in old regimental H.Q. on the road as all telephones are installed there, including new battery 75 line.

I have not time to change all the lines to-night,

but

but hope to move my H.Q. to dug-outs just in front of support trenches to-morrow.

Echelon 'A' has not arrived yet. R.E. officer spared me some sandbags but I want still more. I have taken over 8 boxes of S.A.Ammunition besides 2,000 loose in webbing bandoliers from the Royal Fusiliers, these I am placing in trenches.

*: * :*

Further report by Leicestershire Yeomanry (Lieut W.S.
Fielding-Johnson) on the Trench Line.

The line of trenches taken over by us and occupied by two squadrons run in a N.W. direction from YPRES - ZONNEBEKE railway, extending about 250 - 300 yards.

The trenches wanted repair, but there were no sand bags to hand. The bad state was to a great measure due to previous occupants having made "funk-holes", in consequence of which the earth had fallen in. They were also insanitary, and in many places up to 8 inches in water.

Trenches were about 3'6" in depth, with a parapet <u>sloping well away</u> of loose soil of an additional height of from 18" to 2'. In some cases from the top of front parapet there was a width of 5 to 6 feet, the trench itself being about 2½ feet wide.

The trench was regularly traversed, with a front of 12 feet and a traverse of 6 feet.

Our right rested on the railway but there was no communication to the 3rd Dragoon Guards who continued the line on the other side. Five sandbags lay on the line as though it had been intended to make the trenches continuous.

The line was continuous until it reached our left when there was a gap of 20 yards between our left and the right flank of the Life Guards. Here we discovered that the extreme flank of the Life Guards was set back with a result that some of their men fired over our heads before the discovery was made.

There were partially constructed support trenches which appeared to have been heavily shelled.

As pointed out above there was no communication or trench across railway on our right or to Life Guards on

our

our left. There were no communicating trenches, with the support, although communication round traverses was complete.

There was wire in front but this was said to have been broken by shell fire previously.

Improvement was certainly urgently required.

The support trenches were not completed when bombardment started, although trench party had worked all night.

Field of fire was bad owing to growing crops in front of trenches.

* * * *

Report by 2nd Life Guards on Trench Line.
----

1. The trench line occupied by the 2nd Life Guards on night 13th-14th was sited as in my previous memo, forwarded herewith.

    The frontage of the front line trench was approximately 300 yards.

2. One support trench 200 uards in rear of, and rather to our left of, the front line trench in 1.

3. No - there was a gap caused by an unmetalled track in our right sector, (Note, our line was divided into two sectors). The gap was approximately 15 yards wide.

4. When the Regiment took over these trenches, two communicating trenches had been commenced from either end of the support trench each for a distance of about 70 yards. The right hand communicating trench was linked during the night by the Regiment with the front line, but was hardly fit for practical use by daybreak.

5. In places there were rolls on the "loose French wire".

6. The trenches were as a rule well made except on the right of our left sector. There was insufficient head cover and no loopholes. Nor were there any machine gun emplacements.

7. The trenches were, it is considered, incorrectly sited, as being on the forward slope of the hill in full view of the enemy's artillery observers, who were seen to be directing their artillery fire by means of flares.

    A small "point d'appui" capable of holding four or five men had been made 50 yards to our right of our support trench. This appeared to be of little, if any, practical value.

    In conclusion it is considered that had there been a complete continuous supporting line in lieu of the support

                                                              trench

trench referred to in 2, with communicating trenches
linking up the front and supporting line, a retirement
to the G.H.Q. line could well have been avoided.

*   *   *

Map D.

SECRET.

Copy No: 3.

CAVALRY CORPS OPERATION ORDER NO: 3.

20th May, 1915.

1. Tomorrow night 21st/22nd the following <u>portion of the line</u> will be handed over :-

(a) <u>By 2nd Cavalry Division</u>.... from junction on its left with 4th Division as far as YPRES - VERLORENHOEK Road (exclusive) .... <u>to 4th Division.</u>

(b) <u>By 2nd Cavalry Division</u>.... from YPRES - VERLORENHOEK Road (inclusive) to junction on its right with 1st Cavalry Division .... <u>to 28th Division.</u>

(c) <u>By 1st Cavalry Division</u>.... from junction on its left with 2nd Cavalry Division to BELLEWAARDE Lake (exclusive).... <u>to 28th Division.</u>

Detailed arrangements for these reliefs will be made between Divisional Commanders concerned. Completion of reliefs to be reported to Cavalry Corps and to 5th Corps direct.

2. From 9 p.m. tomorrow night 21st/22nd <u>3rd Cavalry Division</u> will cease to form part of Corps Reserve and may, after that hour, start for its regular billets near HAZEBROUCK. Move will be made in busses under arrangements by 3rd Cavalry Division direct with 2nd Army and 5th Corps.

3. At 9 p.m. tomorrow <u>Corps Reserve</u> (less 3rd Cavalry Division) will come under orders of Major-General KAVANAGH (Headquarters in Chateau in H.11.a.) and will be strengthened by those units of 2nd and 1st Cavalry Divisions withdrawn from the line under para: 1 above. Orders for Corps Reserve will remain as in G.S.659 of 19th May.

4. <u>Accommodation</u> for troops being withdrawn from the line will be allotted tomorrow in huts or houses in vicinity of VLAMERTINGHE.

5. The <u>portion of the line</u> referred to in para: 1 (a) above will pass under command of 4th Division as soon as reliefs are completed. <u>Remainder of Cavalry Corps' line</u> remains under orders of Cavalry Corps till 6 a.m. 22nd May when that portion referred to in paras: 1 (b) and 1 (c) above pass to command of 28th Division (Headquarters at crossroads H.7.c.).

6. At 6 a.m. 22nd May the <u>following troops</u> pass to command of 28th Division :-
  28th Divisional Artillery and Artillery attached thereto.
  151st Infantry Brigade.
  Divisional Mounted Troops 28th Division.
  2nd Northumbrian Field Company.

7. From 6 a.m. 22nd May the following will be the <u>organization of the line</u> remaining under Cavalry Corps:-

(a) <u>Right Sector</u> remains as it now is, under Brigadier-General LONGLEY.

(b) <u>Left Sector</u> will be composed of 9th Cavalry Brigade (2 Regiments) plus one Regiment of Cavalry, one Battalion of Territorial Infantry, and 1st Field Squadron R.E., latter units to be detailed by 1st Cavalry Division and placed under the orders of Brigadier-General GREENLY (Headquarters in I.9.c.3.6.) who will report direct to Cavalry Corps Headquarters.

8.

8. Boundaries of Cavalry Corps area after 6 a.m. 22nd May will be :- right as before : between right sector and left sector from their point of junction to road junction in I.16.b. thence to SALLYPORT Bridge (inclusive) in I.8.d.: left a straight line from N.W.corner of BELLEWAARDE Lake to level crossing I.10.d. thence by MENIN Road (inclusive) to MENIN GATE (inclusive).

9. At 6 a.m. 22nd May, Bridges Nos: 7 - 11 pass to 28th Division: No: 12 to Cavalry Corps left sector: Nos: 13 and 14 to Cavalry Corps right sector.

10. When above reliefs are completed 150th Brigade (less 2 battalions) will be in Corps Reserve: one Battalion remains in right sector: one in new left sector.

Issued at 8-30 p.m.

Brig-General,
General Staff,
Headquarters, Cavalry Corps.

6. 7. 8 Cav Bde.   W.D. 78/19.V.
3" Fd. & Sig. Sqdn.   G 769
S.A.A. Sec. A.C.
A.A. & Q.M.G.

1. From 9-0 p.m. to-night, the 3rd Cavalry Division will cease to form part of the Corps Reserve, and may, after that hour, return to its billets in the HAZEBROUCK area.

2. The move will be made under Brigade arrangements by 'bus.

 Staff Captains of Brigades will meet the D.A. & Q.M.G. at 8-0 p.m. at the Cross roads G.8.d. when busses will be handed over in the following order :-

  6th Cavalry Brigade - 30 busses.
  7th Cavalry Brigade - 27   do.
  8th Cavalry Brigade - 22   do.

3. 'A' Echelon transport will return to the HAZEBROUCK area today under Brigade arrangements.

4. S.A.A.Section, Divisional Ammunition Column, will return independently to its billets today.

5. Orders for the 3rd Signal Squadron and 3rd Field Squadron will be issued later.

6. 3rd Cavalry Division Advanced Report Centre will remain in RENINGHELST until 9-30 a.m. tomorrow, after which hour all messages will be sent to the Report Centre, HAZEBROUCK.

(sd) WHF

Advanced 3rd Cavalry Division.
21st May, 1915.

Major,
General Staff,
3rd Cavalry Division.

G 769

150th Bde.
151st Bde.
4th E.Yorks R.
50th Div.Mtd Troops.
28th   do.

1. From 9-0 p.m. tonight, the 3rd Cavalry Division will cease to form part of the Corps Reserve.

2. At 9-0 p.m. tonight the Corps Reserve (less 3rd Cavalry Division) will come under orders of Major-General KAVANAGH, Commanding 2nd Cavalry Division (Headquarters in Chateau in K.11.a).

Advanced 3rd Cavalry Division.
21st May, 1915.

Major,
General Staff,
3rd Cavalry Division.

G. 797.

28-5-15.

1.   The 3rd Cavalry Division, under the command of Brigadier-General Bulkeley-Johnson, will relieve the 2nd Cavalry Division in the trenches East of YPRES tomorrow evening.

2.   The Division will move in busses as far as VLAMERTINGHE, and thence by march via YPRES and the SALLY PORT.

3.   Thirty-three busses per Brigade will be handed over to Brigade Staff Officers by a Divisional Staff Officer at the Road junction due West of L'HOFFAND, on the St. SYLVESTRE - HAZEBROUCK Road (Map 5 A, HAZEBROUCK) at 11-0 a.m. tomorrow, and will be conducted by them to Brigade areas.

4.   Heads of Brigade busses will pass St.SYLVESTRE Cross roads at the following hours :-
      6th Cavalry Brigade............3-0 p.m.
      8th   do..................3-15 p.m.
      7th   do..................3-30 p.m.

5.   Troops will debuss at the road junction G.6.d. West of VLAMERTINGHE and will immediately march to a rendezvous about H.7.a & c. where they will be formed up by Divisional and Brigade Staff Officers. Arrangements should be made to give the men a meal at this rendezvous.

6.   The relief will commence at 8-30 p.m. at which hour the head of the relieving troops will be at the SALLY PORT where guides (1 officer and 3 N.C.O's per Regiment) will meet them.
      Troops will leave the SALLY PORT as follows :-

Royals   ) 8-30 p.m.
R.H.Guards   )

3rd Drag.Gds   ) 9-0 p.m.
10th Hussars   )

Essex Yeo.   ) 9-30 p.m.
N.Somerset Yeo.)

7.   'A' Echelon Transport and S.A.A.Section of the Divisional Ammunition Column will move to its billetting area of 9th to 21st May, West of VLAMERTINGHE, under Brigade arrangements. Pack animals will proceed to the rendezvous mentioned in para. 5. under instructions from A.A & Q.M.G.
      Officers Commanding 'A' Echelon Transport, O.C. S.A.A.Section Ammunition Column, and the S.S.O.Divisional Troops, will meet the A.A & Q.M.G. at 12-30 p.m. at the road junction ½ mile West of VLAMERTINGHE on the main VLAMERTINGHE - POPERINGHE road.
      'B' Echelon transport will remain in its present billets.
      Units will take with them any -
         (a) Very Pistols and Ammunition on charge.
         (b) Hand Grenades, rifle grenades, etc.
         (c) 2 canvas buckets for anti-gas solution. Empty
             biscuit tins will also be required for this
                                   purpose.

The 2nd Cavalry Division will hand over in the trenches all Very's pistols and periscopes in possession. On relief these must be brought back and returned to the D.A.D.O.S. 3rd Cavalry Division.

8. The O.C. Armoured Motor Cars will detail two cars to be at the disposal of General Bulkeley-Johnson. The Officer in charge should report at the ECOLE DE BIENFAISANCE at 9-0 p.m. tomorrow. The O.C. remaining two cars will report to General Briggs at Farm in H.15.a.c. at 5-0 p.m. tomorrow.

9. The O.C. 3rd Field Squadron, R.E. will report to General Bulkeley-Johnson at 9-0 p.m. tomorrow at the ECOLE DE BIENFAISANCE.

10. At ~~6-0~~ 1-0 a.m. on the 30th May, General Briggs will take over command of the Cavalry Corps sector, the boundaries of which are shown on the 1/10,000 maps which have been issued.
Up till that hour, this sector will be under the command of Major-General Kavanagh, whose Headquarters are at the Chateau H.11a. A report will be furnished to him and to Gen Briggs on completion of the relief.

11. The Advanced Report Centre, 3rd Cavalry Division, will be established at the ECOLE DE BIENFAISANCE (which will in future be referred to as the ECOLE) at 8-30 p.m. tomorrow.
General Briggs' Report Centre will be established at Farm H.15 a.c. from 6-0 a.m. May 30th.

12. Further instructions regarding organization of defences, artillery co-operation, etc., will be embodied in a memorandum which will be issued tomorrow.

28th May, 1915.

M.F.GAGE, Lieutenant-Colonel,
General Staff,
3rd Cavalry Division.

W.D 80

G. 809.

Headquarters,
   Vth Corps.

   With reference to the G.O.C's conversation with Major-General Briggs this afternoon, relative to the importance of the entrenched position at HOOGE, General Briggs would be glad to know if the enclosed copy of an order which has been issued to Brigadier-General Bulkeley-Johnson meets with the approval of the G.O.C. Vth Corps.

(sd) M*Grath*

Advanced 3rd Cavalry Division.   Lieutenant-Colonel,
                                       General Staff,
   29th May, 1915.   for Major-General,
                              Commanding 3rd Cavalry Division.

Adv. 3rd Cav Div.   G X 1200
The Corps Commander approves.

(sd) H.S. Jeudwine

29.V.15.   BGGS

New copy
Watkin Fenhough Maj
G.S.
1.VI.15.

3rd Cavalry Division.

G. 904.

Headquarters,

    3rd Division.

The attached remarks by Major-General Briggs on the 5th Corps communication (attached) are forwarded, together with a copy of the orders issued by Major H.E.R. Boxer, 1st Bn. Lincolnshire Regiment.

[signature]

                              Lieutenant-Colonel,
                                General Staff,
4th June, 1915.   3rd Cavalry Division.

Reference 5th Corps letter G.X 1245; referring to paragraph :-

(1)   It was on the 31st May, not the 1st June, that the Corps Commander saw General Briggs.   At that time the 3rd Dragoon Guards held the HOOGE Fort shown on the attached sketch, which included the stables.   The Corps Commander subsequently directed that the Chateau should be occupied and a redoubt (shown on the sketch) constructed that night; he at the same time insisted on the necessity of holding the HOOGE Fort at all costs.   General Briggs pointed out that though he could hold the HOOGE Fort and the remainder of his line with the force he then had, he would require additional troops to carry out the occupation and maintenance of the extension of his line which was then suggested.

(2)   The report sent in, our G.874 of the 2nd June, to the effect that the line was re-established as before, including the Chateau, stables, and HOOGE Fort, was the result of similiar reports received by General Campbell direct from the trenches, and there was reason to believe that this report was, in fact, substantially correct. Major Mason, 3rd Dragoon Guards, personally saw the King's Dragoon Guards established in the stable at 9-30 p.m. that night, and there was no reason to suppose that the King's Dragoon Guards had not recovered every portion of their line as already reported.   It was not until the morning of the 3rd that it was discovered that neither the Chateau nor the annexe were held by the Lincolns who had taken over from the King's Dragoon Guards and 3rd Dragoon Guards on the previous night, and it was only at 5 p.m. on the same date that General Briggs was informed that the Lincolns did not even hold the stables.

The conclusion is that there was some misunderstanding in the carrying out of the reliefs between the 3rd Dragoon Guards, the King's Dragoon Guards, and the 1st Lincolns.

With reference to paragraph 7, sub-paragraph (b) it is to be noted that the situation at this moment is precisely the same as when the Corps Commander interviewed General Briggs on May 31st, and that all ground then held at HOOGE is now in our possession. As stated above, the loss of the Chateau was apparently due to a misunderstanding which might well occur in a confused situation such as that caused by a counter-attack and reliefs taking place within a few hours of one another.

With reference to sub-paragraph (c), until the receipt of your G.A.215 of June 3rd at 5-15 p.m. it was not known that the Corps Commander was desirous that the two Indian Cavalry Regiments should be employed in the front line. Not only was it then too late to alter the arrangements which had been made for the attack by the Lincolns, but, in addition, General Briggs considered that it would be most inadvisable and unfair on the Regiments concerned to employ them in a night attack against, to them, unknown positions, without any previous reconnaissance on their part.

* * * * *

Reference ZILLEBEKE Sheet 1/10,000.

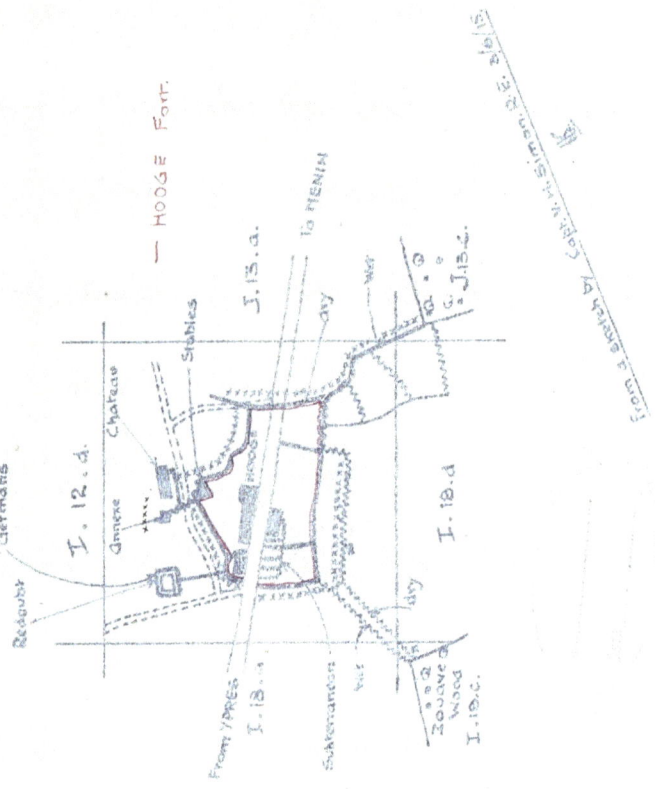

NARRATIVE OF OPERATIONS 25TH/28th SEPTEMBER,
1915.

CONFIDENTIAL

3rd CAVALRY DIVISION.

Narrative of Operations, 25th - 28th September, 1915.

25th Sept.
7.15.am.   On the night of the 24/25th September, the Division was billeted in the BOIS DES DAMES; at 7.15 am. on the 25th Sept. 1st Army telephoned that the Division was to move to a position of readiness at VAUDRICOURT.

10.45.am.   The move of the fighting troops was completed by 10.45.am.

11.15.am.   At 11.15.am. G.O.C. IV Corps, whose Advanced Headquarters were at VAUDRICOURT communicated verbally an order received from the 1st Army that 3rd Cavalry Division was to move forward to a further position of readiness about FOSSE 3; COURONNE DE RUTOIRE, consequent on the progress made by our infantry, which was reported to have reached the approximate line HILL 70 - CHALK PIT Wood - HULLUCH.

12.15.pm.   On arrival at the rendezvous at 12.15.pm., the G.O.C. was informed by Major Lockett (11th Hussars), who had already preceded the advance of the Division in command of Machine Gun Detachments and Mounted Divisional Troops of the IV th Corps, that the enemy was still in possession of a portion of his front line trenches immediately East of LE RUTOIRE, and that our infantry were at present unable to make any forward progress in this portion of the line.

The G.O.C. then had an interview with G.O.C. 1st Division, who corroborated Major Lockett's statement.

Since it did not appear possible, under these circumstances, to effectively co-operate with the infantry, the G.O.C. proceeded to the Headquarters, 15th Division at MAZINGARBE, in order to be in close communication with 1st Army by telephone.

1.30.pm.   At 1.30.pm. G.O.C received a message from 1st Army stating that our infantry had occupied HULLUCH and HILL 70,

and

Sept.25th. 25th   2.

and were attacking CITE ST AUGUSTE. The 3rd Cavalry Division was at the same time directed to advance Eastwards between HULLUCH and HILL 70, and to secure the high ground between HARNES and PONT-a-VENDIN until relieved by infantry. It was also to seize the crossings of the Canal between the latter place, COURRIERES and HARNES.

The actual situation, however, at this hour was not in accordance with that stated in the message, since according to the latest reports from the firing line HULLUCH and HILL 70 were still in possession of the enemy. Moreover, the enemy's fortified (back) line extending from HAISNES via CITE ST. ELIE - HULLUCH to CITE ST. AUGUSTE was still intact.

Since the mission assigned to the 3rd Cavalry Division in the above order, did not seem possible of accomplishment at that time, the G.O.C. telephoned the existing situation to G.O.C. IVth Corps, and requested him to communicate it to the First Army Commander.

The order was subsequently cancelled by the latter, and the 3rd Cavalry Division was directed to stand fast for the present.

Mounted patrols were now despatched towards LOOS and HULLUCH, in order to gain touch with the XXXXX infantry, and to report further on the situation.

3-45 pm.   The patrol despatched towards LOOS reported that at 3-0 p.m. our infantry were engaging the Germans on HILL 70, and were just in possession of PUITS 14 Bis, but were running short of ammunition.

The patrol sent towards HULLUCH found the enemy still in possession of the line from LONE TREE HILL to SOUTHERN SAP, and reported that at 4-10 p.m. the Germans were surrendering in parties of about 200 at that place, and that Cavalry Route No. 7 was clear as far as the German first line trenches.

7-0 pm.   7.P.M At 7-0 p.m. the 3rd Cavalry Division was ordered to off-saddle and bivouac for the night, and to be in readiness to move at 5-30 a.m. the next day. Heavy rain during the late afternoon and during the night.

Sept.26th.   Early on the morning of the 26th, the situation underwent a change. The first intimation of this came from the 7th Division

3.

Sept. 26th.
1-45 a.m.
which telegraphed to the 3rd Cavalry Division at 1-45 a.m. that the Germans had counter-attacked and had forced back a portion of the 7th Division line.

3-5 a.m.
At 3-5 a.m. a message was received from the First Army to the effect that the 1st Corps had been authorised to call on the 3rd Cavalry Division, as a temporary measure, and at 3-20 a.m. a further message was received from the 7th Division (sent at 1-45 a.m.) asking that a Cavalry Brigade might be sent at once to VERMELLES, as it might be required for counter-attack. This Brigade was not employed by the 7th Division.

9-0 a.m.
About 9-0 a.m. a patrol of the 3rd Dragoon Guards, under Lieutenant Katanakis, 3rd Dragoon Guards, was despatched towards THE QUARRIES and CITE ST. ELIE.

10-25 a.m.
At 10-25 a.m. the 15th Division reported that our infantry was retiring in confusion from HILL 70 along the LENS road. Since that Division had no troops available to check the retirement, it asked the G.O.C. if he would hold the 3rd Cavalry Division in readiness to man the original German front line trenches in the vicinity of LENS road redoubt, G.34.a., in the event of the situation developing seriously ?

The G.O.C. pointed out, however, that he was not at liberty to do this without the sanction of the First Army, which he asked the G.O.C. 15th Division to obtain.

10-30 a.m.
At 10-30 a.m. another patrol under Captain Worthington, 3rd Dragoon Guards, with Lieutenant Pank, R.E., had reconnoitred Cavalry Road No. 7 towards HULLUCH and had found all clear up to our new line immediately W. of that place.

11-15 a.m.
At 11-15 a.m. Lieutenant Katinakis' patrol which had been sent towards The QUARRIES and CITE ST. ELIE reported that both these places were held by the enemy.

11-40 a.m.
At 11-40 a.m. the G.O.C. 3rd Cavalry Division was ordered to place two Regiments at the disposal of the IVth Corps " to be used as a mounted reserve, for defensive purposes only". The 6th Cavalry Brigade, under Brigadier-General D.Campbell, was

12-30 p.m.
ordered to detail two Regiments for this purpose, and they were immediately called upon to occupy the LENS road and LOOS road

4.

Sept. 26th.   redoubts, G.34.a. and G.28.b., but as the situation did not permit of the movement of mounted troops so far to the front, the horses were left behind (W. of CORON DE RUTOIRE), and the men marched up.

NOTE.- A report on the movements of these two regiments (3rd Dragoon Guards and 1st Royal Dragoons by the G.O.C. 6th Cavalry Brigade is attached.)

3.30.pm.   At 3.30 pm. an order from the IVth Corps directed General Campbell to proceed with his Brigade to LOOS, which he was to hold until the arrival of the Guards Division. The G.O.C. ordered General Campbell to carry out this task, with two regiments, in accordance with the 1st Army Order of 11.40.am.

4.35.pm.   Subsequently (at 4.35 pm.) the G.O.C. was ordered by the 1st Army to take the remainder of his Division and to hold the original German front line trenches between the VERMELLES - HULLUCH road in the North and LOOS in the South until relieved by the Guards Division. The order was received soon after 5.pm. and the North Somerset Yeomanry of the 6th Cavalry Brigade moved off at 6.pm., and the 8th Cavalry Brigade at 6.30.pm., all dismounted.

On arrival, the Guards Division was found to be already in occupation of the German front line trenches, and at 9.15. pm. the 8th Cavalry Brigade troops commenced to march back to their horses.

In the meanwhile, a Staff Officer of the 3rd Cavalry Division had been sent to get in touch with General Campbell and his situation, with orders to return and report personally to the Divisional Commander at MAZINGARBE. As a result of this officer's report, as communicated to him by General Campbell, the G.O.C. received orders from the 1st Army at

11.30.pm.   11.30.pm., directing him to proceed immediately to LOOS with the remainder of his Division, and to take over command of the defence of that village and of any other troops that might be occupying it.

27th Sept.   The troops of the 8th Cavalry Brigade and the

North

26th Sept. 27th

North Somerset Yeomanry had already marched some 5 or 6 miles backwards and forwards between their horses and the German trenches in accordance with previous orders, and they had now to march back a further 4½ miles to LOOS, consequently, the men being fatigued, the Division was not wholly concentrated in LOOS until 2.45.am on the 27th.

LOOS. *Loos*

Steps were at once taken to place the village in a state of defence. The 3rd Cavalry Division connected with the left of the 141st Brigade, 47th Division at the CHALK PIT, M.6.a. on the right flank, and with the 2nd Guards Brigade at Point 58. G.29.d. on the left, in accordance with 1st Army Orders. The village was shelled by the enemy's artillery at intervals during the night, but the troops holding the perimeter only suffered slightly, as the fire was directed chiefly on the centre of the village.

All the infantry remaining in the village were collected and sent to join their formations.

A thorough search of the village and its numerous cellars was instituted, and steps were taken to collect the wounded and bury the dead of which there were some 160 Germans and many British. 45 Germans were captured in hiding, and 6 field guns and a machine gun were found well concealed in various emplacements in the village.

7.pm. Patrol Work. *7.pm*

At daybreak the situation about PUITS 14 BIS and HILL 70 was very obscure owing to the various contradictory reports which were received. Patrols were consequently sent out to clear matters up in these directions.

11.30.am. *11.30 am*

These patrols reported that small parties of the enemy were found to be holding the house on the HULLUCH – LENS road about H.25.C.d.7., that the wood in

27th Sept. 27th

H.25.a. was clear, and that wounded British soldiers found here had said that no Germans had been there for two days.

The patrols sent towards HILL 70 came in contact with small hostile parties and there was some skirmishing and our men were fired at from the red houses H.31.b.2.9.

3.30.pm. At 3.30 pm. the enemy opened a very heavy fire on their original front trenches in G.28., and as soon as the advance of the Guards Division commenced an intense bombardment was opened on LOOS, large numbers of gas shells bursts, necessitating the use of respirators, and several cases of gas poisoning occurring. The attack on PUITS 14 BIS having been reported successful, the 3rd Guards Brigade attacked HILL 70, suffering several casualties in passing through LOOS.

5.pm. About 5.pm. the bombardment of the village died down. The situation as it was then believed to be was that the attack by the 2nd Guards Brigade had succeeded in gaining PUITS 14 BIS, but had been driven back, and in a subsequent attack gained possession of the Chalk Pit and wood, H.25.a. The 3rd Guards Brigade had succeeded in occupying a line on the N.W. slope of Hill 70.

5.30.pm. In accordance with instructions received from IVth Corps, steps were taken to strengthen the defences of the village, trenches were wired, roads barricaded, and a central keep commenced round the road junction in G.36.a.1.7.

6.pm. The enemy again bombarded the village heavily at 6.p.m. and continued to do so until after dark, when it
8.20.pm. slackened off for a short while but was continued intermittently most of the night.

10.20.pm. Information was received from the IVth Corps that the Division would probably be relieved by a Brigade from the 1st Division on the following night.

About

Sept. 27th.

10.30.pm.
About this hour motor despatch riders arrived with orders from the 1st Army, which were almost simultaneously confirmed by telegram. These orders stated that, according to an intercepted German wireless message, we had broken through the German lines of defence. General BRIGGS was instructed to get into touch with the Guards Division near PUITS 14 BIS; and, should the report that our troops had broken through the German line prove true, to push on with the whole of his Division reinforced with the mounted troops and motor machine guns of the IVth Corps and occupy VENDIN-LE-VIEIL ANNAY-PONTA -VENDIN before daybreak.

A staff Officer was immediately sent off to ascertain if there was any change in the disposition of the Guards Division and in the situation in their front.

11.pm.
Shortly afterwards a Staff Officer arrived from the XIth Corps asking General BRIGGS if possible to come back and see General HAKING (Commanding XIth Corps) as the latter thought he might be able to assist.

General BRIGGS, however, knowing that the Guards had retired from PUITS 14 BIS before dark, did not consider it desirable to relinquish his command as, placed where he was in LOOS, he was enabled to keep in close touch with the situation, his conception of which was not in accordance with what the XIth and VIth Corps apparently believed it to be. He explained the latter to the Staff Officer referred to above who thereupon returned to General HAKING.

11.30.pm.
The Divisional Staff Officer sent to ascertain the situation of the Guards Division returned at 11.30.pm. and confirmed what our observers had already seen and reported, that is to say that the 2nd Guards Brigade in their first attack had captured the Chalk Pit H.25.a.,

8.

Sept. 27th.

and PUITS 14 Bis. The 3rd Guards Brigade had then launched its attack against Hill 70. In the meanwhile the 2nd Guards Brigade had been driven back to the LOOS - HULLUCH Road, had launched a second attack and had succeeded in occupying the CHALK PIT and Wood in H.25.a., but had been unable to secure the PUITS and keep in H.25.c. The 3rd Guards Brigade had established itself on the N.W. slopes of Hill 70 but had not succeeded in taking the crest of the Hill.

Sept. 28th.
12-30 a.m.

A report to this effect was immediately sent to the IVth Corps and it was pointed out that the situation did not permit of the movement indicated in the Army Commander's instructions being carried out.

1-30 a.m.

Subsequently further instructions amplifying the orders of the First Army were received but these became non-effective on account of our above report.

In spite of fairly severe shelling during the night, work on the defences was pushed on rapidly, but after daylight observation from a hostile captive balloon caused its cessation at most points.

During the night, the 47th Division had succeeded in occupying the belt of scrub in M.6.a. This was of considerable importance as it had sheltered hostile snipers and a machine gun which had caused considerable annoyance to the right of our line, as well as against transport etc, moving down the main BETHUNE - LENS road.

At dawn the 6th Cavalry Brigade sent out an officers' patrol under Lieutenant W.O.Berryman, 1st Royals, towards PUITS 14 Bis; this officer returned about 11-30 a.m and was able to deliver a very clear report on the situation. He was able to fix the position of the Guards front line trenches and to report the occupation by the enemy of the houses in H.31.b.2.9. and H.25.c.9.6.

The morning passed fairly quietly but any attempt

on the part of our men to gather into groups was the signal for a shell.

2-30 p.m.   *2-30*   Early in the afternoon, General RAWLINSON arrived and conferred with General BRIGGS on the situation. He also listened to Lieutenant W.O.Berryman's report on the information gained by his patrol. The Corps Commander left about 3-15 pm and shortly afterwards a very heavy fire was again opened on the village which caused the collapse of a large number of houses including that occupied by Divisional Headquarters.

4-0 p.m.   At 4-0 p.m. the Guards again attacked Hill 70 and PUITS 14 Bis but the attack does not appear to have attained much result.

11-0 p.m.   *11.Pm*   Instructions were received for relief and were issued to Brigades, and shortly afterwards the 2nd Brigade, 1st Division, commenced to arrive.

Sept 29th.   Considering the shelling to which LOOS was subjected, the casualties were extraordinarily small, this was due to the fact that the trenches on the perimeter were never seriously shelled, fire being concentrated on the village which was well provided with cellars in which the reserves were able to take shelter whenever the bombardment was severe.

The casualties in the Division were :-

	Killed.	Wounded.	Missing.	Missing believed killed.
Officers.	2.	15.	-	-
Other ranks.	25.	106.	5.	1.

During the time the Division occupied the village, troops had little opportunity for rest, whenever the enemy's fire slackened sufficiently to permit of it, they worked hard (right up to the moment of relief) at improving the defences - in this they received the greatest assistance and help from the 3rd Field Squadron, R.E.

The strain on the Signal Squadron was very severe, in addition to the constant stream of messages which had to be dealt with, the lines were repeatedly broken by shell fire. It was remarkable how rapidly communication was always re-established.

The Medical organization of the Division was severely taxed in coping with the large number of wounded found in and around the place.

Over four hundred serious cases were attended to as well as numerous others which were fit to walk, and very great praise is due to Major HUGHES, R.A.M.C, and the Cavalry Field Ambulances for the way in which they carried out their work.

Headquarters, 3rd Cavalry Division.
November, 1915.

M A Gage
Lieutenant-Colonel,
General Staff,
3rd Cavalry Division.

S E C R E T.

3rd Cavalry Division.

The 3rd Cavalry Division, (less 1 Brigade with Horse Artillery) is placed at the disposal of the First Army.

One Brigade and Horse Artillery Battery is placed at the disposal of the Second Army.

Cavalry Corps Headquarters will be informed as soon as possible which Brigade and Battery is detailed to Second Army.

The two brigades allotted to First Army will move as follows :-

1 Brigade will march by night on the 20th/21st Sept. via CAUCHY -a- LA TOUR, AUCHEL and MARLES - LES - MINES to bivouac in the BOIS des DAMES.

The remainder of the Cavalry Division will march on the night 21st/22nd Sept. by the same route to the same destination.

No troops of the 3rd Cavalry Division to be North of the AUCHY-AU-BOIS - CAUCHY-a-LA-TOUR - AUCHEL - MARLES-LES-MINES Road.

A Staff Officer of the 3rd Cavalry Division to report at the 4th Corps Headquarters tomorrow morning, September 20th, to make the necessary arrangements regarding the bivouac in the BOIS des DAMES.

With reference to the Brigade detailed to the Second Army, further orders will be issued. It will remain in its present billeting area until further orders.

A. F. Home
Brig. General,
General Staff.

G.S.1107.
19 SEP. 1915

W.D. 2/20

App. 2

Reference to attached Sheet 5a

~~1. ...~~
~~7th Cavalry Brigade.~~
~~6th Cavalry Brigade.~~
~~3rd ... Division, ...~~
~~3rd ... ...~~
H.Q. 4th Adv. R.L.s
~~... ... .~~
~~... .~~

1. (a). The 3rd Cavalry Division (less 7th Cav. Bde) is placed at the disposal of the 1st Army.
   (b). The 7th Cavalry Brigade is placed at the disposal of the 2nd Army.

6th Cav. Bde. 2. (a). The 6th Cav. Bde will march to a bivouac in the WOOD des DAMES (G.6) on the night of the 20th/21st Sept. via CHOISY-le-Tour, ASNIER and BAILLY-les-dimes.

6th Cav. Bde.   (b). The remainder of the Division (less 7th Cav.
3rd ... Sqdn. Bde) will march on the night 21st/22nd Sept. by the same
3rd Sig. Sqdn. route to the same destination in accordance with
H.Q. 4th Bde. instructions to be issued later. No troops to be east
...   of a north and south line through ... ..., ...,
               ... before 7 p.m. on either night, nor to pass north
               of the ...---..., ...---..., ..., ...---
               les-dimes Road.

7th Cav. Bde.   (c). Further orders will be issued to 7th Cav. Bde,
                 until receipt of these it will remain in its present
                 billeting area.

3. The 3rd Bde Field Squadron will detail one field troop to come under the orders of the 7th Cav. Bde. This troops will remain in its present billets until further orders.

   The field troops to be allotted to the 6th and 8th Cav. Bdes, will join these brigades on arrival at ...---...

"B" Echelon   4. "B" Echelon transport will be concentrated
Transport.   in the ... regimental billeting areas and will await
              further orders.

                                        [signature]
                                        Lieut. Colonel,
                                        General Staff.

H.Q., 3rd Cav. Divn.
20th September, 1914.

SECRET.

WD 3/20 appx 3
Recd. 9.15 p
Sp 20

3rd Cavalry Division.

Reference para 3 (a) of Operation Order No.1 of today, the 7th Cavalry Brigade will march tomorrow to its new billeting area near STAPLE.

Its head will cross an E. & W. line COYECQUE - FAUQUEMBERGUES at 7 a.m.

All vehicles will be moved by the WIZERNES - ARQUES - CASSEL main road.

It will report it's arrival at STAPLE to Head Quarters 2nd Army at OXELAIRE just south of CASSEL.

R.F.Howe
B.G.
General Staff.

CAVALRY CORPS
GS 1110
20 SEP 1915
HEADQUARTERS, GENERAL STAFF

G.286

Repeated to 7th Cav. Bde.
9-25 pm.

WAT.

SECRET.

WD 4 app 4
9/258
285

8th Cavalry Brigade.
3rd Field Squadron, R.E.
H.Q. IVth Brigade, R.H.A.
H.Q. & H.Q.s.

==

1. The 3rd Cavalry Division (less 6th and 7th Cavalry Brigades) will be concentrated in the vicinity of the cross roads ½ mile North of the F in FONTAINE-LEZ-HERMANS by the time given in the attached March Table.

2. Route from Starting Point to BOIS DES DAMES will be as given in S.3 of todays date.

3. Advanced parties will meet A.A. & Q.M.G. at railway Crossing by R of PLACE A BRUAY (due south of B-IS DES DAMES) at 6.0 p.m. September 21st.

4. 3rd Cavalry Division Report Centre will close at WANDONNE at 10.0 a.m. September 22nd at which hour it will open at LABUISSIERE Chateau.

W.A. Arthur Tooth-ough
Major,
General Staff, 3rd Cavalry Division.

20th SEPTEMBER, 1915.

MARCH TABLE issued with
G.285 of Sep. 20th

UNIT	HOUR OF START	STARTING POINT	DESTINATION	ROUTE	REMARKS
8th Cav. Bde.	CONCENTRATION 1-30 p.m. cross Rd. R F	of FONTAINE -LEZ-HERMANS	BOIS DES DAMES	Rds. Rechinghem Gr.	will leave S.P. at 5.30 p.m.
H.Q. IV Bde. R.H.A.	1-45 p.m.	—do—	—do—	RECLINGHEM- LAIRES- FEBVIN PALFART.	will follow 8th Bde. at
2nd Fd. Cy. R.E.	2.0 p.m.	—do—	—do—	will follow in rear of IV Bde. R.H.Q.	

Copy No. 8

S E C R E T

FIRST ARMY OPERATION ORDER No. 95.

HINGES.
19th Sept.1915.

1. (a).   In conformity with the general plan of operations as notified to Corps Commanders, the First Army will assume the offensive on the 25th September, and advance between LENS and the LA BASSEE Canal towards the line HENIN-LIETARD - CARVIN.
   (b).   The French Xth Army will also take the offensive on the 25th September and advance towards DOUAI. The left of its attack will pass immediately south of LENS.
   (c).   The dividing line between the First Army and the French Xth Army will be the road LENS - HENIN-LIETARD - FLERS, inclusive to the First Army.
   (d).   The Second Army will break the enemy's front near HOOGE and will hold troops in readiness to support the First Army as opportunity offers.
   (e).   The XIth Corps and the Cavalry Corps (less one division) will be in General Reserve.
   The Cavalry Corps will move through the First Army front and secure the crossings over the HAUTE DEULE Canal between DOUAI and COURRIERS (both exclusive) as soon as the enemy's line has been broken.

2.   Corps of the First Army south of the LA BASSEE Canal will attack with the object of securing the line LOOS - HULLUCH, and the ground extending to the LA BASSEE Canal. As soon as possible after piercing this line units will be pushed forward to gain possession of the crossings of the HAUTE DEULE Canal between HARNES and BAUVIN.
   Corps of the First Army north of the LA BASSEE Canal will vigorously engage the enemy in order to prevent him from withdrawing troops for a counter attack.
   Wherever the enemy gives ground he must be followed up with the greatest energy.

3. (a).   The artillery bombardment will commence on the 21st September, and will continue day and night under instructions already issued.
   (b).   The 4th Corps will assault the enemy's trenches between the DOUBLE CRASSIER (inclusive) and the VERMELLES - HULLUCH road (exclusive).
   It will advance with its left on the HULLUCH - VENDIN-le-VIEIL road, and operate so as to secure the passage of the HAUTE DEULE Canal at PONT-a-VENDIN and the LENS - CARVIN road south of ANNAY.
   (c).   The 1st Corps will assault the enemy's trenches between the VERMELLES - HULLUCH road (inclusive) and the LA BASSEE Canal.
   It will advance with its right on the HULLUCH - VENDIN-le-VIEIL road, and operate so as to secure the passages of the HAUTE DEULE Canal from PONT-a-VENDIN to BAUVIN.
   It will also assault the enemy's trenches at GIVENCHY and attack CANTELEUX.

(d)

(d). The Indian Corps will assault the enemy's trenches in the vicinity of MOULIN du PIETRE. It will take advantage of any weakening of the enemy on its front to operate so as to secure the high ground about HAUT POMMEREAU and LA CLIQUETERIE Fme.

(e). The 3rd Corps will assault the enemy's trenches in the vicinity of LE BRIDOUX. It will take advantage of any weakening of the enemy on its front to operate with a view to effecting a junction with the Indian Corps on the AUBERS ridge.

4. The attacks by the 4th and 1st Corps south of the LA BASSEE Canal will be preceded by 40 minutes gas and smoke, in accordance with the directions already issued, and the assault will take place at 0.40.

The attacks by the 1st Corps at GIVENCHY and by the Indian Corps will be preceded by 10 minutes gas and smoke, and the assaults will take place at 0.10.

The attack by the 3rd Corps will take place at daylight. It will not be preceded by smoke unless the hour of zero is suitable.

The hour of zero will be notified later.

G.Os.C. Corps will arrange for smoke to be discharged along the whole of the remainder of their line, commencing at 0.6, and will be prepared to take advantage of any retirement of the enemy in their front and to advance with their whole force in conformity with the general plan of operations.

5. The 3rd Cavalry Division (less one brigade) will be in Army Reserve in the BOIS DES DAMES, in readiness to advance on CARVIN as soon as possible.

6. Adv. First Army Headquarters will remain at HINGES.

R. Butler. Major-General

General Staff, First Army.

Issued at 11 p.m.

Copies to:- 1st Corps.
3rd Corps
4th Corps.
Indian Corps.
No. 1 Group, H.A.R.
No. 4 Group, H.A.R.
No. 5 Group, H.A.R.
3rd Cav. Div.
XIth Corps.
G.H.Q.

No. 1 Wing, R.F.C.
O. i/c Signals.
Intelligence.
D.M.S.
M.G., R.A.
M.G., R.E.
D.A. & Q.M.G.

www.ingramcontent.com/pod-product-compliance
Lightning Source LLC
Chambersburg PA
CBHW081428300426
44108CB00016BA/2322